RECEPTIVE HUMAN VIRTUES

ELIZABETH AGNEW COCHRAN

RECEPTIVE HUMAN VIRTUES

*A New Reading
of
Jonathan Edwards's Ethics*

THE PENNSYLVANIA STATE UNIVERSITY PRESS
UNIVERSITY PARK, PENNSYLVANIA

Library of Congress Cataloging-in-Publication Data

Cochran, Elizabeth Agnew, 1977–
Receptive human virtues : a new reading of Jonathan
Edwards's ethics / Elizabeth Agnew Cochran.
        p.   cm.
Summary: "An examination of the writings on virtues and
ethics of eighteenth-century Puritan Jonathan Edwards"—
Provided by publisher.
Includes bibliographical references (p.   ) and index.
    ISBN 978-0-271-03752-3 (cloth : alk. paper)
    ISBN 978-0-271-04845-1 (pbk. : alk. paper)
    1. Edwards, Jonathan, 1703–1758.
            2. Virtues.
    3. Christian ethics—United States.
    4. Christian ethics—Puritan authors.
            I. Title.

BV4630.C62   2010
241'.0458092—dc22
2010020624

Copyright © 2011 The Pennsylvania State University
All rights reserved
Printed in the United States of America
Published by The Pennsylvania State University Press,
University Park, PA 16802-1003

The Pennsylvania State University Press is a member of
the Association of American University Presses.

It is the policy of The Pennsylvania State University
Press to use acid-free paper. Publications on uncoated
stock satisfy the minimum requirements of American
National Standard for Information Sciences—
Permanence of Paper for Printed Library
Material, ANSI Z39.48–1992.

FOR MY PARENTS
Peter and Lois

Contents

Preface ix

Acknowledgments xi

1
An Ethic of Receptive Human Virtues   1

2
Love as Necessary and Volitional:
Edwards's Account of True Virtue in God   21

3
Charity as a Human Virtue:
The Moral Accountability of a Necessary Nature   40

4
Humility as a Human Virtue:
Imaging God's Mercy Through Creaturely Capacities   62

5
Virtuous Repentance:
Apprehending and Approving God's Moral Excellence   94

6
Justice and Partial Loves:
The Natural Goodness of Incomplete Virtues   124

Conclusion
Virtues, Accountability, and Dependence:
Edwards's Significance for Contemporary Christian Ethics   167

Notes   171

Works Cited   187

Index   195

Preface

Twentieth-century virtue ethics emerged as an attempt to overcome perceived inadequacies in modern moral thought. This discipline has been characterized largely by a return to premodern texts: Aristotle in philosophical circles, Thomas Aquinas in theological circles, and Plato and Augustine in the more recent work of scholars such as Robert M. Adams and Eric Gregory. Theological ethicists are increasingly appreciative of Jonathan Edwards, but Edwards is not generally considered a major player in virtue ethics specifically. It is likely that Edwards has been neglected both because of his Enlightenment context and because, at first glance, many of his ethical writings appear to point toward a view of virtue similar to that of other modern thinkers. *The Nature of True Virtue*, particularly when separated from its counterpart text *The End for Which God Created the World*, seems to characterize true virtue as a singular quality, a narrow benevolence similar to the virtue of David Hume and Francis Hutcheson.

This book argues, however, that Edwards develops a careful and complex theory of the virtues, although he does not treat the virtues systematically. Moreover, Edwards's understanding of the virtues is important for contemporary retrieval because it gives rise to a distinctive view of moral agency and accountability that runs counter to a Kantian tendency to celebrate the autonomous workings of a human will detached from the natural world. Edwards's different virtues come together in the sixteenth sermon of *A History of the Work of Redemption*, which extols the virtues of the incarnate Jesus Christ. In this text, Edwards delineates multiple categories of virtues characteristic of human experience. Using Edwards's sermon as a starting point, this book explores the conception of these virtues that Edwards develops in his broader corpus. In articulating his view of each sort of virtue, Edwards consistently affirms that the triune God is uniquely and supremely virtuous. At the same time, he offers a compelling and nuanced vision of a range of human virtues that speak to the multiplicity of moral experiences characteristic of human existence.

Edwards's human virtues are "receptive": we necessarily receive them from God, and in this sense an Edwardsean moral agent is never fully autonomous.

PREFACE

But Edwards is simultaneously clear that humans are the authors of our own actions, and that we remain authentic moral agents even as our pursuit of the virtues depends fundamentally on God. Edwards radically redefines the character of human responsibility in a world that God providentially oversees. In doing this, Edwards implicitly constructs an ethic that in some ways runs counter to what we might expect of a theologian committed to traditional Reformed notions of original sin, election, and predestination; such a theologian, we might reason, is likely to limit moral agency to only a select few. Edwards's ethic does limit true virtue to the elect, but his account of moral responsibility simultaneously functions to make the virtues more accessible to all people than do conceptions of the moral life based in the notion of human autonomy. Edwards's virtues ground a vision of morality rooted in acknowledging the limitations all humans share, an acknowledgment that is paradoxically crucial to the realization of our human potential.

Acknowledgments

I am indebted to a number of people who have supported my work on this book. I am grateful to Jennifer A. Herdt for her astute and diligent guidance in working through the earliest versions of this argument and for her continued thoughtful feedback as I developed this book manuscript. I also very much appreciate the dedication of Jean Porter, Gerald P. McKenny, and George Marsden, who offered insightful suggestions for further revision. In addition, Oliver Crisp and D. Stephen Long gave me constructive feedback.

In addition to the specific assistance I received on this project, my colleagues (both professors and peers) at the University of Notre Dame provided a supportive and formative intellectual environment that contributed significantly to its success. I particularly appreciate Krista Duttenhaver, John Perry, James Helmer, Carter Aikin, Paul Martens, Matthew Loverin, Maura Ryan, Todd Whitmore, Cody Jones, Kimberly Baker, Mary Hirschfeld, and Deonna Neal.

I also value the intellectual encouragement I have received since joining the theology faculty at Duquesne University. Department chair George Worgul and my colleagues in the Theology Department have supported my work in ways that have been important to my continued development of this project. Bill Thompson-Uberuaga and Bill Wright were particularly helpful conversation partners as I worked on revising the manuscript. Robert Lazu, a doctoral student at Duquesne, provided able assistance with research that enabled me to refine my argument in chapter 1. I am grateful to Duquesne University's McAnulty College of Liberal Arts for providing funding that supported my work in the production phase of this manuscript, and to Ann Vinski, who prepared the index.

Additionally, I wish to acknowledge several people whose contributions have been crucial to this manuscript's completion: Patrick Alexander, director of Penn State Press, who offered essential guidance in my earliest stages of revision; Kathryn Yahner of Penn State Press; and Suzanne Wolk, for careful and diligent copyediting. Two anonymous readers for Penn State Press offered comments and recommendations for revision that were perceptive and insightful.

ACKNOWLEDGMENTS

I also appreciate the feedback I received from colleagues at the 2007 annual meeting of the Society of Christian Ethics, where I presented an earlier version of the fourth chapter.

Portions of this book are derived from two articles that I published previously; both are used with permission: "Creaturely Virtues in Jonathan Edwards: The Significance of Christology for the Moral Life," *Journal for the Society of Christian Ethics* 27, no. 2 (2007): 73–96, published by Georgetown University Press, and "Jesus Christ and the Cardinal Virtues: A Response to Monika Hellwig," *Theology Today* 65, no.1 (2008): 81–94.

The love and support of my family have been invaluable for my completion of this work. I am grateful to my husband, Michael Cochran, my brother, Peter, and my parents, Peter Agnew and Lois Peters Agnew. Not only have my parents been a major source of emotional and spiritual support throughout my life, but they have also played a significant role in my intellectual formation, particularly my formation as an academic writer. This book is dedicated to them.

1

An Ethic of Receptive Human Virtues

Jonathan Edwards's ethic is fundamentally an ethic of receptive human virtues. These Edwardsean virtues are in some ways continuous with the goals and purposes of twentieth-century virtue ethics, which has tended to focus on recovering Aristotle in philosophical circles and Thomas Aquinas in theological circles. Edwards shares ideas in common with both of these thinkers: like Aristotle and Aquinas, he adopts a teleological account of human nature, and he understands virtue to be a habitual disposition that is necessarily related to this human *telos*. But Edwards's theological commitments lead him to an account of the virtues that is simultaneously distinct from his predecessors and contemporaries and that gives him some measure of uniqueness in the history of Christian ethics. The study of Edwards's thought provides Christians with a particularly lucid framework for thinking through questions about divine providence and human responsibility, and his conclusions can be theologically satisfying even for ethicists who stand outside Edwards's own Reformed tradition.

Edwards's distinctive position and its contributions to contemporary ethics can be understood through exploring the "receptive human virtues" that I contend are central to his thought. On the surface, this phrase has two shortcomings: first, Edwards himself does not use it, and second, the very notion of "human virtues" may appear conceptually redundant because the term "virtue" is both etymologically related to humanity and nearly always defined as a human excellence, a perfection characteristic of human nature. But the idea of receptive human virtues captures concisely three significant features of Edwards's ethic that make his position unique and compelling: Edwards's account of the virtues is thoroughly human (in spite of his broadly Neoplatonist inclination to define the virtues most fundamentally as perfections of God); Edwards's account of the virtues treats the virtues as a multiplicity of qualities rather than as a singular entity (even though we might perceive a unity in the virtues he identifies); and Edwards's account of the virtues provides a starting point for speaking about humanity's moral accountability within a theological worldview that strongly affirms the necessity of divine grace for good actions, the limitations of the postlapsarian human condition, and God's providential ordering of the universe. Although I will return to these claims at different points throughout this study, I expand them briefly here in order to consider what is at stake in emphasizing the human character of Edwards's virtues, the multiplicity of these virtues, and the receptive quality of these virtues.

The "Human" Character of Edwards's Virtues

Asserting the "human" character of Edwards's virtues may appear unnecessary. Surely virtues, by their nature, are necessarily human qualities because they are perfections of character intricately connected to the nature and ends of human beings. Virtues are generally understood to be human dispositions that make their possessors good human beings, and that are constitutive of a morally good human life.[1] These characteristics of the virtues are particularly at work in Aristotle and Thomas Aquinas, and we will see that Edwards also adopts this view of the virtues to some degree.

Yet at the same time, Edwards's account of the virtues is complicated by his theological commitments. In recent decades scholars have increasingly emphasized the role Edwards's doctrine of God plays in his virtue ethics. Rather than defining the virtues as excellences proper to human nature, Edwards aligns virtue itself with God's being. To be sure, interpreters of Edwards differ in the divine qualities that they perceive as most central to his view of virtue. William Spohn and Roland Delattre, for example, associate Edwards's virtue with divine beauty.[2] Paul Ramsey links this virtue primarily to love.[3] William Danaher, in turn, suggests that Edwardsean virtues are best understood in terms of the perfections of the Trinity and the relations among its members.[4] Nevertheless, in spite of these differences in emphasis, each of these scholars recognizes that Edwards's doctrine of God provides a foundation for understanding his virtue ethic and his argument that humans pursue the moral life as they participate in God's virtues through the process of sanctification.[5] In this sense, Edwards's virtue theory shares notable features with a contemporary Neoplatonist or Augustinian approach to virtue such as that developed by Robert M. Adams in *Finite and Infinite Goods: A Framework for Ethics*. Adams explains that the claim "God is the good itself" is central to Platonism; in consequence of this claim, God is the exemplar for all goodness and beauty found in creation, and resemblance to God is important for all human excellences.[6]

As an interpretation of Edwards, this study is an attempt to complement, rather than discount, scholarship that presents Edwards's doctrine of God as central to his virtue ethic. Edwards's writings support and confirm these scholars' essential insight that Edwardsean virtues are best understood as representations of divine qualities. At the same time, scholars have not fully explored the implications of such a claim for Edwards's treatment of the virtues as human qualities. This point is important because it suggests the need to develop a more complete account of Edwards's virtue ethic.

One goal of any study of a key historical figure's ideas is to present these ideas in as complete a manner as possible, and while it is legitimate to see the divine character of virtue as a guiding principle for reading Edwards, we must hold this principle in tension with an Edwardsean claim that may initially seem to contradict it. In the sixteenth sermon of his posthumously published collection of sermons *A History of the Work of Redemption,* Edwards acknowledges that there are virtues that God, as God, cannot be said to practice. This sermon identifies several qualities as "virtues" that Edwards develops more fully in his writings as a whole. Edwards's discussions of these human qualities merit our attention because they appear to run counter to current scholarly emphases upon Edwards's doctrine of God. If Edwards indeed identifies virtues that God cannot be said to practice, then in what sense can we affirm that virtues are derived from God's character? I argue that each of Edwards's "human virtues" can be properly understood only in relation to God's own moral excellence, but the defense of such an argument requires careful attention to each of these qualities and a recognition that Edwards's virtues are genuinely human qualities.

Edwards discusses four sorts of moral qualities in humans that I address in this book. The first three sorts of attributes can properly be called "virtues" because they participate fully in the nature of true virtue. The fourth category encompasses attributes that constitute Edwards's view of natural goodness; these might be called incomplete virtues because they have the capacity to be perfected through the infusion of grace. A study of Edwards's account of these different sorts of virtue reveals a nuanced and balanced picture of the human moral life that takes seriously an intricate connection between true virtue and God's being. Edwards conceives both divine and human virtue as love, but he does not understand this love as a narrow benevolence that excludes other praiseworthy qualities. Each of the human virtues has a particular relation to love that reveals one of love's dimensions.

Although the four categories of human virtues permeate Edwards's thought, the first three come together in a striking manner in the sixteenth sermon of *A History of the Work of Redemption*. The *Work of Redemption* is a collection of sermons that Edwards preached in 1739. These sermons describe the salvific accomplishments of Jesus Christ's incarnation and atonement, and the sixteenth sermon focuses specifically on the virtues of the incarnate Christ and their importance for salvation. Christ's virtues play a key role in human salvation for Edwards: salvation is accomplished, in part, by the obedience to God that Christ practiced and also by the virtues that he displayed. It is in this soteriological context that Edwards articulates and specifies the meaning of the human virtues.

In his characterization of Christ's virtues, Edwards reveals a conception of infused human virtues as falling into three categories. First, Christ embodies perfectly the love to God that is "true virtue." As other scholars have noted, this type of virtue is most properly defined as a divine excellence, a moral quality of God embodied in the internal relations among the members of the Trinity. Yet this Christian love can also be called a human virtue insofar as it represents the end for which humans were created. Our natures have been changed by original sin so that we cannot be said to be naturally inclined toward this end, but the redemptive work of Christ enables humans authentically to participate in God's love and, through this participation, to practice true virtue. True virtue is most fundamentally divine virtue; it is God's very nature and the key expression of God's perfect moral excellences. Yet through God's creative and redemptive activity, it becomes a human virtue as well.

The second category of virtue that Edwards recognizes in the *Work of Redemption* comes closer than any other type to an Aristotelian understanding of virtue as human excellence, but Edwards's conception of the specific virtues in this category differs markedly from even the transformed Aristotelianism of Thomas Aquinas.[7] Edwards identifies some virtues as expressly human excellences, that is, excellences proper to created natures rather than to divine nature. Edwards explicitly recognizes that God's divine nature cannot logically be said to practice certain virtues, but God does practice them in Christ's human nature, and Christ's incarnate embodiment of these virtues is the source from which Edwards derives their meaning. Edwards identifies humility and meekness as virtues of this type. Christ's embodiment of a meek and humble love reveals to us the self-giving nature of the meekness and humility that Christians should practice as part of the moral life. These virtues, then, are most properly excellences of created natures, yet their meaning is revealed in Christ, and they image aspects of divine love even though they simultaneously differ from the virtue of love.

The *Work of Redemption* also identifies a third category of human virtues: virtues that presuppose sin. Edwards presents repentance for sin and the denial of lust as examples of this sort of virtue and explains that Christ embodies perfectly all divine and human excellences except for the virtues in this category. Although God does not practice them, these qualities can genuinely be said to be virtuous, for they are habitual dispositions of character that are partly constitutive of human "good" and that benefit those whom God enables to possess them. Through the gift of the spiritual sense that humans receive in conversion, God offers us the power to exercise and cultivate repentance, a disposition through which we regret our sin and recognize our utter dependence upon divine grace. Though repentance is not constitutive of love (for love is proper to God, and God has no sin of which to repent), in humans it is a corollary of love. We can only know and understand our need to repent when we compare our actions to those of God. God's revelation of his goodness gives us the ability to see ourselves as we truly are and to acknowledge our limitations. In revealing his character to us, God illumines our hearts and shows us the nature of divine goodness and virtue. This illumination leads us to love God and, as a consequence of this love, to repent of those qualities in ourselves that are decidedly inconsistent with divine virtue.

In addition to these three categories of virtues laid out in *A History of the Work of Redemption*, Edwards discusses two other qualities at some length in the *Two Dissertations*: justice and partial (or private) loves. Edwards is adamant in insisting that these character traits lack the nature of virtue; they are dispositions that humans are able to pursue through our natural faculties, even after the Fall. In his theology of creation laid out in the *Two Dissertations*, Edwards argues that God has providentially ordered that our natural instincts will lead humans to perform actions, independently of the intervention of God's special grace, of which a truly virtuous disposition would approve. Edwards is careful to contend that the dispositions and actions resulting from these instincts are not truly virtuous because they arise from a motive inferior to love to God. Nevertheless, he also affirms that these actions and dispositions possess a quality of "natural goodness" that gives them a (limited) type of merit such that they function as incomplete virtues. Thus, although these traits lack the nature of true virtue, they are human dispositions and activities that have a capacity to be sanctified and should be considered as part of Edwards's picture of the moral life.

The Multiplicity of Edwards's Virtues

Not only does a study of Edwards's human virtues provide a more complete picture of Edwardsean virtues as human qualities, but it also contributes to contemporary conversations about the status of the virtues in modernity. Many scholars characterize the Enlightenment as a historical period in which traditional theories of the virtues collapsed, leaving a view of "virtue" as a singular quality most often identified as benevolence. Edwards's position affirms multiple human moral qualities as virtues during an era when contemporary historians suggest that virtue theories irrevocably shifted away from theology and toward a prioritization of "benevolence" for its own sake. Because Edwards indeed offers a theory of "the virtues," his work provides a weighty counterexample to standard narratives of the history of virtue such as those developed by J. B. Schneewind and Alasdair MacIntyre.

Schneewind's and MacIntyre's arguments are part of a larger conversation among scholars regarding the proper interpretation of modern moral thought. A number of recent works have attempted to account for shifts in seventeenth- and eighteenth-century moral thought by situating them within a broader narrative about the emergence of secular moral philosophy. Advocates of modern moral thought tend to characterize its central concepts as positive developments that address key moral issues more effectively than earlier modes of thinking, particularly intellectual developments in medieval Christianity, are able to do. Denigrators of modern moral thought, in turn, often characterize modernity's intellectual developments as a loss, or as a wrong intellectual turning that can be righted by retrieving more palatable moral claims from an earlier time. MacIntyre and Schneewind develop positions representative of this conversation, and they are particularly interesting from the standpoint of this study because both thinkers explicitly relate their accounts of the emergence of modern moral thought to historical changes in the idea of the virtues. At the same time, neither thinker addresses Edwards as a figure within his historical narrative, and a study of Edwards's view of the human virtues points to ways in which Edwards's position challenges the standard narratives.

A Critique of Modern Moral Thought: Alasdair MacIntyre's Narrative of Virtue's Historical Developments

In keeping with many contemporary scholars who advocate the recovery of the virtues as a starting point for ethics, MacIntyre understands the Enlightenment as a doomed project that contemporary thinkers can overcome only in one of two ways: we can retrieve premodern ways of thinking (in his work in the 1980s, MacIntyre specifically advocates the recovery of a form of Aristotelianism), or we can accept postmodernism (in the form of Friedrich Nietzsche's thought). As he develops this position, MacIntyre argues specifically that the concept of "virtue" underwent a transition and decline in early modernity. As an eighteenth-century thinker whose account of the virtues is teleological and broad enough to account for multiplicities of human moral experiences, Edwards stands as a counterpoint to MacIntyre's account of this history.

After Virtue: A Study in Moral Theory offers an extended historical narrative of the intellectual context that was formative for Edwards's thought, the intellectual world of Britain and Scotland in the early modern period. This narrative particularly addresses the shifting understandings of "virtue" at work in this context. For MacIntyre, at the root of modernity's failings lies its loss of a sense that virtues are a means through which humans move toward a particular *telos*, an end or purpose. In *After Virtue*, MacIntyre turns to premodern thought to recover a sense of the virtues as historically and socially embodied, arguing that particular historical social formations provide the teleologies necessary to give the virtues coherence. MacIntyre develops a constructive Aristotelian account of the virtues, an account whose central concepts of practices, moral traditions, and the narrative order of a human life are designed to capture "the complex, historical, multi-layered character of the core concept of virtue" and the necessary connection between a given theory of the virtues and a specific social formation.[8]

In the course of developing his criticism of the modern age and his argument on behalf of retrieving a premodern view of the virtues, MacIntyre suggests that one sign of virtue ethics' decline is a modern transition from theories of "the virtues" to theories of "virtue." Premodern virtue theories recognized the virtues as a multiplicity of qualities that were held together in unity and whose primary coherence was based in their relation to a *telos*. Modern virtue theories continue to speak as if there are lists of virtues, but in reality their discourse has shifted so that "virtue" has become a singular entity, and its particular contributions to ethics are subsequently minimized. MacIntyre laments this shift from "the virtues" to "virtue" and links it to the influence of Stoicism on modern thinkers such as David Hume.[9]

Although Edwards engages his philosophical contemporaries and develops particular ideas in a manner consistent with their insights, my study suggests that his view of the virtues is ultimately more consistent with the premodern tradition of the virtues than with MacIntyre's characterization of dominant Enlightenment positions. Edwards shares his contemporaries' emphasis upon love, but he understands human love as closely connected to other virtues as well and, consequently, he characterizes love as part of a theory of the virtues rather than as a unilateral entity that represents a singular moral principle. MacIntyre does not ultimately deny that it is possible for a modern thinker to develop a view of the virtues that is largely premodern—for MacIntyre, Jane Austen is an example of such a figure.[10] But as Jeffrey Stout has observed, MacIntyre tends to associate "premodern" virtue theories rather exclusively with Aristotelianism.[11] Edwards's theory of the virtues is decidedly teleological and is thereby informed by Aristotelian categories to a degree that gives Edwards some common ground with MacIntyre. Edwards's virtues are human character traits constitutive of the end for which humans were created, the purpose of glorifying God and responding appropriately to God's moral beauty.[12] But Edwards's alignment of virtue with God's being leads to a position distinct from that of Aristotle as well, a conception of the virtues as reflections of divine beauty. Humans receive the virtues only through participation in the being of a God who is inherently good.

Schneewind's Characterization of Modern Moral Thought: The Decline of Moral Theology and the Decline of Virtue

In contrast to MacIntyre, who sees the Enlightenment as a time in which morally valuable theories of the virtues were lost, Schneewind presents modern philosophy in a positive light and argues that its rejection of theology was in certain senses inevitably brought about by developments in the theological tradition prior to the eighteenth century. According to Schneewind's narrative of late medieval and early modern Christian thought, the enterprise of moral theology at this time developed in a manner that reveals its instability and that led to the emergence of a Kantian morality that would reject moral theology's authority. Schneewind's argument is important both because it focuses in particular on early modernity as a time of decline for theological ethics and because it implies that both the enterprise of moral theology and premodern accounts of the virtues are inherently unstable. Schneewind's account of moral theology merits further reflection (see chapter 2) because his historical narrative helps to shed light on some of Edwards's interlocutors. But his characterization of the virtues' collapse in modernity is important to consider here briefly because Schneewind's position, like MacIntyre's, underscores the historical significance of conceiving and recovering Edwards as a theorist of the virtues.

Schneewind's account of the virtues challenges contemporary thinkers (such as MacIntyre) who seek to recover notions of virtue as central to ethics. He contends that virtue was not lost in the modern age. Instead, modern thinkers redefined the notion of virtue because they perceived two deficiencies in classical virtue theory. First, Schneewind explains, moderns recognized that classical virtue theories cannot adequately address the needs of a world in which the legitimacy of multiple moral traditions and perspectives is recognized and in which resources are limited. In contrast to theoreticians of virtue who are concerned with humanity's shared dispositions that constitute their moral goodness, modern natural lawyers such as Hugo Grotius saw possible disagreements among moral traditions as a crucial issue for moral reflection and also became concerned with discussing the distribution of resources and the limitations of humanity.[13] Schneewind, pointing specifically to Aristotle, argues that classical virtue theory is of little use in addressing these questions, particularly the question of adjudicating moral disagreements.[14] For Schneewind, Aristotle does not provide tools for discussion among members of multiple moral traditions or recognition of multiple perspectives that might be navigated.

Schneewind implies that a second problem inherent in virtue ethics is its imprecision: an Aristotelian understanding of the virtues is somewhat imprecise in the moral guidance it provides, and it also reserves moral knowledge for persons who have already achieved virtue, which means that moral standards are inaccessible to everyone else. Schneewind contends that Christian moral theology has always been based in law, and that Christian attempts to give a place to the virtues were one of virtue's early "misfortunes." He observes that the seventeenth-century natural lawyers, whom he notes were "serious Christians," except for Hobbes (49), develop moral theories that give a place to "virtue and the virtues" but see them as "secondary to laws or rules" (45). It can be argued, Schneewind explains, that this position has its origins in Aquinas's "attempt to bring classical natural law doctrine and Aristotelian virtue theory into some kind of union" (45) and was strengthened by "numerous Protestant writings" of the time that offer act- and law-centered accounts of morality (45). This latest dichotomy between law and virtue becomes crystallized in the writings of Grotius and Samuel Pufendorf, who displace Aristotelian morality with a law-based morality (48). Yet this displacement, Schneewind contends, does not constitute a rejection of virtue; instead, Grotius establishes a framework, codified by Pufendorf, that distinguishes perfect and imperfect duties, and virtue is subsumed by the latter category (48–49). Perfect duties, duties that are important to the running of society, are very precise. Imperfect duties are less specified; they are essentially expressions of love (49). Schneewind goes on to argue that some form of this Grotian dichotomy is reiterated in the writings of David Hume, Adam Smith, and Immanuel Kant (51–62).

In the course of developing this argument, Schneewind suggests a relation between love (the embodiment of imperfect duties) in modern moral thought and the earlier virtue tradition that echoes MacIntyre's suggestion of a modern move from "the virtues" to "virtue." Whereas MacIntyre laments this move as distorting the earlier tradition, Schneewind suggests that modern views of love allow the tradition to be preserved to the extent that it can be. For Schneewind, the natural lawyers preserve a form of the virtue tradition by allowing love, in addition to law, to have some moral significance (49). Schneewind notes that the ways in which the natural lawyers discuss love parallel earlier conversations about the virtues and essentially accomplish the same things, even though modern natural lawyers have rejected the language of virtue (49). Love, Schneewind suggests, essentially replaces the virtues as a moral category at this time.

The characterization of Edwards as a modern Christian theorist of the virtues suggests a way of reconciling Christian theology with an ancient tradition of the virtues that focuses upon human excellences of character. For Schneewind, Christian thought is incompatible with the concept of virtue; the concept of law is central to its moral thought, and Schneewind sees Aquinas and the modern natural lawyers as conceiving ethics primarily in terms of natural law and as seeking to preserve some form of the virtue tradition alongside this ethic. A close study of Edwards challenges this perception of moral theology, because Edwards presents an ethic for which character, rather than law, is primary. The character of the triune God, as revealed to us in Jesus Christ, is key for Edwards's ethics, and the central moral task for humans is to pursue the virtues that allow us to participate in and assimilate God's perfect moral character in a manner accommodated to human nature. Edwards's moral thought, then, is virtue-based rather than law-based.

At the same time, Edwards's ethic challenges Schneewind's suggestion that the content of the virtue tradition can be reduced to benevolence. Although Edwards gives love a place of prominence within his ethic, Edwardsean love should not be read as a single principle that is parallel to Schneewind's characterization of Kant's categorical imperative (60), but instead as a foundation that unifies a complex view of multiple moral qualities that humans should seek. These qualities all stand in some relation to love, but they are not identical (or reducible) to it: for example, the virtue of humility illuminates a key dimension (but not the sole dimension) of love, and virtuous repentance is a corollary of love. Edwards's virtue ethic thereby indicates that a narrow benevolence is neither the whole of Christian theology nor the whole of virtue, though it is fundamental to each.

MacIntyre and Schneewind represent larger positions in a debate about the viability of modern thought. Because both thinkers are particularly concerned with the virtues' status in modernity, their arguments are important to understanding the historical significance of a study of Edwards's human virtues as an alternative line of thought in modern virtue ethics. Their questions about the historical developments in moral thought about virtue reveal key issues that are at stake in a study of Edwards's ethics.

The Receptive Nature of Edwards's Virtues

Perhaps the most significant contribution a recovery of Edwards can offer to contemporary ethics is a view of moral formation that takes seriously historical Christian commitments regarding the necessity of divine grace in moral action. Edwards is not the only theologian who emphasizes God's providential oversight of the world's affairs, or who strives to avoid the Pelagian heresy that perceives humans as capable of being good through their own merits. But Edwards's position is particularly effective in addressing the morally complicated idea that human morality depends fundamentally upon the activity of the triune God. Any position that emphasizes divine sovereignty stands in danger of undermining human freedom, and yet Edwards develops a view of moral accountability that answers coherently the question of how humans can be authentic moral agents in a world that God oversees. For Edwards, we receive the virtues, and the capacity to grow in virtue, through God's gracious personal intervention. At the same time, we participate authentically in this reception so that we retain a degree of moral responsibility for our virtues.

In developing this view of moral accountability, Edwards adopts a philosophical framework that rejects Aristotle's view of habituation as central to the acquisition of virtue. For Aristotle, humans acquire the virtues through the repeated performance of good acts: "we become just by doing just acts, temperate by doing temperate acts, brave by doing brave acts." Aristotle contrasts the virtues with a human ability to see or hear, which arises from the sense of sight or hearing. "It was not by often seeing or often hearing that we get these senses"; we do not acquire the sense of sight by repeated acts of seeing. Aristotle maintains that, unlike the activities of the senses, we do acquire virtuous states of character by participating in activities that are in keeping with these virtuous qualities. A just human being is "produced" by "doing just acts," and "without doing these [acts] no one would have even a prospect of becoming good."[15]

Edwards scholars attest to Edwards's departures from Aristotle's account of moral formation; for example, Anri Morimoto contends that Edwards's concept of a virtuous disposition "differs from that of Aristotle at one important point: namely, it is not acquired by repeated acts."[16] In chapter 5 I address Edwards's theological concerns about habituation more fully, drawing upon *Original Sin* and *Religious Affections*. For now, it is helpful to situate these concerns briefly in relation both to Edwards's predecessors and to contemporary ethicists in order to underscore Edwards's importance for contemporary theologians who wish to recover the virtues. Edwards's suspicions of Aristotle are largely in keeping with other theologians who perceive habituation to be at odds with a Christian understanding of original sin and the essential place of grace within human moral experience. Such a concern is evident in the writings of Martin Luther,[17] but Edwards would have been even more familiar with arguments voiced by Peter Ramus, a sixteenth-century Huguenot philosopher respected in early New England,[18] and Puritan thinkers such as William Ames and Cotton Mather. Ramus views Aristotelian metaphysics and ethics as antithetical to Christian theology,[19] in part because they encourage humans to conceive virtue as within our grasp, independently of divine assistance. Ames commends Ramus's critique of Aristotle,[20] specifically noting the danger in Aristotle's view "that all virtues are within man's power and obtainable by man's nature, art, and industry."[21] Mark Noll explains that Ames "illustrated a common attitude that combined a measure of respect for Aristotle's natural intellectual gifts with a forceful rejection of what Ames considered his dangerous anthropocentrism," particularly on the subject of virtue.[22] In *The Marrow of Theology*, Ames affirms that virtue cannot be shaped by the workings of the "human mind"; instead, "there can be no other teaching of the virtues than theology which brings the whole revealed will of God to the directing of our reason, will, and life." Although Ames defines virtue as a habit of the will,[23] he uses this term differently from Aristotle, insisting that a habit "can be the product only of regeneration by the Holy Spirit."[24] Likewise, Edwards's contemporary Cotton Mather retains a commitment to the necessity of election for virtue, coupling this commitment with a distrust of Aristotle's moral philosophy.[25] Edwards's critiques of Aristotelian habituation are very much in keeping with this Puritan intellectual context.

The import of Edwards's departures from Aristotelian habituation is underscored by recognizing that several contemporary theologians likewise recognize potential limitations in Aristotle's moral thought even as they advocate an ethic of virtue. Gilbert Meilaender's *Theory and Practice of Virtue* expresses concern that virtue ethics (a discipline focused largely on Aristotle at the time Meilaender was writing) tends toward egoism and a focus on the self.[26] Similarly, Stanley Hauerwas and Charles Pinches recognize the potential problems of recovering an Aristotelian virtue ethic from a Christian perspective. Their 1997 work *Christians Among the Virtues: Theological Conversations with Ancient and Modern Ethics* ultimately advocates Aristotle's virtue theory and characterizes it as a helpful framework for considering the Christian moral life, both because Aquinas sees it as a fruitful starting point for his own virtue theory and because they themselves "think [Aristotle] is more right than wrong about most things having to do with living virtuously." Yet their argument simultaneously acknowledges the challenges that Aristotelianism poses for a Christian account of virtue, particularly in Aristotle's understanding of happiness as an end for humanity and his view of magnanimity as a virtue. Hauerwas and Pinches believe that Christians can transform and interpret these concepts in ways that are consistent with a Christian virtue ethic,[27] but their chapter on biblical virtues does not refer to Aristotle.[28]

To be sure, in spite of these concerns about features of Aristotelian ethics, many Protestant virtue ethicists have chosen to build theories of virtue on MacIntyre's *After Virtue*, which seeks to recover Aristotle for contemporary reflection. Such ethicists argue that MacIntyre's text provides a useful foundation for an account of the virtues tied to ecclesiology.[29] Yet *After Virtue* itself does not purport to present a theological account of virtue, but rather a premodern view that has strong affinities with Thomistic virtue theory only insofar as Aristotle and Thomas Aquinas are consistent with each other. *After Virtue*'s Aristotelianism does not by itself provide grounds for presuming Aristotelianism to be the logical foundation for a Christian virtue ethic; as Jean Porter has noted, there are significant differences between Aristotle's virtue ethic and Thomas Aquinas's account of the infused virtues.[30] MacIntyre likewise recognizes the discontinuity between an Aristotelian virtue ethic and commitments central to Christianity. Although he contends that the New Testament view of the virtues shares a "logical and conceptual structure" with Aristotle's virtue ethic,[31] he affirms notable differences in the content of each account of the virtues:

> At once it is impossible to delay the remark that the most striking contrast with Aristotle's catalogue [of virtues] is to be found neither in Homer's nor in our own, but in the New Testament's. For the New Testament not only praises virtues of which Aristotle knows nothing—faith, hope, and love—and says nothing about virtues such as *phronesis* which are crucial for Aristotle, but it praises at least one quality as a virtue which Aristotle seems to count as one of the vices relative to magnanimity, namely humility. Moreover since the New Testament quite clearly sees the rich as destined for the pains of Hell, it is clear that the key virtues cannot be available to them; yet they *are* available to slaves. And the New Testament of course differs from both Homer and Aristotle not only in the items included in its catalogue, but once again in its rank ordering of the virtues.[32]

MacIntyre's observation does not discount the possibility of reconciling an Aristotelian virtue ethic with a Christian catalogue of the virtues. Yet MacIntyre recognizes that this project is not straightforward, in keeping with the suspicions of Aristotle that some Protestants have articulated. MacIntyre does commend Aquinas's reconciliation of Aristotelianism with the Christian tradition in *Whose Justice? Which Rationality?* But Aquinas's method of accomplishing this reconciliation, as MacIntyre rightly recognizes, is to engage this tradition carefully alongside the works of Augustine, and to acknowledge the ways in which these two moral traditions presume differing views of moral formation.[33] A connection between Aristotelian thought and Christian theology is by no means self-evident.

Ultimately, Edwards develops a Christian account of the human virtues that is not strictly Aristotelian, particularly in its conception of how virtues are acquired. Partly because Edwards overtly rejects Aristotelian habituation, it seems more faithful to Edwards's thought to align his work with certain commitments of Neoplatonist and Christian Platonist virtue theories, as noted above. The influence of Neoplatonism on Edwards is most evident in his central contention that God is the good, and that goodness in creatures is constituted by creatures' resemblance to God. As many scholars have noted, Edwards is also deeply influenced by his contemporaries, and particularly by a form of eighteenth-century British rationalism that was partly a development of certain Neoplatonist claims via the seventeenth-century Cambridge Platonists. Many of Edwards's claims about love echo those of the Cambridge Platonists, as I discuss in chapters 2 and 3. Likewise, his view of moral formation has strong affinities with that of Francis Hutcheson, to whom Edwards appeals intentionally as a means of articulating a model of acquiring virtue that differs from habituation.[34] While features of Edwards's thought are indebted to Aristotelian categories,[35] Neoplatonism and eighteenth-century British philosophical frameworks are more fruitful for understanding Edwards's account of the human virtues.

Some readers of Edwards might be concerned about whether this division of his ethic from Aristotelian habituation threatens to undermine any attempt to view Edwards's ethic as allowing a prominent place for human freedom and moral accountability in the virtuous life. Wilson's *Virtue Reformed: Rereading Jonathan Edwards's Ethics*, which argues for a stronger influence of Aristotelian concepts on Edwards's moral thought, aims partly to demonstrate that an Edwardsean ethic affords a positive place to human moral agency. Wilson's characterization of Edwards's view of "habit" as in keeping with Aristotle's account of virtue seems designed to ensure that humans have an active capacity to shape their own characters. For example, Wilson contends that Edwards draws from "Christian Aristotelianism" to defend the notion that agents are partly able to influence their own dispositions.[36] Wilson's desire to affirm the moral accountability and freedom of an Edwardsean moral agent is consistent with the overall thrust of Edwards's thought, but it is nevertheless the case that Edwards distances his position overtly from Aristotelian habituation, and an account of Edwards's virtue ethics must acknowledge this point.

Indeed, it is precisely in its points of contrast with Aristotelian habituation that Edwards's distinctive views of moral agency and accountability emerge. As this study moves through Edwards's conception of the human virtues, it explores issues of accountability and freedom and considers the success of Edwards's ethic in addressing them. Admittedly, Edwards's commitment to God's complete sovereignty over creation and his affirmation of a traditional Reformed view of original sin present challenges for understanding how his position conceives humans as responsible for their actions. Humans cannot practice true virtue apart from the specific intervention of God's converting grace, and at many points Edwards adamantly insists that this grace is given or denied independently of our actions. Moreover, recent scholarship suggests that Edwards was at least on some level an occasionalist, that is, he believed that God re-creates and causes events at given moments in time. In light of these features of Edwards's thought, it may seem that Edwards affirms God's power to such a degree that he risks denying human freedom and human moral accountability.

Although Edwards's understanding of accountability may not satisfy all contemporary readers, his position nonetheless contributes to Christian virtue ethics in valuable ways. I return to Edwards's view of accountability at several points in this study in order to underscore the ways in which his receptive understanding of virtue is compatible with a conception of moral agents as responsible for their actions. Edwards defends human moral responsibility implicitly by suggesting that our moral agency and freedom reflect God's, an argument that I consider more fully in chapters 2 and 3. He also explicitly addresses the question of whether actions that the Holy Spirit causes in us can legitimately be "our" actions; I explore this discussion in more depth in chapter 5. Together these arguments attest to Edwards's concern to reconcile moral responsibility with theological commitments to the priority of divine grace in the moral life.

Method and Structure

This study is intended not simply to delineate categories of Edwardsean human virtues that previous scholars have not identified but to discuss human moral attributes in a manner that demonstrates Edwards's particular significance for how we understand the status of Christian theology in modernity, as well as the relation between Christian theology and contemporary virtue ethics. In order to develop an argument that is constructive as well as historical, I bring Edwards's position into conversation with other premodern and modern accounts of these virtues for the purpose of highlighting particular features of Edwards's thought. I focus each chapter on one category of human attributes, and each chapter is roughly parallel in structure: I first describe Edwards's view of each virtue or quality, then turn to outside thinkers (either thinkers whom Edwards engages directly or those who pose interesting questions for his thought), and finally return to Edwards's position to show how these comparisons illuminate and challenge it.

AN ETHIC OF RECEPTIVE HUMAN VIRTUES

These historical comparisons do not comprehensively consider all of the intellectual influences on Edwards's thought. Edwards was a widely read scholar conversant with many of the philosophical traditions of his day, and a study of his ideas must of necessity be somewhat selective in the influences it discusses. The comparisons I offer in each chapter function, at points, to underscore the insights Edwards's position offers to contemporary Christian virtue ethicists; engagements with Augustine, Thomas Aquinas, and John Calvin are useful in this regard. Other comparisons, such as those to the Cambridge Platonists and Francis Hutcheson, illuminate the relation of Edwards's position to his intellectual context. British and Scottish thinkers were particularly important for this context as it relates to Edwards's moral thought. George Marsden's *Jonathan Edwards: A Life* indicates that most American colonists in the mid-1700s, including Edwards, thought of themselves as British subjects and took the Scottish intellectual context very seriously.[37] Many of Edwards's treatises central to understanding his ethics were written in the 1740s and 1750s and reflect the Scottish influence to which Marsden alludes. Norman Fiering's *Jonathan Edwards's Moral Thought and Its British Context* also attests to the importance of this intellectual tradition for reading Edwards's ethics, particularly because of its place in Edwards's academic formation.[38]

Another important methodological point relates to the multiple genres of Edwards's writings from which I draw. Although I derive the first three categories of virtue from a single sermon in *A History of the Work of Redemption*, I develop accounts of Edwards's views of these virtues from a variety of texts, including treatises as well as sermons. *The Religious Affections*, *Treatise on Original Sin*, and *The Two Dissertations* are in many ways most central to the definitions of these virtues that I develop. I also refer frequently to Edwards's sermons, including both individual sermons and collections of sermons such as *A History of the Work of Redemption* and *Charity and Its Fruits*. Additionally, I draw at points from Edwards's texts that reflect on the revivals and from his conversion narrative *The Life of David Brainerd*. I note differences among Edwards's texts where relevant, but for the most part I presume continuity among these texts.

This analysis of Edwards's human virtues begins with love. Chapter 2 examines the divine love that is the foundation of all the human virtues. I argue that Edwards's understanding of love as equivalent to the person of the Holy Spirit establishes a relation between virtue and the Christian God that ensures a highly theological view of morality without resorting to the types of voluntarist arguments that Schneewind suggests were the only alternative for modern moralists who wished to secure God's centrality for moral knowledge and action. Edwards's articulation of a position similar to that of the Cambridge Platonists reveals how his view is distinct from the modern voluntarism that Schneewind associates with Luther and Calvin. At the same time, Edwards infuses Cambridge Platonist theology with Trinitarian claims in a manner that allows him both to underscore the intentionality of God's love and to guard against a view of the divine will that exercises power arbitrarily. Edwards's account of divine love is significant for subsequent chapters, both because this love undergirds and empowers the human exercise of the virtues and because it provides a model for understanding moral accountability in terms of the paradigm of freedom and necessity at work in divine actions.

My exploration of Edwards's virtuous love continues in chapter 3, which focuses on Edwards's account of true virtue in humans. This virtue is an image of the divine love discussed in chapter 2, and it is unique among the human virtues in that it participates in this divine love. Edwards draws from the Cambridge Platonists in developing this account of love, but he also departs from them significantly by maintaining a strong commitment to the traditional Christian doctrine of original sin. This departure appears to put the moral accountability of Edwards's virtuous agent in jeopardy; we cannot exercise true virtue apart from the assistance of God's grace, and this gift of grace does not depend on our moral merit. Yet Edwards's position does allow for a moral accountability that images God's own moral agency, just as virtuous human love images God's love.

Virtues that Edwards defines as creaturely excellences are the subject of chapter 4. Edwards identifies several virtues as of this type, but I focus on the virtue of humility because Edwards discusses this quality most extensively. Edwards's suggestion that some virtues are best conceived as excellences of creatures is striking in light of recent interpreters' increasing recognition that Edwards conceives the virtues first and foremost as excellences of God. *A History of the Work of Redemption* challenges us to consider how this thesis intersects with human virtues that cannot be attributed to God. Edwards explicitly argues that qualities such as humility are legitimately virtues, but that God in God's divine nature cannot properly be said to embody or practice them. Drawing upon Christological insights, Edwards develops a compelling account of humility as a creaturely virtue that simultaneously succeeds in tying this category of human virtue to God's being and activity. Ultimately, Edwards's position reveals a closer connection between these creaturely excellences and divine virtue than is immediately apparent. The meaning of Edwards's humility is embodied for humans in the person and work of the incarnate Jesus Christ, whose human nature is the perfect moral archetype of human virtues in this category. This starting point leads Edwards toward a view of humility as an active self-renunciation, a position that puts him at odds with Thomas Aquinas. In turn, Edwards's account of humility reveals continuity between the human virtue of humility and God's merciful practice of virtuous love: the excessive nature of Christ's humility reveals the nature of divine mercy to us. Humility therefore can plausibly be characterized as an image or type of divine mercy, although there are limits to this characterization in the moral practice of humans apart from Christ.

Chapters 3 and 4, then, develop accounts of human virtues that are parallel to virtues that can be attributed to God. In some sense, God can be said to practice both love and humility, the latter through the work of the incarnate Christ. Chapter 5 turns to human attributes that God, even in the person of Christ, decidedly does not possess. These attributes are exclusively human, yet divine virtue is ultimately at work in their practice as well. Their relation to divine virtue is more oblique than in the cases of love and humility, but considering them in light of Edwards's views of creation and sin shows how a connection to divine virtue is nonetheless important to understanding Edwards's definition of these qualities.

Chapter 5 considers human virtues that presuppose sin and that therefore cannot be attributed to God even in the person of Christ. In discussing this sort of virtue, Edwards points to the example of "repentance," which he identifies as a disposition in the regenerate to hate and regret their sin. Repentance cannot be attributed directly to God, but Edwards makes the human apprehension and approval of God's moral perfections essential to its practice. Edwards situates his understanding of virtuous repentance within the broader narrative of conversion so that in the elect, the spiritual sense's apprehension and approbation of God is what brings repentance about. Edwards relies heavily on Francis Hutcheson's moral sense theory in developing his view of the spiritual sense and his account of moral formation. Rather than arguing that our performance of actions forms us in particular dispositions, as Aristotle does, Edwards makes our practice of repentance dependent upon God's self-revelation. It is only through seeing and approving God's moral perfections that humans are able to see their own sin for what it is and, consequently, to repent. It is Hutchesonian "apprehension" and "approbation," rather than Aristotelian habituation, that undergird Edwards's account of moral formation.

Chapter 6 turns to a final category of human virtues, qualities that Edwards associates with "natural goodness." The cultivation of these attributes, which include justice and various particular human loves, does not depend upon the intervention of God's special grace but is instead something that "natural man" is capable of pursuing and achieving. For Edwards, justice and partial loves are not truly virtuous, but neither are they simply Augustinian "splendid vices." Edwards presents justice and partial loves as incomplete virtues, dispositions that lead us toward acts that true virtue approves. These natural dispositions have merit, as they have been ordered by God's providence to help humans to live comfortably together. Therefore, they can be said to contribute to our flourishing and to promote conditions in which true virtue may be exercised and its activity expanded. The idea that these natural attributes are incomplete virtues is consistent with Edwards's broader views of creation and sin evident in *The End for Which God Created the World*. The theology of creation that Edwards presents in this text integrates Calvin's natural law position with the British rationalist tradition as represented in Samuel Clarke. In contrast to Calvin, Edwards does not suggest that the world is completely disordered after the Fall; instead, his focus is on the human will's tendency toward disorder. The incomplete virtues are means through which humans, in spite of original sin, take part in the natural goodness of the rational created world and thereby participate in God's ordering of the world toward God's glory. Edwards's careful treatment of these attributes provides an effective framework for speaking about the moral potential of natural goodness while simultaneously maintaining the primacy of conversion within the moral life.

Together, these different human virtues situate the moral life within a world permeated by God's grace. Each human virtue is achieved through receiving the grace of the triune God who is virtue itself. Yet our reception is not passive. For Edwards, we actively participate in the virtue we receive; this participation makes our moral agency authentic. Our human agency is an image of God's own moral activity. It is fitting, then, to begin this discussion of Edwards's receptive human virtues with a consideration of the divine virtue that is their foundation.

2

Love as Necessary and Volitional
Edwards's Account of True Virtue in God

I suggested in chapter 1 that this study of Edwards's human virtues complements readings of Edwards that focus on the God-centered character of Edwardsean virtues. Because Edwards's human virtues are each necessarily tied to divine virtue in some way, it is helpful to consider Edwards's account of God's virtue more fully before turning to these human virtues. An exploration of Edwards's divine virtue points to a significant difference between Edwards's virtue and Aristotelian and Thomistic virtue theories. Edwards's account of love is more in keeping with Augustine than with Thomas Aquinas. Both Augustine and Aquinas conceive love as the primary virtue, but for Augustine, love unifies all the virtues so that each quality that we might identify as a virtue (qualities such as prudence, justice, or temperance) is both distinct from love and, simultaneously, a form of love that reveals a particular dimension of love's character.[1] Edwards follows Augustine in presenting love as the primary virtue, and the other human virtues, while representing different dimensions of human moral experience, are nonetheless radically related to love, so that their meanings cannot finally be understood independently of love.

Edwards's account of divine virtue provides a starting point for exploring his provocative views of moral accountability and moral agency. For Edwards, the being and activity of a virtuous God serve as a model for understanding human moral agency as authentic even though it does not depend solely on our own choices and decisions. God is both virtuous and good, and yet God may appear to be constrained by God's own inherent virtue because this virtue makes God incapable of doing evil. Edwards's position makes clear that divine virtue does not require the freedom to choose evil. God is necessarily virtuous, but God fully wills and intends God's own virtue through the activity of the Holy Spirit, whom Edwards equates simultaneously with God's will and God's love.

This chapter's exploration of Edwards's divine virtue begins by situating Edwards's position in relation to the Christian Platonist tradition, particularly as this tradition is represented in the Cambridge Platonist movement with which Edwards was familiar. Edwards develops his view of divine virtue by building on the Cambridge Platonists' understanding of God as fundamentally goodness and love, but he augments this position with a rich Trinitarian theology that guards against some of their arguments' possible shortcomings. Edwards's relation to the Cambridge Platonists has significant implications for his conception of moral accountability. Edwards characterizes God's virtuous love as simultaneously necessary and intentional. This view of moral action points to the possibility of reconciling authentic moral agency with some level of necessity.

Edwards and the Cambridge Platonists

For Christian Platonists, as for Aristotelians, virtue is the human *telos*, and Edwards stands with both traditions by affirming that God creates humans for the purpose of pursuing loving dispositions and actions and thereby giving glory to the love and virtue that is God's own being. But several features of Edwards's account of divine virtue demonstrate that Neoplatonist divine exemplarity is the strongest philosophical paradigm at work in his virtue theory. Whereas Aristotelian virtues are excellences proper to human nature, Edwardsean true virtue is an excellence most proper to God. Edwards conceives love as constitutive of divine being, holiness, and, correlatively, virtue. As a quality of divine nature, virtue is something that humans cannot acquire through habituation but only through divine gift. For Christian Platonists, human virtue requires that God imparts God's own nature to us and thereby gives us a virtuous disposition that we can cultivate and strengthen through divine assistance. Consistently with the broader tradition of Christian Platonism, Edwards contends that true virtue in humans is most accurately characterized as a participation in divine being and virtue. It is therefore necessary to consider Edwards's view of divine virtue before we can understand the human virtues.

Edwards's account of divine virtue is illuminated by exploring central arguments of the Cambridge Platonists, who are known to have influenced Edwards. Cambridge Platonism is a seventeenth-century British intellectual movement whose key figures were primarily Anglican divines affiliated with Cambridge University. Benjamin Whichcote, who taught at Emmanuel College when many of the other Cambridge Platonists were students, is commonly considered the movement's founder. Other well-known thinkers affiliated with this movement include Ralph Cudworth, Henry More, John Smith, and John Norris. While individual Cambridge Platonists differed in their particular interests and emphases, the movement can be characterized in general terms as most centrally concerned with affirming God's goodness, and, correlatively, with challenging Hobbesian materialism, atheism, and forms of Calvinist voluntarism that the Cambridge Platonists perceive as potentially compromising divine goodness.[2] The Cambridge Platonists are suspicious of traditional views of predestination and original sin because they believe that these concepts promote the ideas that God is arbitrary and that salvation is completely hidden. As pastors, the Cambridge Platonists fear that these beliefs could lead people to despair, which would in turn put them in danger of ultimately rejecting God and embracing the world.[3] In order to reassure people that religion need not be inaccessible, the Cambridge Platonists affirm a Neoplatonic argument that there is harmony between faith and reason. We have been created with the faculty of reason, and our reason enables us to know God, to participate in God's being, and to discern moral precepts.[4]

To understand the broader implications of the Cambridge Platonists' critiques of Calvin and Hobbes (and Edwards's reactions to them), it is useful to turn to J. B. Schneewind's historical argument about the emergence of modern moral thought. Schneewind identifies two recurring sorts of positions in late medieval and early modern moral theology and philosophy. One of these is "voluntarism"; the other Schneewind calls "intellectualism" or "antivoluntarism." Voluntarists such as Luther and Calvin contend that the moral order was established by an arbitrary divine fiat, so that God's will is the source of morality. For these modern voluntarists, divine law constitutes good and evil rather than perceiving and reflecting it, a claim that emphasizes God's power and sovereignty over creation.[5] But although this sort of voluntarist argument keeps God essential to morality, it risks undermining God's goodness and presenting God as a tyrant. Hobbes, too, is a voluntarist, and his writings reveal a second danger of modern voluntarism: the argument that God's will stands completely outside our categories of "good" and "evil" can make God so transcendent that God becomes completely irrelevant to human moral pursuits. Hobbes suggests that God gives theorems their moral status as law and provides the form of the law of nature. Yet for Hobbes, God is removed from daily moral decisions. After giving theorems their moral status as law, God leaves us to our own devices. Because the transcendent

God has been removed from the daily practice of human morality, the primary framework of Hobbes's moral thought is a system of causes and effects that take place entirely in the material world.[6] Schneewind's identification of these problems with voluntarism is sobering for modern Christian theology. He implies that voluntarism, in spite of its theological difficulties, is the only logical option through which moral theologians might secure God's importance for the enterprise of morality.[7]

In light of Schneewind's identification of Calvin as a voluntarist, my contention that Edwards's account of love has common features with the Cambridge Platonists may seem somewhat surprising. Because Edwards is part of the Calvinist Reformed tradition, and because he follows this tradition by emphasizing divine sovereignty, we might expect him to be more squarely aligned with the modern voluntarism that Schneewind associates with both Calvin and Hobbes rather than with a group of thinkers who opposed Calvin. But the Cambridge Platonists' writings were very important to the intellectual context that shaped Edwards. Their writings had a broad cultural influence on the latitudinarianism that represented the mainstream of Anglicanism and a significant impact on the development of philosophy in Britain. Locke[8] and Shaftesbury[9] read and responded to them extensively, and Edwards is known to have studied the Cambridge Platonists as well.[10] Moreover, if we consider carefully the common concerns of Edwards and the Cambridge Platonists, their similarities are not as surprising as we might initially think. Edwards shares the Cambridge Platonists' opposition to Hobbesian materialism[11] and their interest in engaging current philosophical texts. Additionally, the similarities among their positions reveal that Edwards and the Cambridge Platonists also share a philosophical framework for which the Neoplatonist concepts I have emphasized (that is, the idea that God is fundamentally goodness and virtue, and the belief that human virtue is constituted by a participation in divine virtue) are crucial in developing their challenges to materialism. We will see that both Edwards and the Cambridge Platonists turn to Neoplatonism as a means of defending God's essential goodness and love.

At the same time, Edwards's theological commitments lead him to reject some features of the Cambridge Platonist view of virtue, which makes his position intriguing. Schneewind suggests that thinkers who oppose voluntarism, such as the Cambridge Platonists, tend toward arguments that ultimately and inadvertently make God irrelevant to the moral enterprise.[12] Such thinkers defend God's inherent goodness by arguing that God is subject to the same moral standards of good and evil that oversee humanity. Although antivoluntarists generally affirm God's centrality for moral standards and pursuits by appeals to providence, an unintended consequence of their emphasis on God's subjection to moral law is that later thinkers can build on their ideas to argue that God is unnecessary for human morality.[13] Perhaps perceiving this risk, Edwards builds on promising elements of the Cambridge Platonists' view of virtue and augments them theologically. Edwards's continuity and discontinuity with Cambridge Platonism enables him to present a theologically coherent understanding of true virtue without resorting to the type of modern voluntarist arguments that Schneewind implies are the only alternatives for theologians who wish to speak of morality as an enterprise from which God is not functionally absent.

Edwards's most overt departures from the Cambridge Platonists are evident when we recognize that their concern with affirming God's accessibility and humans' natural capacities to act virtuously sometimes lead them toward claims that tend to undermine the particularity of Christian doctrine, and more specifically the Christian view that humans need grace in order to practice virtue. The element of their thought that most tends toward this problem is a rejection of the traditional Christian understanding of original sin; Edwards certainly departs from them in this respect, as I discuss in chapter 3. Many of the Cambridge Platonists' contemporaries were concerned that their rejection of original sin and their positive theological anthropology effectively created a moral system in which God was unnecessary, just as Schneewind suggests was a tendency in "antivoluntarist" positions. The Cambridge Platonists' successors, second-generation latitudinarians, were able to shift Cambridge Platonism fairly comfortably into a system of thought that was much less doctrinally explicit. Granted, in fairness to the Cambridge Platonists, it is by no means clear that they themselves were subject to this sort of critique: many scholars have effectively argued that they present a strong account of divine grace and divine love that distinguishes them from Neoplatonist predecessors[14] and that presumes some degree of Christian theological particularity.[15] While some scholars remain unsatisfied that the Cambridge Platonists themselves avoid the problems of minimizing the significance of Christian revelation and particularity,[16] it is understandable that Edwards drew from their thought, even as he simultaneously exercised caution with regard to those features of Cambridge Platonism that may be said to have contributed to the development of latitudinarianism.

Although Edwards shares the Cambridge Platonists' concern with upholding God's fundamental love and goodness, his use of Cambridge Platonist concepts is tempered by his concern with guarding against an overly optimistic view of human nature that would risk undermining the dependence of human moral practices upon God's grace. Edwards's most striking differences from the Cambridge Platonists are his Trinitarian theology and his view of original sin. Chapter 3 addresses original sin more fully in relation to human love, but Edwards's Trinitarian theology is central to understanding the divine virtue that is my focus in this chapter. In developing his account of God's moral goodness, Edwards augments the Cambridge Platonist understanding of God as love with a more robust Trinitarianism. This adaptation of Cambridge Platonist thought, in turn, allows Edwards to affirm key Christian theological commitments without resorting to Schneewind's modern voluntarism (an emphasis upon the workings of an unchecked divine will as constitutive of the moral order).

Divine Virtue in the Cambridge Platonists

The Cambridge Platonists' texts demonstrate their concern with affirming God's fundamental goodness, in opposition to tenets of atheism and of certain Calvinist positions (as the Cambridge Platonists perceived them). Ralph Cudworth maintains this characterization of God as inherently good, explicitly contrasting this idea to presuppositions of the modern voluntarists that Schneewind identifies, in his 1647 "Sermon Preached Before the House of Commons":

> Now, I say, the very proper Character, and Essentiall Tincture of God himself, is nothing else but *Goodnesse*. Nay, I may be bold to adde, That God is therefore God, because he is the highest and most perfect Good: and Good is not therefore Good, because God out of an arbitrary will of his, would have it so. Whatsoever God doth in the World, he doth it as it is suitable to the highest Goodnesse; the first Idea, and fairest Copy of which is his own Essence.[17]

Cudworth echoes this claim later in his sermon, affirming that "God which is infinite Goodnesse, cannot but hate sinne, which is purely Evil."[18] These affirmations highlight the Cambridge Platonists' understanding of God as both equivalent to goodness and, correlatively, as not acting according to the measure of an unchecked will.

Like Cudworth, John Smith emphasizes God's goodness in the context of a challenge to voluntarism. In contending that God is essentially and eternally good, Smith develops and defends an argument that God judges all things by his own eternal goodness, rather than by the workings of an arbitrary will:

> But God when he gives his Laws to men, does not by virtue of his *Absolute dominion* dictate any thing at randome, and in such an arbitrarious way as some imagine; but he measures all by his own Eternal Goodness. Had God himself been any thing else than the *First and Greatest Good* of man, then to have loved him with the full strength of all our Faculties should not have been *the First and Greatest Commandment*. . . . God's *Unchangeable Goodness* . . . is also *the Unchangeable Rule of his Will*. . . . Nor does he charge any Duty upon man without consulting first of all with his *Goodness*.[19]

Thus Smith, like Cudworth, affirms God's goodness specifically in conjunction with resisting voluntarism. These passages reveal that the Cambridge Platonists were primarily concerned to uphold God's goodness and saw the rejection of a particular view of God's will as a necessary corollary to this position.

Yet, significantly, the Cambridge Platonists' method of defending God's goodness is not simply to speak in terms of God as overflowing good, but as love. This emphasis differentiates them not only from "classical Protestantism," which stresses God's justice,[20] but also from the general position of philosophical Neoplatonists.[21] Patrides affirms that "the burden of [the Cambridge Platonists'] emphasis was constantly on the principle that God is Love,"[22] and his interpretation is well supported by the Cambridge Platonists' works. For example, Cudworth maintains that God's love is a ray of God's goodness and holiness that we can see reflected in our own hearts. God practices eternal love within the Trinity and directs it toward creatures: "God from all eternity hath loved us." Later in this sermon, Cudworth praises "Divine Love" for all that it accomplishes between God and humanity and among humans as well.[23] Smith likewise presents love as the first of the divine virtues, and a virtue through which we may come to resemble God.[24] He also identifies love with God indirectly by presenting "universal love" as the supreme path through which we may enter God's life.[25] More, too, presents love as particular to God's essence; when the soul participates in a "divine motion," imitating God, this motion is "Love or Goodwill to all Mankind."[26] Divine love is central to Cambridge Platonist teaching on the nature of God's being.

The Cambridge Platonists' affirmation that God is love is not merely a linguistic departure from classical Neoplatonist positions; instead, it is a departure with significant consequences for how God is understood. Neoplatonist philosophy tends to characterize God in terms of an overflowing goodness, which implies that God is so good that this goodness cannot be controlled and shared intentionally. According to this sort of position, God's own nature *compels* God to communicate goodness. But in saying that God is love, the Cambridge Platonists invoke the idea that God acts intentionally, because love is a volitional and willful force.[27] As love, rather than simply as goodness, God can choose to exercise and direct this love in specific ways, both among members of the Trinity and toward creatures. The Cambridge Platonists therefore adapt Neoplatonist claims to affirm that God willfully and intentionally shares the divine nature by exercising virtue toward creatures.

Edwards's Divine Virtue: Trinitarian Love and the Subversion of Modern Voluntarism

Both Edwards's continuity with the Cambridge Platonists and his explicit and implicit departures from their arguments are instructive for understanding his account of divine virtue. Edwards's view of virtuous love as constitutive of God's being builds on Neoplatonism, much as the Cambridge Platonists do, but Edwards develops these arguments in connection with a retrieval of the early Christian understanding of divine love as the person of the Holy Spirit. This development is important for two reasons: first, it functions as a means through which Edwards ensures the Christian particularity of his view of true virtue; second, it establishes a stronger and more explicit connection between virtue and the divine will than is present in the Cambridge Platonists, a connection that has the capacity to subvert features of modern voluntarism. Edwards was concerned to uphold a vision of God that departs less fully from that of Calvin than the Cambridge Platonists' does. George Marsden describes divine sovereignty as the central principle of Edwards's thought and more generally notes various moments in Edwards's life when Edwards was distressed by the undermining of Calvinist orthodoxy.[28] Yet rather than affirming the sovereignty of God's will in a manner that isolates the divine will from divine goodness, Edwards's view of virtue reestablishes an essential link between God's will and God's goodness, and thereby transcends the types of voluntarist and "antivoluntarist" arguments that Schneewind suggests are inevitable in modern moral theology.

In order to understand how Edwards builds upon and theologically enriches the Cambridge Platonists' thought to develop this position, it is useful to begin by noting his arguments regarding God's goodness that seem most clearly consistent with Neoplatonism. One of Edwards's more extended Neoplatonist characterizations of the divine nature takes place in his early sermon "God's Excellencies." This sermon's account of God's perfections employs a logic that is quite consistent with traditional Neoplatonist and Christian Platonist arguments. Edwards begins by affirming that God is greater and more excellent than all created beings. God's excellence, goodness, and holiness are infinite.[29] Any good qualities in creatures come from God, and God must therefore be said to possess them in a more complete sense than creatures do. This insight leads Edwards to conclude that God's very essence is the holiness and beauty whence these excellences spring. Edwards suggests both that God possesses and practices virtues in a more perfect sense than that in which any creature may aspire to practice them, and that God's infinite practice of these excellences serves as a basis for recognizing God's nature as beauty itself. Edwards affirms that because God is the source of all the excellences and perfections of creation, he must contain them in an infinite degree: "All other excellencies proceed from him as the fountain . . . he has made all things that are excellent, and therefore must have given them their excellency and so must have all that excellency in himself, or else could not have given it. . . . He must have all the glories, perfections, and beauties of the whole creation in himself to an infinite degree, for they all proceed from him . . . and [he] is as much more excellent than they all, as the whole sun is than one single ray."[30] The perfections of creation, for Edwards, are infinitely present in God's being.

God's infinite possession of these perfections, in turn, leads Edwards to affirm beauty and goodness as inherent in divine being. After explaining that God possesses excellences in an infinite degree, Edwards proclaims that "God's is an infinite excellency, infinite glory, and beauty itself." Moreover, not only is God's being equivalent to beauty, but it is also equivalent to the category of "excellency," or goodness, itself: "he [God] is an infinite, eternal, and immutable excellency." Edwards concludes this passage by maintaining both that God possesses all earthly excellences in an infinite degree and that the quality of "excellency" is constitutive of his being: "he is not only an infinitely excellent being, but a being that is infinite excellency, beauty, and loveliness."[31] God, for Edwards, is beauty and excellence, and these qualities give him an inherent "loveliness" such that it is fitting for creatures to affirm God's goodness and to love God.

This Neoplatonist characterization of God in "God's Excellencies" is not an isolated phenomenon in Edwards's writings. An examination of Edwards's broader corpus demonstrates that he frequently characterizes God in terms that emphasize the infinite and overflowing nature of divine goodness. Edwards describes God as "the sum of all good" in his sermon "God Amongst His People" and as "an infinite fountain of good" in both his sermon "The Terms of Prayer" and his treatise *The Life of David Brainerd*.[32] This sort of description of God's nature is even more prominent in *The End for Which God Created the World*. In this work, Edwards affirms that God is "the original good, and the fountain of all good," and that God is in some sense constituted by the emanation or communication of his "fullness of good" to the world.[33] God has a "general disposition to communicate good." Though Edwards argues that this emanation is not such that God can be said to depend upon creatures or the created world, the emanation of good is nevertheless important to his account of who God is: "God looks on the communication of himself, and the emanation of the infinite glory and good that are in himself to belong to the fullness and completeness of himself, as though he were not in his most complete and glorious state without it."[34] In both sermons and treatises, then, Edwards appeals to these Neoplatonist images of God as overflowing goodness.

At the same time, like the Cambridge Platonists, Edwards qualifies these characterizations of God's goodness in a manner that guards against a theological concern that God is unable to direct or control this overflow intentionally. Paul Ramsey and William Spohn maintain, in different ways, that Edwards's somewhat Neoplatonist accounts of divine goodness and beauty are tempered by his affirmation that God is love, just as the Cambridge Platonists' affirmation that God is love ensures that they do not portray God simply as overflowing good. Spohn argues that love to God is foundational to Edwards's ethics and that Edwards's account of divine beauty must be interpreted in connection with this affirmation. Spohn ultimately concludes that Edwards's divine beauty is best understood as the beauty of the consenting love practiced among members of the Trinity.[35] Paul Ramsey similarly presents love as the foundation of Edwards's morality, so much so that all earthly beauties are inferior to truly Christian love and holiness; this argument is based in his recognition that Edwards conceives God's being most centrally in terms of love.[36] Edwards thus echoes the Cambridge Platonists not only in his essentially Neoplatonist descriptions of God's goodness and virtue but also in his characterization of God in a manner that guards against conceptions of God's goodness as overflowing without direction.

Yet, unlike the Cambridge Platonists, Edwards does not stop with this affirmation but instead further distinguishes his position from pure Neoplatonism by describing divine love in connection to the doctrine of the Trinity. Stephen Holmes contends that it is Edwards's Trinitarianism, first and foremost, that protects his writings from contemporary suggestions that Edwards presents creation in Neoplatonist terms. God is other than creation, and creation can be said to depend upon God, precisely because God is triune.[37] Holmes's insight is important, and indeed Edwards's Trinitarian emphases distinguish him not only from Neoplatonism but also from Cambridge Platonism. Through his Trinitarian theology, Edwards draws a necessary connection between God's will and God's essential goodness that subverts modern voluntarism more effectively than Cambridge Platonist thought is ultimately able to do. The key to understanding the importance of Edwards's Trinitarian thought for this historical accomplishment lies in the connection that Edwards draws between love and the Holy Spirit. Edwards explicitly connects God's will to God's love. His Trinitarian theology identifies the Holy Spirit as love itself, which necessarily ensures that both God's will and God's activity are intrinsically loving. Consequently, salvation, and the enabling of true virtue, are products of God's will, but the activities of God's will are formed and dictated by love and goodness. God operates through the activity of his will, but this divine will is necessarily and inherently loving.

In recent years, scholars have increasingly recognized both the strong place of love in Edwards's Trinitarian thought and the particular relationship between love, or true virtue, and the Holy Spirit. Amy Plantinga Pauw's *The Supreme Harmony of All: The Trinitarian Theology of Jonathan Edwards* affirms the centrality of love for Edwards in an attempt to complement readings of Edwards that see him as celebrating God's power. Pauw argues that previous scholars have recognized Edwards's emphasis upon love but less frequently connect this love inextricably to the Holy Spirit.[38] Yet this inseparable connection is precisely what Pauw upholds as crucial to a proper interpretation of Edwards. Edwards's writings underscore Pauw's contention that Edwards associates love with the person of the Holy Spirit. In *Charity and Its Fruits* Edwards affirms, "The nature of the Holy Spirit is love," and he identifies the Holy Spirit as God's infinite love in *Discourse on the Trinity*.[39]

Building on this connection between love and the Holy Spirit, Pauw goes so far as to suggest that through his Trinitarian theology, Edwards develops an account of love as "the primary divine attribute."[40] She argues that Edwards gives love and wisdom (or understanding) a distinct place among all the qualities of God, affirming a type of union between love and God's very being. Whereas many of his Scholastic and Puritan predecessors aligned God's being with all of God's perfections,[41] Edwards reserved this alignment only for understanding and love.[42] According to Pauw, this point is significant because Edwards aligns perfections with God's being only when a given perfection can be seen as in a sense equivalent to a member of the Trinity. Edwards explicitly rejects the idea that God's being is equivalent to all of his perfections and, in doing so, "self-consciously departed from" the notion that God's attributes are aligned with his moral excellences. Edwards does allow, nonetheless, for an alignment between understanding, love, and God's being on the grounds that love and understanding are distinct persons of the Trinity; love is the person of the Holy Spirit, and divine understanding is the Son.[43] This argument indicates that attributes such as love hold a special place within Edwards's doctrine of God because they are connected specifically to the essence of a member of the Trinity. As equivalent to the person of the Holy Spirit, love is constitutive of the divine being in a way that exceeds the constitutive nature of many of God's other moral perfections.

This feature of Edwards's doctrine of God has important consequences for how we consider Edwards's position historically in relation to modern voluntarism. There are two related ways in which Edwards's connection between love and the Holy Spirit ensures that his view of human virtue offers a striking alternative to both Hobbesian and Calvinist voluntarism while simultaneously upholding the particulars of Christian theology. First, whereas Schneewind sees both of these forms of voluntarism as presuming a divine will that acts arbitrarily, Edwards's view of divine love suggests that God's being is loving by nature, or intrinsically loving. For Edwards, the affirmation that God is love provides the foundation for understanding God's triune nature. Because these two components of Edwards's theology are intrinsically linked, love is a quality that Edwards attributes to the divine in God's very essence. Love is an eternal state of the divine being; the Godhead subsists in love.[44] This eternal state of love is possible because God's "essence" is "love."[45] Moreover, as Pauw notes, in saying that God's essence is love, Edwards makes a claim specifically about the Holy Spirit. In *The Distinguishing Marks of a Work of the Spirit of God*, Edwards affirms, "Love is that wherein the very nature of the Holy Spirit consists."[46] Edwards's identification of love with the Holy Spirit is important because it shows that for Edwards, God is loving by nature, and specifically God's will (the faculty of the Holy Spirit) is love itself. Through connecting love to the person of the Holy Spirit, then, Edwards presents an account of the divine will not simply as a "will" with the power to operate as it wishes but as a loving will, a will that by its nature operates in love.

A second consequence of the connection Edwards draws between love and the Holy Spirit is that a view of the Holy Spirit as love ensures that God's activity, in addition to God's will, is intrinsically and necessarily loving. The Holy Spirit is not simply divine will; it is also more specifically the impetus of divine acts, and these acts must necessarily be acts of love. Edwards's Trinitarian works describe the Holy Spirit in a manner that emphasizes the dynamism and activity of God's love as it is exercised both among the members of the Trinity and toward the world. These works characterize the Holy Spirit as the active bond of love existing between the Father and the Son and directed from the Trinity to the world: the love of God flowing forth *ad extra* is the Holy Spirit, as is the love of God poured into our hearts.[47] Reiterating these claims, *Charity and Its Fruits* makes the connection between divine love and divine act even more explicit. Edwards affirms a type of equivalence between divine love and divine act so that divine acts *ad intra* and *ad extra* are loving by nature:

> The infinite essential love of God is, as it were, an infinite and eternal mutual holy energy between the Father and the Son, a pure, holy act whereby the Deity becomes nothing but an infinite and unchangeable act of love, which proceeds from both the Father and the Son. Thus divine love has its seat in the Deity as it is exercised within the Deity, or in God towards himself. . . . [Moreover, divine love does not] remain in such exercises [between Father and Son] only, but it flows out in innumerable streams towards all the created inhabitants of heaven; he loves all the angels and saints there.[48]

In connecting love to the person of the Holy Spirit, Edwards emphasizes the ways in which love is constitutive not only of the person of God but also of God's activity.

To be sure, Edwards's focus on love is not always as evident in his writings as I am suggesting. Edwards does write in a Puritan context and is concerned to uphold Calvinist orthodoxy, and there are moments when his depiction of God's nature seems less clearly loving. This is particularly true with regard to his understanding of the situation of the reprobate. Michael McClymond argues that Edwards offers no way of ensuring that God's will lacks partiality in the distribution of salvific grace. For McClymond, Edwards's God is not fully ethical by the standards of British moral philosophers: because the practice of true virtue is connected to divine election, Edwards's God is ultimately partial, bestowing grace on some and withholding it from others.[49]

To some degree, this image of God would appear to represent a type of voluntarism, albeit a voluntarism different from the modern positions that Schneewind describes. For Edwards, God's will does not dictate the content of morality, but it decrees who may practice virtue, and there are moments when Edwards characterizes the distribution of grace as arbitrary: God's "grace is a sovereign thing, exercised according to the good pleasure of God."[50] Several of his sermons follow the traditional Reformed practice of associating God's damnation of the reprobate with God's justice rather than God's love. Perhaps the clearest example of this demarcation occurs in his 1728 sermon "The Torments of Hell Are Exceeding Great." This text suggests that God's redemption of the elect demonstrates God's love, while the unhappiness of the reprobate reveals God's just anger: the salvation of the elect glorifies God's "mercy and love," and the damnation of the reprobate glorifies God's "jealousy and justice."[51] Justice is important to Edwards's soteriology; the central thesis of his 1735 sermon "The Justice of God in the Damnation of Sinners" is "'Tis just with God eternally to cast off, and destroy sinners."[52] Edwards cannot always be said to prioritize God's love as the exclusive constitutive feature of his essence.

At the same time, some elements of Edwards's writings suggest that he actively desires to reconcile his understanding of the damnation of the reprobate with his understanding of God as love, underscoring Pauw's suggestion that love has a sort of constitutive ontological priority in Edwards's understanding of divine being. For example, in some of his sermons, Edwards argues both that the reprobate are offered mercy and that mercy is more natural to God than condemnation. In "The Justice of God in the Damnation of Sinners," Edwards defends God's justice in damning the reprobate through an argument that suggests that the reprobate have been recipients of God's mercy. It is not that God's love is exclusively reserved for the elect, but the reprobate, too, receive it. The difference lies in their response:

> Why should God be looked upon as obliged to bestow salvation upon you, when you have been so ungrateful for the mercies he has bestowed upon

you already? God has tried you with a great deal of kindness, and he never has sincerely been thanked by you for any of it. God has watched over you, and preserved you, and provided for you, and followed you with mercy all your days, and yet you have continued sinning against him. . . . God notwithstanding this ingratitude, has still continued his mercy; but his kindness has never won your heart. . . . God has kept you out of hell, and continued your day of grace, and the offers of salvation, this so long a time; and that, it may be, while you did not regard your own salvation so much as to go in secret and ask God for it. . . . As God has multiplied mercies, so have you multiplied provocations.[53]

The idea that God acts with love toward the reprobate is also present in Edwards's 1727 sermon (preached again in 1756) "Impending Judgments Averted Only by Reformation." Edwards here contends that God's mercy is made evident through his regular practice of giving people an opportunity to reform before passing judgment on them. God shows justice in punishing sinners,[54] but Edwards goes so far as to affirm that God *prefers* to show mercy, when he can do so without being unjust, because mercy is more proper to God's nature than justice:

> God has no pleasure in the destruction or calamity of persons or people; he had rather they should turn and continue in peace. He is well-pleased if they forsake their evil ways, that he may not have occasion to execute his wrath upon 'em. He is a God that delights in mercy, and judgment is his strange work. . . . God don't usually give up a people to dreadful judgments except they are irreclaimable; though they have grievously sinned, yet he is ready upon repentance to forgive. If calls and warnings and threatenings, or corrections, will reclaim them, he is ready to pardon and will turn away from his fierce anger.[55]

This passage suggests that mercy comes more readily to God than damnation and destruction because mercy is more proper to God's being. While God's love is best revealed in the act of saving the elect, then, a closer look at Edwards's soteriology indicates that love is so central to Edwards's view of God's voluntary activity that Edwards contends that even the reprobate receive God's love. Edwards demonstrates his concern to affirm love as a constitutive attribute of God by revisiting the theme of divine love with regard to the breadth of God's activity, even though he may not do so to a degree that fully satisfies contemporary readers.

A similar argument is at work in Edwards's *Miscellany 704*, which further indicates Edwards's wish to present God's activity (even his condemnation of the reprobate) as consistent with his love. Oliver Crisp suggests that Edwards presents God, in *End* and in some of the *Miscellanies*, as eternally decreeing election, but as decreeing reprobation only after the Fall. Crisp contends that Edwards avoids drawing "Arminian conclusions" from this argument; Edwards is adamant that God's decision to condemn the reprobate does not *depend* on creatures' sinful actions, although it is consequent on them.[56] In support of Crisp's point, *Miscellany 704* does indeed affirm that God's decision to damn the reprobate for the sake of justice is not coeternal with his plan to glorify and communicate his love:

> God's decree to glorify his love and communicate his goodness, and to glorify his greatness and holiness, is to be considered as prior to the creation and fall of man . . . the designing to communicate and glorify his goodness and love eternally to a certain number, is to be considered as prior in both those mentioned respects—to their being and fall—for such a design in the notion of it presupposes neither. But nothing in the decree of reprobation is to be looked upon as antecedent in one of those respects to man's being and fall, but only that general decree that God will glorify his justice, or rather his holiness and greatness, which supposes neither their being nor sinfulness.[57]

Damnation, then, is not part of the eternal plan of Edwards's God. Had creatures not sinned, God presumably would have found other ways of glorifying his holiness and justice.

Furthermore, Edwards speaks of God as "permitting" sin. Although Crisp argues that his emphasis on divine sovereignty suggests that we should read this term in Edwards as akin to the more volitional term "ordain" and consequently contends that Edwards has difficulty in avoiding presenting God as the author of sin,[58] Edwards nonetheless chooses the term "permission" in explaining how Adam's sin came to be. In *Original Sin*, he allows that the specifics of God's activity are a "mystery" and that Christians may well have difficulty in reconciling God's permitting of sin with God's "holiness and righteousness." Nonetheless, Edwards assures his readers that "God has no hand in [Adam's sin], any otherwise, than in not exerting such an influence, as might be effectual to prevent it."[59]

This passage seems to challenge Crisp's argument; Edwards suggests that God caused Adam's sin only in choosing *not* to intervene through grace to prevent the sin's occurrence. Crisp's critique may indicate that Edwards is unable to resolve the logic of this position perfectly with his overall emphasis upon divine sovereignty, but it is nevertheless the case that Edwards does describe God's activity with regard to Adam's sin in terms of permission. These texts indicate that Edwards desires to affirm both that God, prior to sin, did not require the damnation of some of his creatures, and that God did not cause sin. God's reasons for not saving all persons remain a "mystery" in Edwards's terms, but at the very least it seems clear that Edwards gives priority to a conception of God's being and activity as necessarily loving.

Edwards's God, then, is a loving God, and Edwards prioritizes this love both in his account of divine salvific activity and in his account of the Holy Spirit's role in divine virtue. Edwards's depiction of the virtue of love, in turn, gives rise to a particular view of moral agency that is instructive for this study. Just as the human virtues respond to and participate in God's love, so does their practice image God's own practice of virtue, which is simultaneously necessary and volitional.

Necessity and Intention in Edwards's Account of Divine Freedom as an Alternative Picture of Moral Agency

In Edwards's view of divine virtue, we see the beginnings of a virtue theory that conceives moral agency in an apparently paradoxical manner. On one hand, Edwards presents virtue in God as *necessary*: love is so constitutive of God's being that Edwards's God cannot act in an unloving manner. On the other hand, Edwards presents God's virtue as *intentional*. God's goodness is not merely an unwieldy and uncontrollable amalgam; instead, it is a love that God actively directs and embraces. Edwards underscores the active nature of God's love by aligning this love with the Holy Spirit, so that God's love is one with God's will.

Edwards's emphasis upon divine intention may appear at cross purposes with his suggestion that goodness and love are necessary to God's being. But I will ultimately argue that Edwards offers a view of moral accountability that allows for *both* necessity *and* intention, and that this understanding of accountability can enrich contemporary virtue ethics. For Edwards, moral accountability does not require a freedom that allows an agent to choose actions neutrally. Edwards presents divine moral agency as an archetype for human moral agency, and it is therefore important to discuss his view of divine freedom prior to considering human moral agency in subsequent chapters.

Edwards's *Freedom of the Will* offers insight into this position that God is fully intentional even as God is, in some sense, constrained by his own nature. In keeping with many Christian thinkers, Edwards maintains that God is incapable of doing evil but that God is nonetheless free. A proper view of freedom, derived from this understanding of God's nature, acknowledges that there is a type of "necessity" in God's moral activity that does not contradict true freedom. For Edwards, it is both necessary and meritorious that God acts consistently with God's dispositions and character. Indeed, God's virtue requires this type of necessity.[60] Edwards explains that God's will acts freely, but this freedom is not a "liberty of indifference" *precisely because* this "liberty of indifference" would run counter to God's virtue. In arguing against the Arminian claim that necessity undermines an agent's moral merit or demerit, Edwards argues that God is meritorious even though he is subject to a type of necessity. Edwards affirms that God is morally praiseworthy even as he is necessarily virtuous:

> The infinitely holy God, who always used to be esteemed by God's people not only virtuous, but a Being in whom is all possible virtue, and every virtue in the most absolute purity and perfection . . . I say, this Being, according to this notion of Dr Whitby, and other Arminians, has no virtue at all: virtue, when ascribed to him, is but an empty name; and he is deserving of no commendation or praise; because he is under necessity, he cannot avoid being holy and good as he is.[61]

Edwards is careful to explain that God's virtue is not "rewardable" *only* because he is incapable of benefiting from creatures or being rewarded by them: God "is infinitely above all capacity of receiving any reward or benefit from the creature." Though not "rewardable" in this sense, God's moral excellence nevertheless deserves human praise and thankfulness, *even though* excellence is a necessary part of God's nature.[62] Underscoring this point, Edwards argues that the acts of the incarnate Christ's human soul were necessarily holy but are still truly virtuous and commendable:

> How strange would it be to hear any Christian assert, that the holy and excellent temper and behavior of Jesus Christ, and that obedience which

he performed under such great trials, was not virtuous or praiseworthy, because his will was not free *ad utrumque*, to either holiness or sin, but was unalterably determined to one . . . that Christ was worthy of nothing at all on account of them [i.e., his virtues], worthy of no reward, no praise, no honour or respect from God or man, because his will was not indifferent.[63]

The concept of God's will that Edwards presumes and defends in this treatise, then, is that of a will that is simultaneously constrained and free.

Virtue, for Edwards, requires that an agent's actions are simultaneously free and consistent with her dispositions. This combination of necessity and intention is important to Edwards's characterization of God as moral agent. And as we proceed with our discussion of the human virtues, we will see that these virtues presume a model of moral agency consistent with Edwards's view of God's moral activity. Human actions are constrained in particular ways, but humans are nonetheless moral agents who can legitimately be held accountable for their actions. Necessity and intention are logically consistent in Edwards's view of moral accountability, and this consistency arises because of the strong parallels between the human virtues and divine virtue in Edwards's thought.

3

Charity as a Human Virtue
The Moral Accountability of a Necessary Nature

It is appropriate for a discussion of Edwards's human virtues to begin with "true virtue," or Christian love. Edwards prioritizes this virtue above the others and conceives it as mirroring and participating in the divine virtue that was the subject of the previous chapter. Edwards's characterization of true virtue as a reflection of God's perfections underscores the continuity of his thought with the Christian Platonist tradition, and with many ideas particular to the Cambridge Platonists. Reading Edwards alongside the Cambridge Platonists provides a foundation for recognizing ways in which Edwards's position gives rise to a model of moral accountability in humans that reflects and echoes the agency at work in the divine nature.

In developing these claims, this chapter first summarizes Edwards's view of "true virtue" or charity and then demonstrates how a comparison between Edwards and the Cambridge Platonists is instructive for recognizing its intellectual context. As with divine virtue, Edwards's account of human virtue draws heavily from the Cambridge Platonists but guards against possible theological pitfalls in their positions by coupling Neoplatonist arguments with a robust conception of original sin. I conclude by returning to the issue of moral accountability addressed in chapter 2. I recognize some of the possible challenges for recovering Edwards's view of moral responsibility and begin to develop an argument on behalf of the merits of his view.

Charity in Edwards

Because the nuances of Edwards's understanding of human love are complex, it is helpful to provide an overview of the "true virtue" or charity that is this chapter's focus before situating Edwards's understanding of charity in relation to the Cambridge Platonist movement. In *The Nature of True Virtue*, Edwards affirms that the Christian scriptures see love as central to virtue: "It is abundantly plain by the Holy Scriptures, and generally allowed not only by Christian divines but by the more considerable Deists, that virtue most essentially consists in love."[1] Consequently, he defines true virtue in terms of love or benevolence. He further distinguishes this truly virtuous benevolence from other loves—loves that are not fully of the nature of true virtue—and for this reason I will speak of Edwards's true virtue as "virtuous benevolence," "truly virtuous love," or "charity" to distinguish it from the human loves that chapter 6 addresses. For Edwards, charity differs from other loves primarily in terms of its object: whereas most natural human loves are directed toward particular individuals in particular relationships with us, the object of truly virtuous love is "universal existence" (8:541) or "Being, simply considered" (8:545). We exercise true virtue or charity when we love "Being in general" and give our "consent and good will" to the system of universal existence (8:540–41). Charity leads us to seek the good of the universe and of the particular beings within it: "The *first* object of a virtuous benevolence is *Being*, simply considered: and if Being, *simply* considered, be its object, then Being *in general* is its object; and the thing it has an ultimate propensity to, is the *highest good* of Being in general. And it will seek the good of every *individual* being unless it be conceived as not consistent with the highest good of Being in general" (8:545). Our benevolence for the universe as a whole will therefore lead us to love beings within it, and to do so in a manner consistent with their existence in the universe.

Having suggested that the distinctiveness of true virtue lies in its object, Edwards goes on to explain that true virtue in both God and humans is, first and foremost, love to God. True virtue will be exercised in a manner proportionate to the existence and goodness of its object, and God is the being with the greatest existence and the greatest degree of love and goodness. Edwards explains that God, as the being of greatest existence and greatest moral excellence, will logically be the primary object of benevolence:

> From what has been said, 'tis evident that true virtue must chiefly consist in love to God; the Being of beings, infinitely the greatest and best of beings. This appears, whether we consider the primary or secondary ground of virtuous love [that is, whether we consider "being" or "goodness"]. It was observed that the *first* objective ground of that love, wherein

true virtue consists, is Being, simply considered: and as a necessary consequence of this, that being who has the most of being, or the greatest share of universal existence, has proportionably the greatest share of virtuous benevolence. . . . But God has infinitely the greatest share of existence, or is infinitely the greatest being. So that all other being, even that of all created things whatsoever, throughout the whole universe, is as nothing in comparison of the Divine Being. And if we consider the *secondary* ground of love, viz. beauty or moral excellency, the same thing will appear. For as God is infinitely the greatest being, so he is allowed to be infinitely the most beautiful and excellent. (8:550–51)

After establishing that true virtue lies chiefly in love to God, Edwards goes one step further and contends that no benevolence can be considered truly virtuous if it is disconnected from this love to God.[2] We may exercise love toward other objects and beings, but if we do not make these affections "subordinate" to our "supreme regard to God," these loves will tend to oppose loving God and to set themselves up as idols: independently of love to God, a natural human love "exalts its private object above the other great and infinite object" and thereby "puts down Being in general" (8:556). True virtue or charity is not *opposed* to the love of particular beings; indeed, it gives rise to these particular loves. But in order for a human love to be classified as true virtue or charity, it must have God and the world God created as its "*direct* and *immediate* object" (8:541).

Edwards's defense of charity as love to God is noteworthy not only because it distinguishes charity from other human loves but also because it further reiterates the parallel relation between Edwards's divine virtue and his view of true virtue in humans. Edwards defines and explains true virtue in humans through considering God's virtue. Human charity is love to God because divine love is fundamentally love to Godself. True virtue in both God and humans is a universal love exercised in a manner proportionate to the existence and virtue in its object, and it is therefore appropriate for God to be the primary object of both divine and human virtuous love: "From hence also it is evident that the *divine virtue*, or the virtue of the divine mind, must consist primarily in *love to himself*, or in the mutual love and friendship which subsists eternally and necessarily between the several persons in the Godhead, or that infinitely strong propensity there is in these divine persons one to another" (8:557). In God, this divine self-love gives rise to God's love of his own creatures: "Virtue in its most essential nature, consists in benevolent affection or propensity of heart toward Being in general; and so flowing out to particular beings, in a greater or lesser degree, according to the measure of existence and beauty which they are possessed of. It will also follow from the foregoing things that God's goodness and love to created beings is derived from and subordinate to his love to himself" (8:557). God exercises true virtue supremely; his love to himself serves as the foundation for his love to creation.

Human charity, Edwards then explains, should aspire to image God's exercise of this virtue. "The most proper evidence" that we are practicing love in a manner consistent with true virtue lies in the degree to which our loves coincide with God's. We measure our own charity by considering "the coincidence of the exercises of our love, in their manner, order, and measure, with the *manner* in which *God* himself exercises love to the creature in the creation and government of the world, and the way in which God as the first cause and supreme disposer of all things, has respect to the creature's happiness, in subordination to himself as his own supreme end" (8:558). Just as virtue in God consists in a disposition to love God that gives rise to a disposition to love creatures, so it is the case that for humans, "a virtuous love in *created* beings, *one to another*, is dependent on, and derived from love to *God*" (8:557). We need not be "*sensibly*" aware, at each moment we practice true virtue, that love to God is the disposition that motivates us (8:558), but human love nevertheless images God's love. For Edwards, then, charity is fundamentally a love to God that gives rise to love to creatures, and Edwards's development of this argument shows the continuity between true virtue in God and human charity.

Human Virtue in the Cambridge Platonists

Because human charity is an image of divine charity, it is not surprising that the philosophical paradigms important for understanding Edwards's account of divine virtue are also at work in his account of truly virtuous human love. It is instructive to situate Edwards's charity in relation to the Cambridge Platonists' understanding of virtuous love in humans. Edwards embraces certain features of the Cambridge Platonists' view of human love and enhances them theologically, just as he does with the Cambridge Platonist understanding of divine virtue.

The Cambridge Platonists tend to portray humans as able to pursue virtue because we are constructed to be able to know and do the good. Whichcote's "The Use of Reason in Matters of Religion" suggests that all humans possess an "inner light," or the "light of our reason," which guides us in ethical behavior and judgment. Reason and nature are the measures of virtue and vice;[3] therefore, when we do not seek virtue we are going against our very being. Sin does not run counter simply to God's commands in scripture but also to our inner light.[4] The faculty that Whichcote sometimes describes as a conscience, coupled with feelings of happiness and unhappiness, can guide us in knowing virtue, because when we sin we are made unhappy. This unhappiness lies in a recognition that we are participating in activity that goes against our nature: "There is a secret Harmony in the Soul, with the Rule of Righteousness; there is no Displacency, Offence, or Reluctancy: And there is an Antipathy arising at the Appearance of Evil, as unnatural to it: But a Complacency in Good, as the eldest and first Acquaintance."[5] Indeed, in developing his account of the connection between virtue and happiness, Whichcote goes so far as to suggest that heaven and hell begin on earth and are experiences tied to the human conscience; sin produces in us a type of remorse that places us in hell.[6] Partly because of the association between virtue and happiness, reason and the conscience, in all humans, are able to know what virtue is.[7] Our created natures therefore ensure that we may know how to pursue virtue and avoid sin, and the link between virtue and happiness provides motivation to act virtuously. There is a congruence between virtue and our "inner light" of human reason.

Edwards echoes some of the Cambridge Platonists' positive claims about human nature, particularly insofar as these claims relate to the question of how we know moral truths (as opposed to how we perform moral actions). Edwards builds upon Cambridge Platonist thought to develop an account of true virtue as a means through which humans are able to pursue and fulfill the ends for which they were created. By drawing from Cambridge Platonist emphases, Edwards is able to offer a view of virtue that is rooted in God's being but that simultaneously gives a significant place to the doctrine of creation such that Edwards, like the Cambridge Platonists, believes that a virtuous life brings about happiness. Many of the Cambridge Platonists, however, move from this positive theological anthropology to a corollary claim that Edwards explicitly rejects, the suggestion that we may have natural capacities to *do* what is good.[8]

The Cambridge Platonist view of human sin runs counter to the traditional Calvinist (and Augustinian) view of original sin, and is representative of a strand of thinking more broadly consistent with tendencies in Anglicanism in Edwards's time, as well as with the positions of Scottish moderates such as Francis Hutcheson and Joseph Butler. Whichcote developed a conception of sin as "reversible," a view that stands in contrast to a conception of original sin as a condition from which persons are unable to escape. Such an idea does not necessarily undermine orthodox Christian thinking, for it is in some sense simply a positive statement about the power of Christ's redemption; Christ's obedience is part of what makes sin reversible.[9] After we have been regenerated, Whichcote suggests, we no longer can be said to "sin," even if we have shortcomings: "Neither are the Infirmities of the Regenerate, call'd *Sin*: Tho' these are Sins that requires God's Forgiveness, and are a true Cause for us to be Humble, and Modest, and to depend upon God: But they do not . . . denominate a Person *a Sinner*. The Scripture tells us. That *those that are born of God do not commit Sin*; that is, in this Sence; no one that is regenerate, doth pass into the contrary Nature: It is unnatural."[10]

Alongside this sort of claim, however, Whichcote frequently presents the reversibility of sin as a claim about the power of the human person to overcome leanings toward sin through personal introspection. Building on the idea that humanity has an innate tendency toward goodness, Whichcote suggests that humans can develop a rational awareness of the wisdom in practicing love universally; this capacity is based in our possession of the candle of the Lord.[11] This point is implied in "The Use of Reason in Matters of Religion," when Whichcote suggests that sin is something we willfully choose rather than something we inherit. Here he acknowledges the existence of "habituated sinners" but suggests that these are persons who choose to sin: "Therefore *Vertue*, in every kind, is according to the Sense of Humane Nature, the Dictates of Reason and Understanding, and the Sense of Man's Mind. And *Vice*, in every kind, is grievous, monstrous, and unnatural. A Man forces himself, when he is vicious; and a Man kindly uses himself, when he acts according to the Rules of Vertue. And this is so true, that all but those that have abused themselves, all but habituated Sinners, understand that *Vertue is conservative to the Nature of Man*."[12] Whichcote here indicates that our natures can know and recognize the benefits of virtue. Virtue is "natural" to us, and there is not an "original sin" as such that clouds our knowledge. This point is emphasized by his use of the word "habituated" to describe sinners; we become sinners by performing sin habitually rather than by being born into it.

Edwards is known to have been particularly familiar with Henry More's writings, which were influential in colonial America. It is worth noting that More is perhaps the exception to the Cambridge Platonists' general rejection of the Augustinian view of original sin. More indicates that he believes that humans are affected by original sin, functioning as a force or tendency that genuinely limits humanity's capacities to act morally. In his "Hymn upon the Resurrection of Christ," More suggests not only that Christ's resurrection was a "triumph" that conquered "Hell, Death, and Sin," but also that humans require the grace of God's spirit to overcome the sin to which we naturally are bound: "Teach us our Lusts to mortify / In virtue of thy precious Death: / That while to Sin all-dead we lie, / Thou maist infuse thy Heav'nly breath."[13] At one point he goes so far as to define the human tendency toward evil explicitly as original sin: "Original Sin [is] that over-proportionated Proneness and almost irresistible Proclivity to what is evil."[14] Though C. A. Patrides suggests that "tradition-bound Protestants, we can be certain, would have been scandalized by More's 'almost,'"[15] this point is nevertheless interesting because it suggests that More stands as a bridge figure between the other Cambridge Platonists and Edwards insofar as his position moves toward reconciling Cambridge Platonism with certain aspects of more traditional Calvinism.[16] Because Cambridge Platonist concepts were mediated to Edwards largely through More, Edwards received them in a form that he is likely to have found more palatable than positions more resistant to Calvinist and Puritan views of original sin. Nevertheless, Edwards takes even More's position one step further, embracing particular features of Cambridge Platonist thought but drawing them into a virtue theory within which a Calvinist doctrine of original sin (and, correlatively, the claim that human virtue requires the intervention of grace) has a more prominent and explicit place.

Edwards's True Virtue as the Fulfillment of Created Human Natures

Chapter 2 argued that Edwards's true virtue is a divine attribute constitutive of the Holy Spirit, God's will. This account of God's virtue builds upon and expands theologically a Cambridge Platonist understanding of divine love. Yet, like the Cambridge Platonists, Edwards does not ultimately present this virtue as exclusively an activity of the divine being. Humans, too, are called to practice true virtue as a means of pursuing the ends for which they are created and redeemed. In *The Nature of True Virtue*, Edwards affirms that the exercise of true virtue is the end for which God has created humans: "For the true virtue of created beings is doubtless their highest excellency, and their true goodness, and that by which they are especially agreeable to the mind of their Creator. . . . Therefore they are good moral agents whose temper of mind or propensity of heart is agreeable to the *end* for which God made moral agents" (8:559).

The similarities between Edwards's understanding of human true virtue and the human virtue of the Cambridge Platonists demonstrate the ways in which Edwards shows precisely how charity, though constitutive of God rather than of creatures, is the means through which humans fulfill their created *telos*. At the same time, Edwards departs from the Cambridge Platonists in his strong affirmation of original sin and his consequent situation of true virtue in a soteriological context. As fallen creatures, humans are not able to reach their created *telos* through their own excellence, because this excellence has been tarnished by sin. True virtue in humans is instead a participation in divine virtue, and in God's very being, through the redemption accomplished in Christ and the work of the Holy Spirit. Both Edwards's commonalities with the Cambridge Platonists and his departures from their thought reveal that Edwards's virtuous love is simultaneously the very being of God and the means through which humans fulfill the ends for which they were created. These emphases underscore Edwards's alignment with the Christian Platonist tradition and are important for understanding and appreciating his distinctive view of moral accountability.

Two features of Edwards's account of true virtue particularly demonstrate how true virtue is the ultimate fulfillment of human nature. The first of these is that Edwards, in a manner similar to the Cambridge Platonists, sees charity as participating in God's being, and he ties this participative virtue to the doctrine of creation. The second is that Edwards affirms a degree of congruity between virtue and our natural ends by presenting virtue as a means through which humans are made happy. Edwards's connection of virtue to happiness shows a recognition, very much in line with the Cambridge Platonists and with others of Edwards's contemporaries who resist modern voluntarism, of the moral order as in some sense inherent in the natural order. When rational beings act virtuously—and indeed, when they practice the true virtue that is constitutive of God's being—they are acting in a manner that is in keeping with their created natures and ends.

Virtuous Human Love as Participating in God's Nature

Like the Cambridge Platonists, Edwards conceives virtuous human love as participating in divine virtue. To some degree, this participation is most fully realized after our redemption.[17] Yet Edwards is still willing to link this participative virtue, at points, to creatures' created states in a manner that highlights his general consistency with the Christian Platonist tradition. Most notably in *The End for*

Which God Created the World, Edwards follows the Cambridge Platonists in connecting human goodness to our status as creatures made in God's image, rather than exclusively to the process of redemption. Roland Delattre notes that Edwards's view of creation in *End* develops the term "emanation" in a manner that conveys God's communication of his goodness, and creatures' subsequent participation in this goodness, as a consequence of creation.[18] And indeed, in *End*, Edwards suggests that creatures are able to act morally only because God communicates his knowledge, holiness, and joy to creatures in the act of creating them, and that as creatures love God (the essence of true virtue), they participate in that knowledge and are conformed to God's likeness.[19]

Edwards suggests that God's praiseworthy quality makes it fitting that other beings know, love, and take joy in God's goodness. In presenting this claim, he offers an account of creatures' moral dispositions—knowledge, love, and joy—as emanations of God's own: "From this view it appears another way to be a thing in itself valuable, that there should be such things as the knowledge of God's glory in other beings, and an high esteem of it, love to it, and delight and complacence in it: this appears I say in another way, viz. as these things are but the emanations of God's own knowledge, holiness, and joy" (8:443). Through his fullness, God communicates his moral dispositions to creatures, giving them knowledge of morality and enabling them to emulate and partake in God's own moral dispositions. It is this process that Edwards seeks to represent through the term "emanation," as a more specific textual analysis demonstrates.

A central part of God's emanation is the communication of divine knowledge, knowledge of God's goodness and therefore of the content of morality: "One part of that divine fullness which is communicated, is the divine knowledge." This knowledge, for Edwards, is the creatures' knowledge of God. God communicates to creatures his own knowledge, so that creaturely knowledge "is most properly a communication of God's infinite knowledge which primarily consists in the knowledge of himself." Specifically God communicates to creatures the knowledge of his own "glory" and "perfections" (8:441). In giving them this knowledge, God provides them with a foundation for recognizing the nature of virtue (God's own being) and even for pursuing a truly virtuous disposition, because the knowledge of divine perfections enables creatures to understand how it is fitting to love and honor God: "the communication itself is no other, in the very nature of it, than that wherein the very honor, exaltation, and praise of God consists" (8:442–43).

Not only does divine emanation establish a possibility for humans to practice truly virtuous love, but it also serves as a means through which God more actively imparts virtue to creatures. Because it is God rather than creatures who is most properly associated with virtue, creatures could not be virtuous simply through having the substance of morality revealed to them. God must give them the ability to partake in a virtue that is more proper to God's being than to their own. Through the "communication of God's holiness . . . the creature partakes of God's own moral excellence, which is properly the beauty of the divine nature." By communicating his goodness to creatures, God instills in them a holiness that they exercise "in love, which is the comprehension of all true virtue; and primarily in love to God, which is exercised in a high esteem of God, admiration of his perfections, complacency in them, and praise of them" (8:442). God communicates morality to creatures both so that they can apprehend God as the being to whom love is most centrally due and so that they are enabled, in spite of their creaturely limitations, to respond to God with the love that is due him.

In the process of emanation, closely intertwined with the doctrine of creation, God communicates himself to creatures so that they may know and participate in God's own love. He offers them knowledge of morality by revealing to them his own nature, his own goodness and holiness. Moreover, he enables them to cultivate moral dispositions in themselves by imparting his goodness to them. In a sense, then, emanation is more than one-sided communication; it is, instead, a communication that allows for creatures' participation in divine goodness. Through this divine communication, creatures participate in God's virtue and become conformed to the likeness of God, who is virtue itself: "the good that is in the creature comes forever nearer and nearer to an identity with that which is in God" (8:443). Divine emanation is an act through which God communicates and imparts his goodness to creatures and elicits their responsive moral formation.

Virtuous Love and Christian Happiness

Edwards's discussion of Christian happiness and its relation to virtue functions as a second line of argument through which Edwards connects human virtues to our natural ends. In Edwards's day, the relation of virtue to happiness was a contested issue, with consequences for how we understand the nature of moral motivation. With the Cambridge Platonists, many of Edwards's contemporaries and immediate predecessors accept the belief that a virtuous life will make a person happy. These thinkers distinguish between virtuous motives and motives of self-interest, and they suggest that the world is constructed in a manner such that virtuous motives and actions will bring about happiness. Shaftesbury, for example, suggests that virtue makes people happy because the pursuit of virtue coincides with our own interests. He explains that humans do not pursue virtue only for the sake of happiness. Instead, they are constructed to desire the good of the moral system of which they are a part, and happiness follows from the successful pursuit of this desire.[20] Joseph Butler likewise suggests that virtue brings about happiness. Virtue and self-interest generally coincide, but the pursuit of self-interest cannot make us happy in the manner that virtue can.[21] The idea that virtue and happiness are related is a means through which thinkers such as Shaftesbury and Butler establish a particular view of the natural world as ordered so that virtue benefits its possessors and brings about their happiness, a view that resonates with Edwards's understanding of the world as providentially ordered by a loving God. Edwards presents the coincidence of virtue and happiness as a sign of God's goodness rather than as a motive to virtue: it is virtuous to follow divine commands, but because God is good, God commands us in a manner that will bring about our happiness.

In emphasizing human "happiness" as a part of virtue, Edwards may, at first glance, appear decidedly inconsistent with many ancient theorists of virtue. As a subjective quality or disposition, happiness is at odds with the eudaimonism central to ancient virtue theories, even though eudaimonia is often misleadingly translated as "happiness." As Julia Annas explains in *The Morality of Happiness*, eudaimonia is best construed in terms of objective flourishing or perfection rather than exclusively as an individual's subjective satisfaction or pleasure. Annas contends that eudaimonia, a central component of both Aristotelian and Stoic accounts of virtue, is defined in relation to a moral agent's final end, a good that "unifies and organizes" all "other aims and goods." The concept of eudaimonia helps to specify our final end and encompasses the activity we undertake in the pursuit of that end. Eudaimonia therefore differs from happiness as a subjective feeling, for even though it "implies a positive view of one's life" as an agent considers her life retrospectively, it also is tied to our final end, which arises from an objective reality.[22] Ancient theorists would contend that subjective fulfillment should follow from the attainment of our ends, but a modern emphasis on "happiness" runs the risk of allowing subjective fulfillment to displace objective flourishing as a standard by which to judge the morality of actions and dispositions.

Edwards indeed focuses on the notions of "happiness" and "pleasure" as parts of virtue, but the connection he draws between human happiness and divine providence does not elevate the subjective quality of happiness as a moral standard, nor does it necessarily stand at odds with ancient eudaimonism. His account of happiness is strikingly similar to the position of the Roman Stoics, whose ideas Edwards would have encountered indirectly through thinkers such as John Calvin and Francis Hutcheson. To be sure, Annas is suspicious of the Roman Stoics, arguing that their conception of "cosmic nature . . . as a first principle within ethics" runs counter to mainstream Stoic eudaimonism.[23] Michael Gass, however, challenges Annas on this point, arguing that the Roman Stoic position that it is morally good to assent to divine providence is logically consistent with eudaimonism. According to Gass, the Stoic emphasis on virtue as sufficient for happiness is a logical complement to the suggestion of later Stoics that a virtuous life is "characterized by a voluntary and beneficial subjection to the rule of divine reason." Gass argues that the Roman Stoics were coherent in their belief that eudaimonism is compatible with a view of morality as involving a conscious harmonization of one's activity with nature's aims. He concludes that it is plausible to see the Romans' elevation of assent to God's providence as an ultimate culmination of eudaimonistic reflection on one's end.[24]

For Edwards, the concept of "Christian happiness" functions as part of an account of divine providence that echoes the Roman Stoics in its claim that humans are made subjectively happy through the exercise of true virtue, the *telos* toward which they are objectively ordered. "Happiness" describes the state of mind appropriate to a virtuous individual who consents to God's providential (and loving) ordering of the world. Edwards's defense of the meritorious nature of virtuous happiness is tied to his understanding of the nature of God's moral agency. In *End*, Edwards observes that God, the supremely virtuous being, takes joy in God's own virtue and imparts that joy to creatures: "Another part of God's fullness which he communicates is his happiness." Both divine and human happiness consist in an appreciation of divine goodness and virtue that leads to feelings of joy. God rejoices in God's own goodness, and God likewise enables creatures similarly to rejoice in God's being and providential work. God's happiness "consists in enjoying and rejoicing in himself, and so does also the creature's happiness." God communicates this happiness to the creature. Moreover, this joyful disposition of praising God is itself morally praiseworthy because it is a sign that our hearts respond favorably, and with approval, to God's goodness.

God approves of and is pleased with the "heart's exalting, magnifying, and glorifying God."[25] Perfectly modeled in God's own virtue, Edwards's Christian happiness functions as a sign that an agent has the moral maturity to recognize and approve God's goodness and to celebrate it. Feelings of happiness are subjective in that they reside in a subject, but they follow from assent to an objective reality, an assent to divine goodness that objectively merits a joyful response.

Edwards's sermons exhorting Christians to happiness further show how divine joy is a model for the morally praiseworthy joy associated with virtuous human love. Many scholars believe that "Christian Happiness," dated to 1720 or 1721, is "Edwards's first formal sermon, composed for his licensure or delivered as an academic exercise."[26] This sermon defends the thesis that "a good man is a happy man, whatever his outward circumstances are."[27] Edwards's development of this claim demonstrates his concern to show that happiness results from our recognition of God's goodness in the ordering of the world, and, specifically, in God's benevolent design of the moral laws:

> Hence learn the great goodness of God in joining so great happiness to our duty. God seems to have contrived all methods to encourage us in our duty. . . . How much the goodness of God shines forth even in his commands! What could the most merciful being have done more for our encouragement? All that he desires of us is that we would not be miserable, that we would [not] follow those courses which of themselves would end in misery, and that we would be happy; and God, having a great desire to speak after the manner of man, that we should not be miserable but happy, has the mercy and goodness that he forwards us to it, to command us to do those things that will make us so.[28]

Edwards's suggestion that the relation of virtue to human happiness is evidence of divine goodness echoes the Cambridge Platonists as well, and is another means through which Edwards emphasizes God's love rather than God's arbitrary power, as I discussed in chapter 2. God's goodness, Edwards explains, leads him to make commands that are consistent with our created natures so that following them will benefit us. That God has chosen to act this way, in spite of his power, is a mark of his mercy.[29] For Edwards, the cultivation of virtuous love emulates and partakes in God's nature, and it brings us joy just as it brings joy to God.

Edwards's reiteration of this theme in his 1723 sermon "The Pleasantness of Religion" demonstrates even more pointedly that feelings of happiness follow from the objective attainment of our *telos*, as well as from our appreciation of God's benevolent nature. In this text, Edwards argues that an agent who is truly virtuous (one who is affected by "true religion") will feel pleasure precisely because this religion enables humans to fulfill the purposes for which God created them. We see that this is so because the body and soul of the "godly" act peaceably together so that their consciences are at peace:

> But the godly [in contrast to "the wicked man"], taking those delights [that is, the delights of the created order] according to reason and conscience, his internal man consents to his external in the enjoyment of them and partakes with him therein, and it is a pleasant feast that the body and soul enjoy together. His reason, the highest faculty of the man, gives him leave and his conscience commends him in it, and there is no such perplexing disturbance in his breast as the wicked have; but all is done with peace and without the sting of conscience. The reasonable creature never feels better and more easy when he acts reasonably and like according to the nature of a man, and like consistent with himself.[30]

This passage is striking because it underscores a link between true virtue and our *telos* and because it hints that human faculties will be uneasy if they are not acting virtuously. Edwards does not suggest here that we may act virtuously independently of grace, but he does suggest that our faculties are uneasy when we act viciously. Virtue is consistent with our natures and the purposes for which they are created, and we feel delight and happiness when we know that we are pursuing these ends.

Edwards, then, aligns virtue with a happiness that follows from an objective moral recognition of divine virtue. While this alignment differentiates Edwards's account of happiness from other modern views of happiness as mere subjective fulfillment, his use of the terms "happiness" and "pleasure" requires that we note concerns raised by some of his contemporaries about affirmations of coincidence between virtue and happiness. One concern is practical: if virtue makes us happy, then it becomes difficult to know whether virtuous actions are motivated by genuinely virtuous motives or by self-interest. Even though Shaftesbury and Butler wish to elevate virtuous motives above motives of self-interest, their positions imply that self-interest can motivate us to act virtuously, a claim that raises questions about whether and how virtuous motives can be distinguished from motives that lack virtue. Edwardsean works such as *The Religious Affections* and

The Distinguishing Marks of a Work of the Spirit of God aim to address this concern; Edwards seeks to discern signs that truly virtuous and spiritual affections are at work in a given individual's actions.

A second concern relates to the necessity of divine law for human virtue. Some of Edwards's contemporaries, such as Samuel Clarke, argue that if virtue produced happiness necessarily, then both virtue and self-interest would lead us to pursue it, and there would be no need for the divine law, with its prospects of eternal reward and punishment. Clarke contends that if virtue and happiness coincide, this coincidence would be sufficient motive to act virtuously. But we do not always act virtuously, and this is because virtue does not always bring about happiness. True virtue, for Clarke, often involves self-sacrifice, or even death. Clarke concludes that we are motivated to pursue virtue only because God gives us additional sanctions in order to ensure that we will live virtuously in spite of the suffering that virtue sometimes entails.[31] In developing this argument, Clarke works to ensure that God's law is necessary as a motivator for moral action.

It is important to note these concerns because they show how Edwards's views of creation and sin lead him toward an account of human virtue that is largely in keeping with the Stoic view of continuity between virtue and happiness, but that is simultaneously nuanced by a desire to affirm the particularity of the Christian tradition as central to morality. Like Clarke, Edwards acknowledges that suffering is often a part of virtue; in chapter 4 I show that Edwards uses the life of Christ as the model for the virtue of humility, and he thereby brings certain forms of suffering into close relation with the practice of virtue. But at the same time Edwards is comfortable suggesting that the life of true virtue, or the life of "religion," brings about happiness, as the elect recognize that their virtue is a means through which their wills are conformed to the activity of a benevolent God. In drawing this connection between true virtue and happiness, Edwards characterizes this virtue as a means through which creatures fulfill the ends for which this God created them. At the same time, perhaps aware of the concern raised by thinkers such as Clarke, Edwards guards against a suggestion that happiness alone can be a proper motive to virtue. A strong account of original sin is one means through which he affirms the importance of God for moral activity and motivation.

Sin and Its Implications for Edwardsean Charity: Revisiting the Issue of Moral Accountability

Edwards self-consciously departs from the Cambridge Platonists in his desire to reconcile his account of virtue with a traditional Christian doctrine of original sin. As Delattre rightly recognizes,[32] Edwards affirms that human true virtue depends upon the redemptive work of Christ, and the sanctifying activity of the Holy Spirit. In doing so, he reintegrates virtue with a traditional Calvinist view of salvation for which justification is prior to, and necessary for, sanctification.[33] Apart from Christ, we cannot be sanctified and therefore cannot truly practice virtuous love. Although true virtue makes us happy, the happiness we feel in this virtue is subsequent to our conversion. Thus, alongside the emphases that Edwards shares with the Cambridge Platonists—affirmations that humans are created for the end of loving God and that this virtue brings about their happiness—Edwards simultaneously hastens to affirm our subjection to sin and our correlative inability to fulfill these natural ends apart from the direct assistance of divine grace that brings about conversion. An understanding of Edwardsean true virtue must take Edwards's position on sin as well as creation into account. Edwards holds a positive view of the ends for which we were created, and true virtue is in part a means through which we fulfill those ends. At the same time, we cannot fulfill these ends through our own merits, and so true virtue must come to us externally and as a gift, which raises questions about its authenticity.

Edwards's Defense of Original Sin

Edwards's account of original sin is generally consistent with the traditional Reformed view of this doctrine. Stephen Holmes suggests that Edwards's *Treatise on Original Sin* is (with the exception of one idea in it that most commentators consider to be "misconceived") "little more than a solid restatement, mainly built on Biblical exegesis, of the mainstream Christian position."[34] In affirming and defending the traditional view of original sin, Edwards departs from the Cambridge Platonists by embracing a doctrine that has theological implications for his understanding of truly virtuous human love.

Although Edwards conceives true virtue as humanity's natural *telos*, he perceives our moral capacities that practice this virtue to be inhibited by sin. We are created for the purpose of loving and glorifying God, but original sin limits our ability to pursue the truly virtuous life. Original sin affects our hearts, wills, and dispositions, the seats of virtue; for Edwards, original sin involves both the imputation of Adam's sin to his descendants and a recognition that our hearts are consequently corrupt.[35] We are unable to overcome this deeply ingrained depravity through our own efforts, and we therefore require the assistance of divine grace in order to practice charity: "That is to be looked upon as the true tendency of the natural or innate disposition of man's heart, which appears to be its tendency when we consider things as they are in themselves, or in their own nature, without the *interposition of divine grace*. Thus, that state of man's nature, that disposition of the mind, is to be looked upon as evil and pernicious, which, as it is in itself, tends to extremely pernicious consequences, and would certainly end therein, were it not that the free mercy and kindness of God interposes to prevent that issue" (3:109). In our hearts there is naturally a "moral depravity," an "evil tendency or propensity" that affects our wills and dispositions (3:110).

Edwards's contention that original sin involves wills and dispositions raises questions about whether this sin also affects our intellects—in other words, one might ask whether Edwards believes that it is possible for sinful human intellects to *recognize* goodness and virtue and understand their nature and meaning, even if humans cannot willfully *pursue* virtue apart from God's intervening grace. *Original Sin* is less clear on this point. Certainly its primary emphasis is on the corruption of human dispositions and actions rather than on intellectual faculties, and in chapter 5 we will see that Edwards presents conversion as a change in disposition rather than an intellectual event. Moreover, other Edwardsean texts suggest that Edwards, like the Cambridge Platonists, wishes to affirm that God's activity is "reasonable" in a manner that humans can appreciate. For example, his sermon "All God's Methods Are Most Reasonable" defends the rational nature of divine providence, election, and redemption.[36]

At the same time, Edwards's understanding of sin leads him elsewhere to question the capacity of our reason to understand God's activity; God's actions are objectively reasonable, but humans apart from conversion cannot see this. Although there are moments when Edwards seems to contend that even sinful humanity can apprehend God and God's virtue (and thereby "know" this virtue, in a sense) independently of a special act of God's grace, Edwards places limits on this knowledge. *True Virtue* affirms that divine virtue possesses a beauty that humans may naturally appreciate, but it also indicates that humans cannot see God's more powerful spiritual beauty until they are given a spiritual sense. Edwards's 1736 sermon "All That Natural Men Do Is Wrong" demonstrates that he places great weight on this lack of spiritual understanding in terms of what it means about our ability to know God, and to know the meaning of virtue, without divine assistance. In this sermon, Edwards affirms that apart from the intervention of God's grace, we lack understanding of God's being (and hence of virtue) and are incapable of learning this understanding even when we are taught:

apart from grace, humans "don't understand, i.e., they neither know God nor know how to seek or serve him. Natural men, many of them, are taught concerning God and his ways, but they are without understanding. They neither know nor will they learn."[37] At the very least, then, grace is required for us to exercise affective knowledge (and hence approval) regarding virtue, but it appears that even our cognitive knowledge of virtue is limited apart from God's special revelation. I make this case more fully in chapters 4 and 5, which argue that Edwards understands our knowledge of virtue to be imperfect apart from divine illumination, which occurs both in God's self-revelation in the incarnate Jesus Christ and in God's encounter with an individual at the moment of her conversion. It is possible that Edwards views original sin as impairing our ability to know God and to know the meaning of virtue, although Edwards's view of these inabilities may be grounded in his belief in humans' utter dependence upon God (even independently of the Fall) rather than in his view of sin.

Recognizing precisely what is accomplished in redemption adds to our understanding of Edwards's original sin in a manner that has implications for how we conceive humans' created capacities to know and pursue virtue prior to the Fall. Edwards is adamant that Christ's redemption is the "fruit of God's love to mankind" and that it saves the elect "from *deserved* destruction" (3:354). The nature of this salvation, Edwards says, is that it "changes" our natures, so that we are "regenerated, or born again"; from this account of conversion, we know that sin has affected our natures to such a degree that a change in needed in order for virtue to be practiced (3:361). It is finally unclear whether this regeneration restores our natures to the state in which God created them originally, or whether it adds to our natural created capacities and elevates us beyond them. But Edwards does explicitly connect this regeneration to virtue and holiness. In redemption, Edwards explains, we are *"created anew, or made new creatures"* (3:369). In conversion we turn "from sin to God" (3:362), and this turning is the means through which "men come to have the character of true Christians" (3:363). Virtuous love is not something of which we are naturally capable; because of Edwards's view of original sin, we live righteously only through being given "a new heart and spirit" in which "habits of true virtue and holiness" are instilled (3:365).

In contrast to the Cambridge Platonists, then, Edwards holds a view of original sin such that our natures must experience conversion in order to pursue (and, to some degree, to know) a life of virtue. The Cambridge Platonists affirm the necessity of Christ for salvation, but Edwards believes that a strong doctrine of original sin is essential in order to ensure this necessity. Edwards's view of sin demonstrates that even though the exercise of true virtue is central to the end for which we were created, our natures are such that they require the interposing work of divine grace in order for a given individual to overcome the inhibitions that sin places upon her. This argument poses difficulties that demonstrate the need to address the issue of moral accountability in Edwards.

Virtuous Love, Salvation, and the Divine Will

Edwards's integration of the concept of virtue with a recognition of the severe nature of original sin ensures that God does not become extraneous to the moral life. Even though true virtue is consistent with our natural ends, humans cannot pursue true virtue independently of God, both because God is himself true virtue in a way that humans are not and because their moral faculties are damaged. Edwards's understanding of sin leads him to conceive humans as unable to practice virtue apart from God, though they may to some degree know and approve virtue simply through the created faculties that God gave them. The merit of this position is that it preserves God's centrality to the human practice of morality. At the same time, the danger of this position is that it introduces a type of voluntarism (albeit different from Schneewind's voluntarism) into our understanding of ethics: God's will does not establish the meaning of morality independently of God's love, but God's will does decree *who* may be moral in a manner that may appear arbitrary from a human perspective. For Edwards, because of our sin, we cannot practice virtue independently of a specific and personal encounter with God in which God instills in us a spiritual sense that enables our pursuit of virtue. I discuss the mechanics of the spiritual sense more fully in chapter 5, but for now it is important to recognize that Edwards's view of sin leads him to conceive our natural capacities to pursue virtue as limited to such a degree that we are powerless to pursue true virtue independently of divine mercy. Edwards's account of true virtue is therefore tied closely to his view of salvation, which poses challenging questions for its recovery by contemporary Christian ethicists.

As the means through which creatures tainted by sin fulfill the purposes for which they were created, Edwards's true virtue, or Christian love, is intricately connected to the process of human salvation. True virtue is something that humans receive as an act of grace. This link between true virtue and salvation is evident in Edwards's 1738 series of sermons, *Charity and Its Fruits*. These sermons on 1 Corinthians 13 affirm both the importance of love for Edwards's account of morality and the need for humans to be able to receive God's salvific grace in order to practice this love. These sermons affirm that Christian love, or charity,[38] is the content of true virtue. Edwards makes two observations that seem to lead him to designate this type of virtue as "true virtue": first, this virtue is the means by which people receive salvation, and second, the possession of this type of virtue distinguishes Christians from "natural men" (8:130). Edwards connects this virtue both to salvation and to Christian distinctiveness in each of the first two sermons in his series. In the first sermon he affirms, "All that virtue which is saving, and distinguishing of true Christians from others, is summed up in Christian or divine love" (8:131; see also 147). The second sermon reiterates that Christian love is the sum of all the saints' virtue that is "distinguishing" and "saving" (8:149). Edwards goes so far as to suggest that the presence or absence of love is the means by which an action can be tested to determine whether it is truly Christian.[39] Without love, even a seemingly meritorious activity is worthless because it lacks this salvific quality: Edwards notes that "many of the heathen have been eminent for moral performances. Some of them have been eminent for justice, and others for their great deeds which they have done for the public good" (8:176), but it is love (and specifically Christian love) that God requires of us (8:180). Edwards sees love as a sign of whether a person is Christian or not, and, correlatively, as a sign of whether one has received salvation.

Having presented this true virtue as a sign of human salvation, Edwards reiterates the necessity of God's gracious activity in order for Christian love to be genuinely exercised. God's granting of grace to a human moral agent is a necessary condition of her ability to act in a virtuous manner. "True grace and holiness" are proper qualities of human hearts, but only if we receive them; they are not qualities that we may acquire through our natural abilities (8:158). God must give us grace in order for us to practice love, which is the "summary comprehension of all saving grace" (8:151). *True Virtue* is consistent with *Charity and Its Fruits* on this point, declaring that apart from God's grace, humans cannot practice true virtue, although it is possible that they might perceive and approve it.[40] This argument ensures that God alone is the author of human salvation and of the virtuous love that is evidence of this salvation. If it could be said that humans can practice true virtue apart from God's grace, this would undermine God's sovereignty. It would imply not only that humans can participate in God's virtuous being independently of God's willing and enabling this participation, but also that humans can earn their salvation through practicing virtue independently of God. Edwards sought to guard against both of these conclusions that would make God extraneous to humans' moral activity.

At the same time, even as Edwards's affirmation of humans' dependence upon God's grace ensures that God is essential to the moral life, it also poses potential problems for contemporary thinkers who wish to engage with Edwards's virtue ethic but do not share his commitments to Dortian Calvinism. As I noted in the previous chapter, Edwards's God does not bestow grace and enable the practice of true virtue universally. Instead, according to Edwards, God's bestowal of grace functions selectively. This Edwardsean claim, in turn, raises concerns about whether God acts arbitrarily in enabling some persons to practice true virtue and denying other persons this capacity. I argued in chapter 2 that God's will is essentially loving, and that a conception of the divine will as fundamentally loving can help ameliorate concerns about God's partiality. But a related concern remains: is the human practice of virtue authentic? If humans cannot practice virtue without the assistance of God, it may appear that Edwards's view of human love allows no place for human agency. In the next section I return to the argument about moral accountability that I began to develop in chapter 2. Humans, Edwards maintains, are in a sense the authors of their own actions, even as God is a cause of our virtue, and we can see how Edwards develops and defends this position through remembering that God's activity provides a model for understanding the human virtues.

Moral Accountability and the Authorship of Actions

Edwards's commitment to a view of truly virtuous love as consequent on God's grace raises questions about the authorship of charitable actions in humans. If God ultimately chooses who can practice true virtue and instills in the elect the power to be virtuous, how can virtue be legitimately ascribed to these human agents? It could be argued that if we are unable to cultivate virtue through our own devices, humans are not clearly accountable for their actions. People who do not act virtuously simply lack God's grace and we should pity them; by the same token, people who act virtuously are simply acting in accordance with dispositions that God has instilled in them and merit no praise. In presenting the cultivation of virtuous love as to some degree out of our control, Edwards's position may appear to tend toward the sorts of despair and atheism that the Cambridge Platonists worried was a consequence of Calvin's emphasis upon divine inscrutability and our inability to know God's will.

In chapter 2 I argued that Edwards's view of divine virtue provides a model for understanding truly virtuous love in humans. We now begin to see this argument's consequences for Edwards's view of moral accountability and the authorship of actions. God's virtue, for Edwards, is realized as God acts in a manner consistent with God's own nature. God is meritorious not only because he performs good actions but because these actions reveal his true nature. God is necessarily good: God cannot change his own dispositions or act in a manner contrary to his nature. And God, Edwards affirms, is nonetheless praiseworthy.

Because human morality reflects God's morality, it follows that humans, like God, are accountable for acting in accordance with their dispositions. Developing an argument that prefigures a position later advanced by David Hume, Edwards suggests that human action has a measure of necessity: there is necessary congruity between actions and dispositions. But it does not follow, Edwards contends, that these actions lack merit. Rather, merit must be understood in terms of living in accordance with God's purposes. In a sense, God enables humans to exercise and pursue meritorious virtues, because God's grace bestows upon humans a spiritual sense apart from which charity could not take place. But humans remain responsible for acting in a manner consistent with their virtuous dispositions.

Edwards is not alone in presenting a virtue ethic that struggles with questions of fairness and accessibility. Bernard Williams has recognized that "moral luck" and contingency influence an agent's ability to know and cultivate virtue even on Aristotelian terms;[41] this argument has given rise to subsequent considerations of the role of contingency and fortune in Aristotelian and Thomistic ethics.[42] Edwards's ethic may not be fully satisfying in its account of moral agency in humans, but his view is intriguing in its suggestion that humans can see themselves as morally accountable even when struggling with circumstances that are out of our control. As we consider additional human virtues, we will return to the issue of moral accountability in order to gain a fuller sense of Edwards's conception of the authorship of actions, and this exploration will help to underscore Edwards's significance for contemporary Christian ethics.

4

Humility as a Human Virtue
Imaging God's Mercy Through Creaturely Capacities

Chapter 3 describes how Edwards's truly virtuous human love images and takes part in divine virtue. By characterizing true virtue as an excellence proper to and constitutive of God's being, Edwards offers an account of Christian love as the fulfillment of the purposes for which humans were created. Humans are able to exercise this virtue in spite of original sin, but they need the assistance of God's special grace in order to do so. God graciously imparts his nature to the elect, and, in doing so, gives them the capacity to love as God intends for creatures to love. Divine and human love, then, are related through participation: humans pursue true virtue as they participate in God's moral excellence.

This understanding of true virtue in humans provides a useful counterpoint for considering a second category of human virtues in Edwards: those virtues that are excellences proper to humans, rather than to God as divine being. Edwards defines these virtues that are creaturely excellences in relation to the person and work of the incarnate Jesus Christ, in whom divine virtue and these human excellences exist in unity. Christ serves as the moral exemplar and perfect embodiment both of the true virtue that is proper to God and of those virtuous qualities that Edwards deems "proper excellencies of created natures." Edwards explains that qualities such as humility and meekness are legitimately considered "virtues" even though they cannot be attributed to the divine being as divine being; in the case of these virtues as well as true virtue, however, the incarnate Jesus Christ is able to practice and embody them perfectly. Christ's divine nature is the moral archetype for true virtue, and his human nature is likewise the moral archetype for the human virtues that are excellences particular to creatures. Edwards's account of the human virtues that are rooted in Christ's incarnation underscores his position's general continuity with the Christian Platonist tradition, particularly as this tradition is represented in Augustine.

This chapter begins with a discussion of Edwards's views of sin and redemption, which undergird his account of Christ's exemplarity of the virtues. I then turn more pointedly to Edwards's view of humility, which he derives from Christ's activity during the incarnation. By presenting Christ as the paradigm of humility, Edwards conceives this virtue as involving not a simple avoidance of pride but a more radical rejection of one's legitimate earthly honors. After considering the importance of Christ's moral exemplarity for the content and meaning of Edwards's humility, I compare Edwardsean humility to Augustine's and Aquinas's understandings of this virtue in order to underscore the departures of Edwards's position from even the Christianized Aristotelianism of Thomas Aquinas. Edwards's depiction of Christ as moral exemplar offers a second model of the relation between divine and human virtue: whereas true virtue in humans participates in God's being, the most perfect forms of the virtues that are creaturely excellences are images or types of divine mercy. Edwards's account of the human virtue of humility therefore reveals and highlights dimensions of divine love that humans are called to incorporate into their own moral practices.

Christological Exemplarity in Edwards's Virtue Ethic

The incarnate Christ embodies and reveals both true virtue and the virtues that Edwards describes as moral excellences of created natures. Unlike love, which is constitutive of the divine being, humility as Edwards conceives it is a quality more proper to creatures than to God: "For though the divine nature be infinitely abhorrent to pride, yet humility is not properly predicable of God the Father, and the Holy Ghost, that exist only in the divine nature, because it is a proper excellency only of a created nature."[1] Yet because Christ is fully human as well as fully divine, he exhibits and practices both sorts of virtues. God as God cannot practice humility, but in Christ divine virtue is joined to these created excellences. For Edwards, therefore, the incarnate Christ is a moral exemplar of both divine virtue and those creaturely virtues that can be considered human perfections. Edwards's account of Christ's moral exemplarity establishes a foundation for understanding his Christological view of humility.

The Redemptive and Revelatory Quality of Christ's Virtues

Edwards affirms Christ's moral exemplarity in the context of exploring the nature of redemption, a theme central to his theology.[2] According to Edwards, Christ accomplished redemption both through the atonement (which achieves a "satisfaction" for sin) and by exhibiting righteousness or merit (which accomplishes a "purchase" of salvation).³ In turn, it is in the context of exploring Christ's righteousness and the purchase of salvation that Edwards discusses Christ's virtues: the redemptive "merit" of the incarnate Christ consists in his obedience and his virtue. Edwards is careful to explain that Christ salvifically displays his righteousness *both* through actions of obeying laws ("all laws of God that ever have been given to mankind, both the law of nature and also all political commands that were ever given to man") *and* through the manifestation of virtues. Christ exercised "every possible virtue" in the course of "doing the work that he had to do here in the world for our redemption." Edwards implies here that Christ's obedience to the law was important as a means of fulfilling the covenant humans had broken. But true "righteousness," such as that which Christ possessed, involves the perfect exercise of virtues as well as the obedience of laws,⁴ and Edwards devotes an entire sermon in the *Work of Redemption* to delineating the specific virtues Christ practiced. Christ's virtue is a cornerstone of Edwards's theology because it is a central means through which human salvation is achieved.⁵

Not only does Christ's exemplarity play a role in the redemption accomplished in the incarnation, but it is also important for the salvation of particular humans because it reveals the content of the moral life to us. Edwards's sermon "The Excellency of Christ" suggests that Christ's embodiment of the virtues is intended to empower humans (or at least the elect, who have this capacity because of their spiritual sense) both to know the virtues' character and to feel love and approval for them, as well as for Christ, who practices them. Humans, Edwards explains, may best love Christ and know the meaning of goodness by recognizing in Christ good qualities that are particular to our own natures. We humans are not properly equipped to see and comprehend God in his full glory. Therefore, even though the full glory of God dwells in Christ as a member of the Trinity, Christ reaches human creatures more appropriately through excellences fitting to them. In doing so, he "acquaints" us with virtues proper to us and invites our affections as these virtues "dazzle our eyes":

> As the glory of Christ appears in the qualifications of his human nature, it appears to us in excellencies that are of our own kind, and are exercised in our own way and manner, and so, in some respects, are peculiarly fitted to invite our acquaintance, and draw our affection. The glory of Christ as it

appears in his divinity, though it be far brighter, yet doth it also more dazzle our eyes, and exceeds the strength and comprehension of our sight: but as it shines in the human excellencies of Christ, it is brought more to a level with our conceptions, and suitableness to our nature and manner.[6]

By embodying human excellences, Christ is able to reveal God's glory to humans and simultaneously to demonstrate the true meaning of human moral excellence.

Original Sin underscores this point. Edwards offers Christ's revelation of the virtues to us, and our subsequent failure to pursue virtues, as evidence of the essential depravity of human nature after the Fall and our consequent need for conversion in order to comprehend properly the human excellencies that Christ reveals to us. Were it not for this depravity, Christ's moral example would certainly have influenced humans more fully: "There has been given to the world an example of virtue, which, were it not for a dreadful depravity of nature, would have influence on them that live under the gospel, far beyond all other examples; and that is the example of Jesus Christ." Edwards goes on to say, as he does in "The Excellency of Christ," that providing an example of perfect virtue was part of God's purpose in the incarnation: "God, who knew the human nature, and how apt men are to be influenced by example, has made answerable provision. His infinite wisdom has contrived that we should have set before us the most amiable and perfect example, in such circumstances as should have the greatest tendency to influence all the principles of man's nature, but his corruption."[7]

Christ has qualities that would lead humans instinctually to follow him if their natures were not depraved. He is of their nature yet superior to them, and he is also their friend: "Men are apt to be moved by the example of others like themselves, or in their own nature; therefore this example was given in our nature. Men are ready to follow the examples of the great and honorable: and this example, though it was of one in our nature, yet it was one of infinitely higher and more honorable than kings or angels.... Men are very apt to follow the example of their friends; the example of Christ is of one that is infinitely our greatest Friend."[8] A second purpose of Christ's embodiment of divine and human moral excellences, then, is to provide knowledge of creaturely moral excellences to humans by offering a perfect example of their practice. For Edwards, Christ's moral exemplarity is central to the redemption of humanity as a whole and to the salvation of individual humans.

Creaturely Virtues and Original Sin

Edwards's suggestion that the virtues are revealed in the incarnate Christ's person and work demonstrates the distinctiveness of his account of creaturely virtues. Although these virtues are in one sense proper to creatures, they are not "natural" to creatures, because we need Christ's revelation in order to understand them. Like love, humility is consistent with the purposes for which we were created. We were created to glorify God, and humility logically guards against any self-assertion that would inhibit our ability to exercise the love to God that is a primary virtuous disposition. Yet, although humility is an excellence proper to creatures, the knowledge and practice of this virtue require God's gracious revelation in Christ.

As with truly virtuous love, humans cannot truly know or practice the virtue of humility independently of God's self-revelation, and because of original sin, humans also require conversion and the gift of the spiritual sense in order to understand and practice it. Just as humans need divine grace to fulfill their created *telos* of practicing true virtue, so do they need God's grace to be able to pursue the virtues that are excellences of their nature. *Religious Affections* suggests that a proper understanding of these virtues, as well as an ability to practice them, requires God's grace. Edwards emphasizes the difficulty of pursuing a life of humility apart from a "Christian" disposition: "'Tis an exceeding difficult thing for a wicked man, destitute of Christian principles in his heart, to guide him, to know how to demean himself like a Christian, with the life, and beauty, and heavenly sweetness of a truly holy, humble, Christlike behavior. He knows not how to put on these garments; neither do they fit him." A Christlike disposition is important for the practice of humility because our dispositions guide our actions; therefore, a spiritual disposition given to us by divine grace (such as that which we receive at conversion) will guide us most effectively in the practice of humility: "Thus it is that a spiritual disposition and taste teaches and guides a man in his behavior in the world. So an eminently humble, or meek, or charitable disposition, will direct a person of mean capacity to such a behavior, as is agreeable to Christian rules of humility, meekness, and charity, far more readily and precisely, than the most diligent study, and elaborate reasonings, of a man with the strongest faculties, who has not a Christian spirit within him."⁹ Edwards does not rule out the possibility that a human might be able to practice some measure of humility apart from conversion, but he suggests that this practice will be imprecise at best. Although humility is an excellence proper to human nature, the human knowledge and practice of humility nevertheless depend decisively upon divine grace.

Because these creaturely excellences are received through grace, they are imbued with a holiness that gives them a spiritual beauty and that distinguishes them from the qualities that function as incomplete virtues. (These incomplete virtues are the subject of chapter 6.) Whereas we are capable of cultivating "naturally good" dispositions through our natural faculties alone, the humility infused in us through God's grace partakes more completely in Christ's moral beauty than these natural dispositions do. Edwards explains that Christ's beauty lies in his essential holiness, and the saints are beautiful to the degree that the "moral image of God" is in them, giving them holiness. This holiness, in turn, extends to the human nature of Christ as well as to the divine, and Edwards specifically alludes to the human virtues of Christ as signs of the holiness of Christ's human nature: "Herein does primarily consist the amiableness and beauty of the Lord Jesus. . . . All the spiritual beauty of his human nature, consisting in his meekness, lowliness, patience, heavenliness, love to God, love to men, condescension to the mean and vile, and compassion to the miserable, etc. all is summed up in his holiness."[10]

Edwards does not specifically include "humility" in this list, but he does mention qualities that he at points seems to equate with "humility"; I develop this argument regarding "meekness" and "condescension" later in this chapter. The human virtues that are perfections of Christ's human nature, then, possess a quality of holiness, a type of spiritual beauty that distinguishes them from dispositions in which we can be morally formed through the activity of our natural faculties alone. Though they are particular to our natures, their pursuit requires divine grace.

Christ as the Moral Exemplar of the Virtues

As part of his theology of redemption, Edwards characterizes Christ as a moral exemplar in whom divine and human excellences coincide perfectly. In the *Work of Redemption*, Edwards explains that the incarnate Christ exercised "every possible virtue and grace" that does not presuppose sin,[11] virtues directed toward God, himself, and other humans (9:320). And so in Edwards's Christ we see the perfect embodiment of both true virtue and humility.

Edwards's Christ reveals the nature of the true virtue constitutive of God's very being. In the *Work of Redemption*, Edwards affirms that Christ exhibited a superlative love to God, a "holy fear and reverence toward God the Father," and although he was not subject to temptation, he withstood temptations to abandon the worship of God. Edwards underscores the noteworthiness of Christ's determination to continue in the worship of God by observing that even the angels that fell succumbed to the temptation to abandon God's worship (9:320–21). Not only does Christ's love for God exceed that of angels, but Edwards also affirms that Christ's demonstration of love surpasses that of all ordinary humans and even of saints: "The angels give great testimonies of their love to God in their constancy and activity in doing the will of God. And many saints have given great testimonies of their love, who from love to God have endured great labors and sufferings. But none ever gave such testimonies of love to God as Christ has done, none ever performed such a labor of love as he, or suffered so much from love to God as he" (9:321). Edwards concedes that "some of the saints," such as Paul and John, manifested love remarkably, but he concludes that "the love to men that Christ showed when on earth as much exceeded the love of all other men as the ocean exceeds a small stream" (9:323). True virtue is exhibited perfectly in Christ, and Christ's virtue surpasses that of any creature.

The perfect love of Christ is a theme also central to many of Edwards's sermons and to his revival text *The Distinguishing Marks of a Work of the Spirit of God*. Edwards consistently affirms the great love and compassion that the incarnate Christ practiced, and his sermon "The Sorrows of the Bereaved Spread Before Jesus" suggests that Christ "has the same compassion now that he is ascended into glory."[12] Likewise, both "The Excellency of Christ" and *Distinguishing Marks* present Christ's character as epitomizing true virtue for humans in a manner that suggests that Christ's love reveals the very nature of virtue to humans. In "The Excellency of Christ," Edwards affirms that Christ manifests virtue to us: as God incarnate, he exhibited perfect virtue to the world. Because Christ is God, he possesses all of God's attributes and excellences, and the incarnation reveals these excellences to us, conjoined in a single person.[13] Recognition of Christ's revelation of love is used as the basis for moral exhortation in *Distinguishing Marks*. Edwards suggests that we should look to Christ as the primary exemplar of what it means to exercise love morally: the love for which Christians should strive "we may see best in what appeared in Christ, in the example he set us, when he was here on earth."[14] For Edwards, it is clear that Christ reveals true virtue to us, and serves as an exemplar whose loving character we should seek to emulate. In Christ, divine virtue is perfectly represented and revealed.

In the person of Christ, moreover, this divine virtue is conjoined to perfect manifestations of creaturely virtues such as humility, which Christ's human nature embodies perfectly. Edwards's sermon "The Excellency of Christ" affirms that although Christ is equal with God, he simultaneously feels and exhibits "the deepest reverence toward God," a reverence that is fitting to him "as he was one that had taken on him the human nature."[15] Edwards further develops this argument in the *Work of Redemption*. He explains that because Christ's humanity was joined to a divine nature,[16] he had more reason to be proud than any other creature, and yet his humility surpasses that of all creatures:

> Christ, though he was the most excellent and honorable of men, yet was the most humble. Yea, he was the most humble of all creatures. No angels nor men ever equaled him in humility though he was the highest of all creatures in dignity and honorableness. Christ would have been under the greatest temptation to pride if it had been possible that anything could have been a temptation to him . . . the man, Christ Jesus, [was not] at all lifted up with pride with all those wonderful works [such as] raising the dead. (9:321)

Though he is God as well as human, Christ models creaturely virtues such as humility more completely than creatures do. Indeed, Christ, as God-man, embodies these virtues "perfectly": "Every virtue in him was perfect" (9:320).[17] Christ embodies and reveals the essence not only of divine love but also of creaturely humility.

Edwardsean Humility as Self-Renunciation

Because Christ's moral exemplarity is important to Edwards, he characterizes human excellences such as humility as reflections of Christ's dispositions:

> There is character for character: such kind of graces, such a spirit and temper, the same things that belong to Christ's character, belong to theirs [the elect's]. That disposition wherein Christ's character does in a special manner consist, therein does his image in a special manner consist. Christians that shine by reflecting the light of the Sun of Righteousness, do shine with the same sort of brightness, the same mild, sweet, and pleasant

beams.... It would be strange if Christians should not be of the same temper and spirit that Christ is of; when they are his flesh and his bone, yea are but one spirit (I Cor. 6:17), and live so, that it is not they that live, but Christ that lives in them.[18]

This claim is striking because it leads Edwards toward a view of humility that stands in contrast to the way this virtue has sometimes been understood in the Christian tradition. Edwards's humility lies not simply in opposition to pride but also in a necessary renunciation of the self, modeled after the incarnate Christ's self-renunciation. After explaining Edwards's distinctive understanding of humility and self-renunciation more fully, I compare Edwards's account of this virtue to the positions of Augustine and Aquinas. This comparison helps to situate Edwards within the broader context of the Christian and philosophical traditions and to highlight the particular contributions and possible limitations of Edwards's position.

Edwardsean Humility as Resistance to Pride

Edwards defines humility in multiple ways throughout his corpus. One of the most frequent definitions he offers is that humility is the opposite of pride, a definition that is consistent with other thinkers in the Christian tradition. An opposition between pride and humility is implied in "The Excellency of Christ," when Edwards suggests continuity between humility and an "abhorrence of pride."[19] Similarly, in *Distinguishing Marks*, Edwards contends that humility is opposed to the devil's nature because the devil's character "above all things, consists in pride and malice."[20] Many of Edwards's sermons reiterate this contrast between pride and humility. For example, "Keeping the Presence of God" calls pride a corruptor in which "the image of the devil chiefly consists" and suggests that only "real humility" can save us from this sin.[21] "Continuing God's Presence" exhorts Christians to witness to Christ by practicing humility and, concomitantly, avoiding pride.[22] "Mary's Remarkable Act" exhorts Christians to humble themselves, and part of the practice of humility involves "subduing" our "pride and self-righteousness."[23] *A History of the Work of Redemption* likewise opposes pride and humility. Christ's avoidance of "temptations to pride" is a hallmark of his humility (9:321). These textual examples indicate that, for Edwards, the avoidance of pride is at least part of what constitutes humility.

Edwards offers a more complete definition of the pride that we should avoid in *Some Thoughts Concerning the Present Revival of Religion in New England*, a defense of the religious revivals that Edwards wrote in 1742 and 1743. He argues that "spiritual pride" is one cause of problems or errors that can occur in relation to these revivals. Edwards likens pride to a disease through which a moral agent perceives herself to be greater than she is.[24] Pride is the "first sin that ever entered into the universe" and a quality that "the best of us" have "in our hearts" (4:415). This pride is dangerous because it prevents us from seeing ourselves as we are and leads us to believe that we are not in need of external instruction; for Edwards, pride is

> the chief inlet of smoke from the bottomless pit, to darken the mind, and mislead the judgment: this is the main handle by which the Devil has hold of religious persons, and the chief source of all the mischief that he introduces, to clog and hinder a work of God. This cause of error is the mainspring, or at least the main support of all the rest. Till this disease is cured, medicines are in vain applied to heal other diseases. 'Tis by this that the mind defends itself in other errors, and guards itself against light by which it might be corrected and reclaimed. The spiritually proud man is full of light already; he don't need instruction, and is ready to despise the offer of it. (4:414)

Whereas a humble moral agent "easily receives instruction" and participates in careful self-examination of her moral qualities (4:414, 417), a person affected by spiritual pride is unable to see herself rightly and to subject herself to others where appropriate.

Spiritual pride, moreover, is a powerful force. Spiritual pride is hidden and functions in secret ways: "Spiritual pride in its own nature is so secret, that it is not so well discerned by immediate intuition on the thing itself, as by the effects and fruits of it" (4:417–18). Even the exercise of humility, its opposite, can be distorted by pride and used to its own advantage, for a moral agent can be proud of her humility and thereby undermine that humility's practice: pride "perverts and abuses everything, and even the exercises of real grace and real humility, as an occasion to exert itself" (4:417). Spiritual pride is therefore to be avoided at all costs. This avoidance is difficult; just as pride is the first sin, so is it "the last thing in a sinner that is overborne by conviction, in order to conversion; and here is the saint's hardest conflict" (4:415–16). Yet its avoidance is crucial to our spiritual well-being and must take place in order for us to practice humility and emulate the "Spirit of the Lamb of God" (4:416).

While Edwards strongly exhorts Christians to avoid pride, both his presentation of Christ as exemplar of this virtue and his claim that God does not practice humility suggest that Christ's humility cannot be defined solely in terms of the avoidance of pride. God is not subject to pride, and if humility were solely the avoidance or absence of pride, then this virtue could be attributed to God. Edwards explains the incongruity of ascribing pride to God in *The End for Which God Created the World*. For Edwards, God logically cannot be subject to pride because God is the being to whom glory is most properly given. As the greatest being, God cannot esteem Godself higher than God is. Consequently, unlike creatures, in whom pride threatens to undermine the practice of virtue, God is a being for whom self-love is equivalent to virtue. Indeed, for Edwards, God is the only being in whom virtue and self-love can be said to coincide. When God loves creatures, he loves himself: "God's virtuous disposition, appearing in love to holiness in the creature, is to be resolved into the same thing with love to himself."[25] Edwards contends that God's happiness and pleasure are connected to divine self-love, love among the persons of the Trinity.[26] Edwards contends that "universal benevolence in the highest sense" is essentially equivalent to "benevolence to the Divine Being";[27] virtue, in God, is therefore love to himself. This view is confirmed in Edwards's conclusion that God's primary motive in creating is to glorify himself, and that this motive is meritorious.[28] In contrast to creatures, God may seek God's own good and be assured that God is simultaneously seeking the general or public good.[29] It is fitting for God to receive glory, and it is therefore impossible that God's self-glorification could be considered excessive or inappropriate. Edwards thereby presents God as logically incapable of pride. God avoids pride and could therefore be said to exercise humility if this virtue were simply the avoidance of pride.

Nonetheless, Edwards affirms that "though the divine nature be infinitely abhorrent to pride, yet humility is not properly predicable of God the Father, and the Holy Ghost, that exist only in the divine nature."[30] Humility, then, must be more than simply the absence of pride. And indeed, a closer examination of Edwards's conception of Christ's perfect humility reveals that this humility involves a radical renunciation of Christ's own righteousness and a disposition of self-abasement. Whereas Edwards's view of true virtue suggests that a virtuous life can bring about happiness, his view of humility requires an agent's willingness to suffer, and even to suffer unjustly. Humility is not simply the avoidance of pride; it is a deeper act of self-renunciation.

Perfect Humility as the Renunciation of Self: The Distinctively Christological Character of Edwards's Humility

A closer examination of Edwards's portrayal of humility suggest that his interpretation of Christ's actions leads him to understand this virtue in a manner that involves not simply the avoidance of pride but a more extensive denial of self and submission to suffering. The *Work of Redemption* connects humility to self-abasement. Edwards argues that submitting to low circumstances, when appropriate, is a testimony to one's humility.[31] Christ manifests his humility by consenting to being made low. Speaking of the incarnate Christ's redemptive suffering, Edwards affirms, "Was this not a wonderful manifestation of humility when he cheerfully and most freely complied with this abasement" (9:322). Virtues, Edwards contends, are most striking in times of trial, and so Christ's humility and other virtues are most evident in his most extreme experiences of suffering:

> All the virtues that appeared in Christ shone brightest in the close of his life under the trials he met with then. Eminent virtue always shines brightest in the fire, pure gold shows its purity chiefly in the furnace. It was chiefly under those trials that Christ underwent in the close of his life that his love to God, his honor of God's majesty, and his regard to the honor of his law, and his spirit of obedience, and humility, and contempt of the world, and his patience, and his meekness, and spirit of forgiveness, and love toward men appeared. (9:323–24)

In presenting a willingness to undergo suffering as evidence of perfect humility, Edwards indicates that true humility requires openness to self-abasement.

By drawing this connection between humility and self-resignation, Edwards underscores the excessive character of Christ's humility. Christ's extreme humility is made manifest in his failure to claim the honors due to him. Christ avoids feelings of pride even though his status puts him in a situation in which a certain type of pride might have been legitimate. Christ was "infinitely honorable" and knew it, but he humbly and willingly subjected himself to treatment unbefitting his station and identity: "though he knew he was the heir of God the Father's kingdom, yet such was his humility that he did not disdain to be abased and depressed down into lower and viler circumstances and sufferings than ever any other elect creature was; so that he became least and lowest of all" (9:322). Christ's suffering was undeserved, and Edwards suggests that this undeserved quality increases its moral excellence. He affirms this point more generally in praising the virtuous meekness that Christ displayed in the atonement; this meekness, like humility, is demonstrated well in conditions of suffering. In praising Christ's meekness as an embodiment of this virtue in its perfect form, Edwards implies that the virtue is greater because the suffering is undeserved:

> None ever met with so great provocations as he did. The greatness of provocation lies in two things, viz. in the degree of opposition by which the provocation is given, and secondly in the degree of the unreasonableness of that opposition, or in its being very causeless and without reason, and the great degree of obligation to the contrary.... Now if we consider... how causeless and unreasonable these abuses were, how undeserving he was of them, and how much deserving of the contrary, viz. of love, and honor, and good treatment at their hands... no man ever met with a thousandth part of the provocation that Christ met with from men. And yet how meek was he under all. (9:323)

It is not Christ's suffering that it most central to Edwards's affirmation of Christ's humility, then, but his willingness not to demand the praise he deserves. By elevating Christ as an exemplar whose actions define the ideal forms of the virtues of humility and meekness, Edwards suggests that the most perfect forms of these virtues are made evident in actions consistent with a denial of one's own merits and desert.

This argument is echoed in Edwards's discussion of humility in the lives of Christians. In *Some Thoughts Concerning the Revival*, Edward draws a contrast between the behavior of a spiritually proud person and the behavior of a humble person; his account suggests that a mark of humility is the denial of such good as may be present in one's heart. Whereas pride makes us see ourselves as better than we are, humility requires that we view ourselves as less than we might be so that we strive to eradicate those things we would wish to change in ourselves: "Pure Christian humility disposes a person to take notice of everything that is in any respect good in others, and to make the best of it, and to diminish their failings; but to have his eye chiefly on those things that are bad in himself, and to take much notice of everything that aggravates him." Seeing oneself as excessively low, and as lower than others, is a mark of humility, whether one is actually lower than others or not: "The eminently humble Christian has so much to do at home, and sees so much evil in his own heart, and is so concerned about it, that he is not apt to be very busy with others' hearts; he complains most of himself, and cries out of his own coldness and lowness in grace, and is apt to esteem others better than himself, and is ready to hope that there is nobody but what has more love and thankfulness to God than he, and can't bear to think that others should bring forth no more fruit to God's honor than he."[32]

Edwards reiterates this point in *Religious Affections*, arguing that the truly humble tend not to recognize their own humility, whereas the proud and the hypocrites falsely perceive themselves to have merit that they lack. Humility shares with pride the feature that an agent does not see herself as she truly is, and in the case of a humble agent, she esteems herself lower than she should:

> An eminent saint is not apt to think himself eminent in any thing; all his graces and experiences are ready to appear to him to be comparatively small; but especially his humility. There is nothing that appertains to Christian experience, and true piety, that is so much out of his sight as his humility. He is a thousand times more quick-sighted to discern his pride, than his humility: that he easily discerns, and is apt to take much notice of, but hardly discerns his humility. On the contrary, the deluded hypocrite, that is under the power of spiritual pride, is so blind to nothing as his pride; and so quick-sighted to nothing, as the shews of humility that are in him.[33]

These characteristics of humility are not strictly reflective of Christ's own humility because Christ is not deceived about his own merits. At the same time, they share with it a type of self-renunciation and a denial of merits that one may have. Christ's humility is exercised through the intentional renunciation of his merit; human humility is also exercised through willful renunciation, but because pride preys upon us, it is safer for us not to risk acclaiming our own merits at all but instead to practice self-deception about them.

For Edwards, then, both pride and humility are on some level disproportionate. Pride involves a failure to recognize our sinfulness and leads us to think of ourselves as better than we are. Edwards affirms that pride is sinful, but he simultaneously argues that the proper exercise of humility may likewise require that we esteem ourselves inaccurately in proportion to our merits. A comparison of Edwards's account of humility to the positions of Augustine and Thomas Aquinas demonstrates the centrality of Edwards's Christology for this argument. Like Augustine, Edwards defines humility in terms of the actions of Christ and therefore sees renunciation as central for its practice; Aquinas, in contrast, is less willing to see self-deception as consistent with virtue.

The Incarnation and the Natural Order: Augustine and Aquinas on Humility

A consideration of Augustine's view of humility reveals striking commonalities with Edwards's Christologically rooted position. Augustine, like Edwards, presents Christ as embodying humility perfectly and revealing it to us. Peter Brown explains that it was not uncommon for Christian writers in late antiquity to uphold saints as moral exemplars and specifically to present Christ in this way; Christ was, for many of these writers, a moral paradigm of holiness.[34] Both Gerald W. Schlabach and Albert Verwilghen observe that Augustine presents humility as a morally significant enterprise that humans can pursue through an imitation of Christ, who models it perfectly. Schlabach characterizes the incarnation as itself "God's humility" and suggests that in the *Confessions*, Augustine affirms his need for "the humility of Jesus Christ" in order to "assent to God's truth."[35] Verwilghen offers a more extensive treatment of Augustine's account of Christ's relation to humility. He explains that Philippians 2:6–11 is important to Augustine's thought and that humility, as it is embodied in this Christological hymn, is an important theme for Augustine's Christology and his soteriology. The events of Christ's life show us how to live humbly, and we can seek God through following the *via humilitatis* that we observe in Christ: "Christ in his annihilation provides us with the *forma servi*. This was the model and the secret for walking in the only path, the *via humilitatis*, which will lead to the Father. . . . Humility is the path by which God, in His Son, 'abased himself in the form of a servant' and 'was obedient unto death, death on the cross' so that sinful humanity could know and imitate it. The humbled Son was, for Augustine, the 'model of humility' which defined Christian behavior." Christ, Verwilghen explains, carries out the salvific plan of the merciful God, and in doing so, he gives humans access to the "mystery" of humility.[36] These scholars' arguments point to the importance of Christ's humility in Augustine's moral thought.

Many of Augustine's own writings underscore this contention that Christ is the model for Augustine's humility. In *Tractates on the Gospel of John* 51, Augustine presents Christ as perfectly embodying humility in a manner that does not compromise his divinity. As the archetype of humility, Christ is our moral teacher: "For the true teacher of humility is Christ, who humbled Himself, and became obedient unto death, even the death of the cross. But He does not lose His divinity in teaching us humility; in the one He is the Father's equal, in the other He is assimilated to us."[37] Like Edwards, Augustine opposes humility to pride and recognizes pride as the first sin. *Of Faith and the Creed* explains that humans must return to God through humility because they fell through pride.[38] Christ possesses such humility that he "deemed it worthy of Him to assume the entire nature of man."[39] Consequently, in his own person Christ offers us an example of the humility through which we return to God.[40]

Augustine's understanding of the nature of humility is in many ways similar to Edwards's view. Because Christ is the moral exemplar of this quality, humility involves a self-renunciation (for Augustine, a "self-abasement")[41] that goes beyond the simple avoidance of pride. We can recognize the distinctiveness of this account of humility, in turn, when we compare it to Thomas Aquinas's position. While Edwards and Augustine develop Christ-centered approaches to defining humility, Aquinas derives an understanding of humility as a human virtue whose character is defined by appealing more immediately to norms perceived in creation. For Aquinas, humility is a part of temperance,[42] and pride is its opposite. In this respect Aquinas and Edwards are similar. Yet Aquinas defines these attributes differently from Edwards, and in a manner consistent with upholding "magnanimity" as a virtue as well. Edwards suggests that the perfect humility of Christ involves the renunciation of the accolades that were his due. In contrast, Aquinas explains that humility is a virtue that guards against a false or unjust pride, a pride disproportionate to an agent's status: "Pride is so called because a man thereby aims higher than he is." The danger in pride is not that an agent will request his due but that she will exceed it and thereby go against reason: "right reason requires that every man's will should tend to that which is proportionate to him. Therefore it is evident that pride denotes something opposed to right reason, and this shows it to have the character of sin." Pride, then, is defined by its excess: it is "inordinate love of one's excellence."[43]

Aquinas's definition of pride allows him to affirm that some recognition of one's own excellence can be meritorious as long as this recognition stands in accord with right reason. Aquinas therefore follows Aristotle in identifying magnanimity as a virtue. Yet Aquinas does not simply reiterate Aristotle's view of magnanimity; instead, he subtly transforms Aristotelian magnanimity in theologically significant ways. Mary M. Keys contends that whereas Aristotelian magnanimity is "the virtue of claiming the greatest of honors, when one rightly judges oneself deserving of them," so that the chief concern of the magnanimous man is his own greatness, Aquinas focuses instead on the ways in which magnanimity can lead us toward good actions that serve the community and God.[44] This focus is evident in Aquinas's *Summa theologiae*, which suggests that an agent practices magnanimity when she recognizes the honors that she legitimately possesses, and offers them to God. Aquinas explains that humans possess some good qualities as gifts from God and some poor qualities as a result of their natural weakness, and magnanimity involves esteeming both rightly and using them appropriately: "There is in man something great which he possesses through the gift of God; and something defective which accrues to him through the weakness of nature. Accordingly magnanimity makes a man deem himself worthy of great things in consideration of the gifts he holds from God: thus if his soul is endowed with great virtue, magnanimity makes him tend to perfect works of virtue; and the same is to be said of the use of any other good, such as science or external fortune."[45] Pride represents an inordinate belief in one's own goodness, but magnanimity is an agent's proper esteem of her own abilities that prevents her from exercising poor stewardship with regard to the skills God has given her. Whereas Aristotle's magnanimity perceives one's merit as a cause for praising oneself legitimately, Aquinas's magnanimity perceives one's merit as a cause for praising God, who is the ultimate source of this merit.

Aquinas explicitly argues that humility is opposed to pride but not to magnanimity. Humility and magnanimity, indeed, are complementary virtues, for both ensure that an agent esteems and uses her gifts in a manner consistent with right reason. Humility guards against excessive or unmerited pursuits of the mind, magnanimity against its inordinately low pursuits: "A twofold virtue is necessary with regard to the difficult good: one, to temper and restrain the mind, lest it tend to high things immoderately; and this belongs to the virtue of humility; and another to strengthen the mind against despair, and urge it on to the pursuit of great things according to right reason; and this is magnanimity."[46] Both humility and magnanimity are concerned with guiding the mind to act in accordance with right reason so that a moral agent will act in a manner appropriate to her abilities and her level of virtue. This characterization of the virtues ensures that humility and magnanimity are not opposed: "Humility restrains the appetite from aiming at great things against right reason: while magnanimity urges the mind to great things in accord with right reason. Hence it is clear that magnanimity is not opposed to humility: indeed they concur in this, that each is according to right reason."[47] For Aquinas, then, humility is a virtue that guards against an excessive pride, but not against a rightly felt pride that encourages agents to use their gifts properly.

The Significance of Edwards's Differences from Aquinas

The distinctions that Aquinas posits among pride, magnanimity, and humility highlight the Christological foundations of Edwards's account of virtue, as well as its differences from both Thomistic and Aristotelian views of what it means for a virtue to be a creaturely excellence. Insofar as Edwards's humility is perfectly embodied in Christ, it seems decidedly unconcerned with promoting an account of virtue as in keeping with right reason. The incarnate Christ's virtue was greater, for Edwards, because it involved his subjection to circumstances that were unreasonable. It would have been just and reasonable for Christ, as God, to resist treatment that was not fitting to his status; after all, Edwards's *True Virtue* contends that it is reasonable, fitting, and virtuous for God to glorify himself above all because God is the being most worthy of being glorified. In submitting to being reviled, the incarnate Christ renounces honors that are due to him as God; God should most properly be exalted. Edwards does not distinguish pride from magnanimity, and yet in praising Christ's renunciation of legitimate pride as a feature of humility, he clearly opposes humility both to what Aquinas calls pride *and* to what Aquinas calls magnanimity. Edwards's presentation of Christ as a moral exemplar of the virtue of humility leads him to define this virtue in a manner strikingly different from Aquinas's conception of humility.

The differences between Edwards and Aquinas point to different starting points for their virtue ethics and the consequences of these starting points. Aquinas's understanding of human excellences builds on the natural order, whereas Edwards derives his understanding of these virtues from the life of God in the incarnate Christ. Edwards thereby appears to capture more straightforwardly a reconciliation of Christian thought with virtue ethics than theologians who begin with Aristotelianism. In addition to the historical Protestant concerns about Aristotelian habituation that I mention in chapter 1, a 2002 work by Daniel Harrington and James Keenan, *Jesus and Virtue Ethics*, points to a struggle among theologians to draw together the moral thought of scripture (and the life of Jesus in scripture) with the moral concept of virtue as Aristotle defined it. Keenan and

Harrington seek to draw these traditions together, and in doing so they highlight the ways in which biblical theology and virtue ethics are generally seen as two distinct traditions of thought.[48] By situating the virtues in Christ, Edwards ensures that his own theory of the virtues is scriptural and theological.

Nevertheless, contemporary proponents of virtue ethics might well be uneasy about the ways in which Edwards's position implicitly yet decidedly involves rejecting even Aquinas's understanding of magnanimity. It may be that Aquinas, by starting with a systematic view of virtue that distinguishes pride and magnanimity, offers certain nuances in his account of virtue that an Edwardsean (or more broadly Augustinian) position fails to capture as fully. Both Edwards's Christ and any moral agent who pursues a humble life by following Christ's example might fail to be virtuous in Aquinas's terms. Is this a failing in Edwards's position? It is worthwhile to explore this question by considering more carefully whether a humble Edwardsean moral agent is subject to what Aquinas calls the sin of pusillanimity.

Pusillanimity and Fortitude in Augustine and Edwards

Aquinas presents pusillanimity as a vice that is an opposite of the virtue of magnanimity; an agent who is not magnanimous risks falling into the sin of pusillanimity. Pusillanimity is the failure of a moral agent to act virtuously in keeping with her own abilities, either because she does not understand these abilities or because she is afraid to use them.[49] Aquinas offers evidence for pusillanimity's sinful character from both scripture and human nature. We have a natural inclination to avoid pusillanimity, and, moreover, the master who gives talents to his servants in the Gospel is angry at the servant who buries his talent in the ground (Matt. 25:14–30): "Now everything has a natural inclination to accomplish an action that is commensurate with its power: as is evident in all natural things, whether animate or inanimate. Now just as presumption makes a man exceed what is proportionate to his power, by striving to do more than he can, so pusillanimity makes a man fall short of what is proportionate to his power, by refusing to tend to that which is commensurate thereto. Wherefore as presumption is a sin, so is pusillanimity." Pusillanimity, then, is the sin of "littleness of soul," an agent's "failure" to reach her potential and to use the gifts God has provided her.[50]

Augustine's and Edwards's views of humility may seem to risk pusillanimity. They deem it virtuous to renounce one's position and abilities, and in doing so they appear to suggest that Christ and the moral agents who follow him are pusillanimous. It is not immediately clear that this overlooking of pusillanimity is a failure in Augustine or Edwards; it could just as easily be argued that Aquinas's position on pusillanimity is problematic because it risks understanding Christ's actions in scripture as sinful. But because there is scriptural warrant for Aquinas's view of pusillanimity, and because Augustine and Edwards likewise derive their understandings of virtuous humility from scripture, it is important to consider whether Augustine's and Edwards's positions can be reconciled with the scriptural claim that we should exercise proper stewardship with regard to our talents and spiritual gifts. Both Augustine and Edwards implicitly address this concern in their accounts of fortitude.

For both Augustine and Edwards, the humble activity of Christ and his followers is not pusillanimous, indicating a "littleness of soul" that reflects an ineffective or inadequate use of one's gifts. Instead, Christ reveals to us that the exercise of humility *is* the proper use of one's gifts. In *On the Trinity*, Augustine explains that God accomplishes our redemption through "righteousness" rather than "power," in order to subvert the workings of the devil, who has led humans to seek power disproportionately:

> But since the devil, by the fault of his own perversity, was made a lover of power, and a forsaker and assailant of righteousness,—for thus also men imitate him so much the more in proportion as they set their hearts on power, to the neglect or even hatred of righteousness, and as they either rejoice in the attainment of power, or are inflamed by the lust of it,—it pleased God, that in order to the rescuing of man from the grasp of the devil, the devil should be conquered, not by power, but by righteousness; and that so also men, imitating Christ, should seek to conquer the devil by righteousness, not by power.[51]

Power, Augustine goes on to explain, need not be completely rejected, because it is not intrinsically evil. But we must recognize that it is inferior to righteousness, and therefore humans do well to join themselves with righteousness, wherein true power consists: "Not that power is to be shunned as though it were something evil; but the order must be preserved, whereby righteousness is before it. For how great can be the power of mortals? Therefore let mortals cleave to righteousness; power will be given to immortals. And compared to this, the power, how great soever, of those men who are called powerful on earth, is found to be ridiculous weakness, and a pitfall is dug there for the sinner, where the wicked seem to be most powerful."[52] Augustine connects this righteousness to fortitude in On the Morals of the Catholic Church, when he suggests that love to God is the root of fortitude and that this love leads us to "bear all things rather than forsake God."[53] In righteousness and virtue, then, there is a type of strength that it is morally proper to pursue.

Edwards makes this point more explicitly in his discussion of the human virtue of meekness. Meekness is not identical to humility, but it is closely enough related that it is useful to consider it in relation to this question of pusillanimity. As with humility, Edwards deems meekness a virtue and a moral excellence of humans that Christ exhibits perfectly. He distinguishes the two in the Work of Redemption by suggesting that humility and patience are virtues a moral agent cultivates respecting herself, and meekness is a virtue that an agent exercises toward others. Yet he defines Christ's meekness partly in relation to the attribute of humility, suggesting some sort of close relationship between the two qualities: "Christ's meekness was his humble calmness of spirit under the provocations that he met with." Additionally, the signs Edwards describes as evidence of the two virtuous dispositions are similar; as with humility, Christ's patient resignation to suffering is evidence of his meekness in the midst of the suffering Christ endured: "how meek was he under all, how composed and quiet his spirit, how far from being in a ruffle and tumult; when he was reviled he reviled not."[54] Distinguishing Marks draws an additional parallel between the two qualities by suggesting that meekness and humility are each dispositional attributes that describe the nature of the love that the incarnate Christ practiced: "The love that appeared in the Lamb of God was not only a love to friends, but to enemies, and attended with a meek and humble spirit."[55] These passages point to a relation between meekness and humility in Edwards's thought.

This similarity is important because it helps us to engage the question of pusillanimity. On one hand, it should be noted that Edwards's view of original sin logically prevents a human moral agent from being pusillanimous. Because of sin, the natural powers that we could be said to possess through creation are so distorted that it could be argued that we have no moral expectation to make use of our natural abilities; instead, we should cleave to God's righteousness, as Augustine argues. But Edwards addresses the issue of pusillanimity even more directly (though without appealing to the term) in his discussion of meekness in Religious Affections. After defending meekness as a virtue, he raises the question of whether upholding meekness requires that we reject a potentially praiseworthy form of boldness or self-assertion: "here some may be ready to say, is there no such thing as Christian fortitude, and boldness for Christ, being good soldiers in the Christian warfare, and coming out bold against the enemies of Christ and his people? To which I answer, there doubtless is such a thing."[56] He argues that we must look to Christ in order to understand what true fortitude is and how we may properly assert our gifts for the sake of God's glory. The incarnate Christ shows us how to exercise fortitude effectively:

> The directest and surest way in the world, to make a right judgment, what a holy fortitude is, in fighting with God's enemies, is to look to the captain of all God's hosts, and our great leader and example; and see wherein his fortitude and valor appeared, in his chief conflict, and in the time of the greatest battle that ever was . . . when he . . . exercised his fortitude in the highest degree that ever he did . . . even to Jesus Christ in the time of his last sufferings. (2:350–51)

Christ's example demonstrates that true strength, and the proper use of abilities that we may possess, lies in meekness. Passionate or violent self-assertion is a sign of weakness (2:350), but the exercise of humility and meekness is our strength: "But how did he [Christ] show his holy boldness and valor at that time? Not in the exercise of any fiery passions . . . but in not opening his mouth when afflicted and oppressed, in going as a lamb to the slaughter, and as a sheep before his shearers, is dumb . . . not shedding others' blood; but with all-conquering patience and love, shedding his own" (2:351).

Indeed, Edwards goes on to refer to the example of Christ's disciple who attempted to wield the sword prior to Christ's arrest, and observes how Christ "meekly" rebukes this disciple. He concludes that Christ models for us the contours of a Christian warrior in this instance. Christ's meekness is not passive submission; it is instead the action of a true soldier. In rebuking the sword-handling disciple, Christ exhibits the virtues supremely: "And never was the patience, meekness, love, and forgiveness of Christ, in so glorious a manifestation, as at that time. Never did he appear so much a lamb, and never did he show so much of the dovelike spirit, as at that time. If therefore we see any of the followers of Christ, in the midst of the most violent, unreasonable and wicked opposition, of God's and his own enemies, maintaining under all this temptation, the humility, quietness, and gentleness of a lamb, and the harmlessness, and love, and sweetness of a dove, we may well judge that here is a good soldier of Jesus

Christ" (2:351). By appealing to Christ's example, Edwards explains that meekness and humility are the strength we are to exercise. True virtuous boldness, or fortitude, lies in these Christian virtues that Christ embodied perfectly.

This discussion of boldness may not appear to answer the questions of pusillanimity fully. To the extent that it does not, it seems likely that this failure lies in Aquinas's and Edwards's fundamentally different accounts of human nature. Edwards's view of original sin leads him to resist seeing human nature (as we currently observe it) as providing norms for our behavior, whereas Aquinas is more comfortable affirming God's revelation of the proper norms for creation in human creatures themselves, though this revelation has been somewhat marred by sin. Nevertheless, Edwards's defense of the boldness exercised in meekness shows that he is concerned to present humility as an active self-renunciation rather than a more passive and indifferent submission to fate.[57] Humble Christians choose to submit themselves to God and to resign themselves to suffering, and, in doing so, they embody their affirmation of the proper order of the world and of their own affections. Virtue and goodness are central to the being of the Trinitarian God, and the task of creatures is to praise God, in part, by recognizing their own weakness in comparison to God and by clinging to the only being who is truly righteous. Edwards affirms that humans should actively and willfully pursue virtue, and this pursuit is the means through which humans use their natural inclinations and faculties properly.

Human Excellence as an Image of Divine Mercy

Edwards's presentation of Christ as the moral archetype of divine virtue and of this category of human virtues has implications not only for how we understand the meaning of these human virtues, but also for the broader question of how divine virtue is related to human virtue in the incarnate person of Christ. Chapter 3 suggests that true virtue in humans participates in the being and love of the Holy Spirit, but this participation does not immediately appear evident as we consider virtues that are perfections of created natures. Yet a closer examination of Edwardsean humility reveals that Edwards's account of this category of human virtues complements the preceding chapter's argument and underscores Edwards's general continuity with the Neoplatonist exemplarist tradition. Even though humility is an excellence that the divine nature cannot practice, this creaturely virtue functions as an image or type of divine mercy. Two of Edwards's arguments particularly demonstrate this intricate relation between humility and divine mercy. First, Edwards argues that the incarnate Christ's simultaneous embodiment of divine and human perfections unifies these perfections. Second, Edwards attributes to the divine nature a quality called "condescension" that is markedly similar to humility, and this condescension functions as one manifestation of divine mercy.

Two Diverse Excellences: Christ as a Unity of Divine and Human Virtue

Edwards establishes the unity of divine virtue and the human moral excellences by locating them radically in the person of Jesus Christ. For Edwards, the incarnate Jesus Christ is a unity of the divine and human natures and, correlatively, a unity of divine and human virtue. "The Excellency of Christ" explains that in the divine and human natures of Christ, "two diverse excellencies" are unified: the infinite majesty characteristic of God and the "superlative humility" that exceeds that of other creatures.[58] In Christ, God intentionally chooses to become flesh and to assume its potential weaknesses. "The Sweet Harmony of Christ" affirms that Christ became human so "that he might be as they [his people] are." He assumed their human nature "in its weak, broken state to be like them," and thereby assumed a nature "subject to affliction and temptation" and to "those disadvantages that are the fruits of sin."[59] At the same time, in becoming flesh Christ also develops the capacity to practice human excellences. Christ retains his divinity, but alongside this divinity he can embody the excellences proper to humanity. Though Christ is equal to God, he simultaneously honors and loves God with a reverence appropriate to his human nature.[60] In Christ, divine excellences and creaturely excellences are brought together.

Edwards is forthright in cautioning that the congruence of divine and human excellences in Christ does not diminish the perfection of Christ's divine excellences. In "The Excellency of Christ" he acknowledges that affirming a category of excellences distinctive to human creatures might risk compromising a Christian view of God as goodness itself and as having all goods properly connected to God's own being. He maintains that the incarnate Christ contains all human perfections but that these cannot logically be said to add to his divine perfections: Christ's human excellences "indeed are no proper addition to his divine excellencies." Divine excellence, Edwards explains, is "infinite." Christ possesses human excellences as well because these are means through which humans may perceive his greatness, but human excellences do not add to the excellent qualities of the divine: "Christ has no more excellency in his person, since his incarnation, than he had before; for divine excellency is infinite, and can't be added to: yet his human excellencies are additional manifestations of his glory and excellency to us, and are additional recommendations of him to our esteem and love, who are of finite comprehension."[61] Edwards, then, strives to uphold Christ's perfect possession of human excellences (and, as a necessary counterpart to this claim, to affirm that there exist qualities that can properly be called excellences of creatures) while simultaneously showing that these excellences do not add to or compete with the virtue and merit of God.

Yet although Edwards is explicitly concerned to protect the integrity of Christ's divinity, his depiction of Christ as the archetype of divine and creaturely virtues necessarily brings these virtues into close relation so that the divine nature can, in a limited sense, be said to embody perfect humility. This is particularly evident when we recall that Edwards situates his defense and explication of Christ's perfect virtue in the context of redemption. Christ's virtues function, in part, as a means through which redemption is accomplished, and consequently cannot be entirely detached from Christ's divine nature, even in the case of creaturely virtues. Edwards is clear that the incarnate Christ's activity upon earth was redemptive only because Christ is God and because Christ's activity can therefore be attributed to the divine nature. In discussing the salvific character of the atonement in "The Free and Voluntary Suffering and Death of Christ," Edwards explains that the atonement accomplished redemption only because it is an intentional act *of the divine God* in Christ: "The life that was laid down was not the life of the divine nature; but notwithstanding it was the life of a divine person that was laid down. . . . The offering up the life of Christ, though it was only of the human life, yet the offering was made by Christ not only as man but as God-man. It is that which renders the act meritorious, because it is not only the act of Christ as man, but also as God."[62] While Edwards is speaking here of the atonement rather than specifically of Christ's virtue or merit, the point is nevertheless significant because it indicates that he believed that Christ's divinity must be at work in all activity of the incarnation in order for human redemption to be accomplished through it. Because virtue, in turn, is part of redemption, the virtues that Christ redemptively possesses and exemplifies must in some sense be possessed and exemplified by Christ's divine nature.

Indeed, because both the atonement and the practice of virtue are part of Christ's redemptive and meritorious activity, Edwards's discussion of the interplay between the divine and human natures during the atonement can compellingly be viewed as a model for how Edwards is likely to have conceived the relation between Christ's divine and human natures in the practice of creaturely virtues. Edwards affirms that it was only Christ's human nature that was killed, just as it was only Christ's human nature that can fully be said to have practiced humility: "it was not the divine life but the human life of that person [Christ] that was laid down." At the same time, however, he is quick to maintain that the action undertaken by Christ at this point was an act of his divine nature as well as of his human nature: "there was the act of Christ as God in it as well as man. It was not only the human nature of Christ that was concerned in offering up that sacrifice to God." Edwards reiterates this point because he implicitly recognizes that an activity that is redemptive must be accomplished by God: "If Christ had offered the sacrifice only as man, and it were to be looked upon as the act of the manhood, it would not have been meritorious, nor would it ever have availed for our salvation."[63] It therefore follows that, as part of redemption, Christ's meritorious practice of creaturely virtues must in some sense be an activity of God.

In one sense, it is Christ's humanity that enables him to practice those virtues most properly ascribed to creatures. Had Christ not become human, he could not have assumed these human excellences. At the same time, however, Edwards emphasizes the unity between human and divine in Christ to such a degree that it would be artificial to deny any link between Christ's divine nature and the virtues that the incarnate Christ practices. Indeed, such a denial would be damaging to Edwards's soteriology. Even if Christ's divine nature is technically unable to practice a virtue such as humility, the unity of the divine and human natures in Christ's salvific activity would make it questionable to rely too heavily on a distinction between virtue practiced by the human nature of Christ and virtue practiced by the divine nature. By explaining that it is Christ's human nature to which humility is properly attributed, Edwards avoids the potential problem of undermining Christ's divinity, but he also ensures that God, in Christ, is the moral exemplar even of this virtue. A characterization of Christ as moral exemplar of humility locates the perfections of divine and human virtues in the person of the incarnate Christ and thereby establishes an intricate connection between creaturely virtue and the divine virtue that is constitutive of God's being.

Merciful Condescension as Divine Humility

The incarnation thus allows for a type of unity between divine and human virtues. A closer look at humility, in turn, reveals more specifically the ways in which divine and human virtue are drawn together in the person of Christ. Edwards presents this unity in terms of a typology: human excellences are types or images of God's own virtue, even though these human excellences (in their precise contours) are qualities that God cannot strictly possess. The incarnation reveals that virtues that appear most proper to creatures in fact retain a particular relation to true virtue in God, and, correlatively, to God's being. An exploration of the relation of Edwards's humility to the divine quality he calls "condescension," which is one specific component of divine mercy, demonstrates the typological relation of divine virtue to human excellences.

As we saw in the previous section, "The Excellency of Christ" affirms that Christ's human excellences do not add to his divine excellences because his divine perfections are infinite. In the course of defending this argument, Edwards suggests that Christ's human virtues are images of his divine excellences. Though the glory of Christ appears in both divine and human excellences, Christ's human excellences are really only reflections of his divine perfections: "his human excellencies are but communications and reflections of his divine; and . . . this light [of Christ's human excellencies], as reflected, falls infinitely short of the divine fountain of light, in its immediate glory." Human excellences retain some qualities of divine excellences, but only in a limited sense: human excellences have "a semblance of the same divine beauty [of divine excellences], and a savor of the same divine sweetness."[64] These statements suggest that Edwardsean virtues that are in one sense creaturely are, in another sense, reflections of divine virtue that are meritorious because they mirror divine beauty.

Edwards further develops a view of creaturely virtues as images of divine virtue through descriptions of a certain kind of humility that God does practice, a "condescension" that can best be understood as an expression of divine mercy. Edwards attributes condescension to Christ's divine nature, and it is plausible to contend that the parallels between divine condescension and earthly humility point to a typological relationship between humility and divine mercy. In "The Excellency of Christ," Edwards praises a quality, which he calls condescension, that seems remarkably similar to humility, but that differs from humility in that it is proper to the divine nature. Condescension, as Edwards describes it, is a merciful disposition that is expressed through a type of self-renunciation, just as humility is. Both condescension and humility involve a willingness to subject oneself to a low state. God, whose nature is inherently good, practices condescension as an ultimate manifestation of the divine mercy constitutive of his being. As an act of self-renunciation, this divine condescension is parallel to the virtuous humility that Christ practices, and, like Christ's humility, models for us the merit of self-renunciation.

Edwards's willingness to attribute "condescension" to God is striking because it suggests that condescension, unlike humility, is compatible with divine self-glorification. Condescension involves an awareness of one's own desert, and an intentionality in foregoing that desert, that exceeds even the intentionality of the humility practiced by Christ's human nature. Christ's human nature renounces its desert, but the deserts it renounces are limited because Christ's human nature is simply human. To some degree, even Christ's humility functions as an acknowledgment of what is true: the human nature of Christ is not God, and it is therefore not worthy of honor as God is. But in practicing condescension, Christ's divine nature renounces the deserts of a divinity, a renunciation even more excessive and unmerited than that which Christ's human nature practices as part of humility. Just as Christ's humility exceeds that of creatures, so does Christ's condescension exceed his humility, and in doing so demonstrates the excessive and unmerited character of divine mercy. Indeed, though Edwards does not say as much, it could be suggested that condescension is the means through which God glorifies himself most fully: just as Christian fortitude is exercised in humility, so is the glory of God exercised in condescension.

Edwards does not specifically compare humility to condescension in "The Excellency of Christ," but he does praise Christ's practice of both qualities in a manner that suggests that the incarnate Christ practices humility and condescension through the same activities. Christ's meritorious condescension is revealed in the very act of becoming human and subjecting himself to low circumstances while human: the conjunction of excellences in Christ "appears in what Christ did in taking on him our nature. In this act his infinite condescension wonderfully appeared; that he that was God, should become man; that the Word should be made flesh, and should take on him a nature infinitely below his original nature! And it appears yet more remarkably, in the low circumstances of the incarnation. . . . His infinite condescension marvelously appeared in the manner of his birth." Condescension here is a morally excellent quality embodied by Christ's divine nature in its assumption of human nature. As Edwards discusses the specific events of the incarnation, however, he conjoins condescension and humility in a manner that highlights the parallels between them. Christ's willingness to live in discomfort is a manifestation of both his condescension and his humility: "Christ dwelt on the earth in mean outward circumstances, whereby his condescension and humility especially appeared."[65] These passages suggest an account of condescension as a divine quality that creaturely humility mirrors.

Recognizing the relation between humility and divine condescension is helpful for specifying the particular nature of Christ's exemplarity of both of these virtues. For Edwards, Christ perfectly embodies both divine virtue and the virtues that are creaturely excellences. Indeed, Christ's embodiment of humility will never be matched: Christ "is not only become man for you, but by far the meekest and most humble of all men, the greatest instance of these sweet virtues, that ever was, or will be."[66] In making this point, Edwards is recognizing a fundamental difference between Christ's practice of these creaturely excellences and the manner in which God's creatures are logically able to practice them. Christ's perfect humility involves the renunciation of honors that he deserves, both because of his sinlessness and because of his status as God's son. Our humility, in turn, may involve the renunciation of honor that we in one sense deserve, but at the same time, Edwards's view of original sin is such that we do not strictly deserve *any* moral merit or honor for ourselves because we cannot practice virtue independently of God. Moreover, even prior to the Fall, our finitude prevents us from deserving as much honor as God does; as I observed in chapter 2, Edwards affirms that love is due to beings in proportion to their existence and virtue, and God surpasses his creatures in both. In the strictest sense, then, only Christ practices humility in its most perfect form, the renunciation of honors that he truly deserves. It is this form of humility that is most fully an image or type of divine condescension (and thereby, ultimately, of divine mercy), although the humility of the elect can be seen as less perfectly imaging this divine quality.

This argument that Christ's perfect humility images divine condescension is underscored by *A History of the Work of Redemption*, in which Edwards goes so far as to describe as "humility" the same divine quality that he calls condescension in "The Excellency of Christ." He affirms that Christ demonstrates humility in his willingness to descend from a loftier place than the angels to a lower place: "The proper trial and evidence of humility is stooping or complying with those acts or circumstances when called to it that are very low and contain great abasement. But none ever stooped so low as Christ, if we consider either the infinite height that he stooped from, or the great depth to which he stooped" (9:322). While Edwards does not attribute this descent specifically to the divine nature, it must be the divine nature to which he refers, for Christ's human nature did not descend from an "infinite height." Moreover, Edwards deems various activities of Christ—Christ's willingness to submit himself to the torture and ridicule of violent humans and to be wrongfully accused—"manifestations of humility" and suggests that Christ's divinity heightens the significance of his willingness to undergo humility. Christ's humility is greater because of his righteousness and because he does not deserve suffering, and it is Christ's divinity, rather than simply the moral character of his human nature, that secures his infinite worthiness: "Such was his [Christ's] humility that though he knew his infinite worthiness of honor, and of being honored ten thousand times as much as the highest prince on earth, or angel in heaven, yet he did not think it too much when called to it to be bound as a cursed malefactor, and to be the laughing stock and spitting stock of the vilest of men" (9:322). Christ's divine nature, then, is not inactive in his practice of humility. In the *Work of Redemption* Edwards presents an account of humility that must logically be practiced by divine and human natures together, for it is Christ's divinity that gives him the merit and desert that makes his humility greater.

Recognizing that God in Christ practices condescension is significant for Edwards's theory of the virtues because it reveals a close relation between excellences proper to creatures and the virtue of God. Creatures embody the excellences proper to their natures when they practice humility by following the example of the incarnate Christ. Yet the true nature of Christian humility is revealed to be a component of Christ's character, and of humans only insofar as God has created them in his image. Creaturely humility, as it is embodied in its most perfect form in Christ, is an image or type of divine condescension, and this condescension, in turn, is a component of God's mercy. It is divine mercy that motivates the incarnation, God's supreme act of condescension. In the *Work of Redemption*, Edwards affirms that love for the church is Christ's motive for redemption: "All this great work [redemption] is for them [the church]. Christ undertook it for their sakes, and for their sakes he carries it on from the fall of man to the end of the world. 'Tis because he has loved them with an everlasting love" (9:526). God's act of redemption is evidence of his constant and faithful mercy exercised toward the church: in considering redemption "we may see the stability of God's mercy and faithfulness to his people, how he never forsakes his inheritance, and remembers his covenant to them through all generations" (9:525). Edwards's sermon "Sinners in Zion" similarly presents the incarnation as a supreme act of mercy: the sin of those who are in the church is particularly grievous because those who exercise it "sin against so much greater mercy. They have the infinite mercy of God in giving his own Son often set before them. They have the dying love of Christ, have this mercy, this glorious Savior, and his blood and righteousness, often offered to them."[67] "The Sorrows of the Bereaved Spread Before Jesus," a sermon with a different tone, exhorts those who are mournful to turn to Christ for comfort; his incarnate life has given evidence of his disposition to be merciful and loving: "By the bowels of his mercies, the love and tenderness of his heart, he is disposed to help those that are in affliction; and his ability is answerable to his disposition."[68] In condescending to become incarnate, God in Christ is exercising the mercy proper to his divine being. Condescension is a means through which mercy is practiced.

Humility, then, is linked to divine mercy through its typological relation to divine condescension. This connection between humility and mercy, in turn, draws together the virtues that are excellences of creatures and the true virtue that is God's very being. Edwards's humility is a type of divine mercy, an expression of love that involves the active renunciation of self in favor of others. A humble moral agent renounces her own worth and gives of herself excessively. Moreover, she is inclined to esteem others better than they deserve and thereby, in a sense, to forgive their sins, or at least to treat them with love even though they may not be said to deserve it. In these actions, a humble moral agent images the inherently merciful God. This God is revealed to us most fully in Christ's incarnation, but as we saw in chapter 2, mercy and love are constitutive of God's very being. The creaturely practice of humility is the reflection of this divine character trait, an image of divine mercy. Thus even these virtues that Edwards defines as human excellences can be understood properly only in relation to God's being; these human virtues are types or images of divine virtue.

In his account of humility, Edwards demonstrates that he recognizes that certain virtues can more aptly be called excellences proper to creatures than excellences proper to God. At the same time, Edwards builds on Augustine to develop an understanding of these virtues that presumes an integral relation between these human moral ideals and God's being. Whereas an Aristotelian virtue ethicist would understand human excellences in relation to the biology of human nature, Edwards believes that even these virtues can only be truly understood in relation to God's being and activity. The incarnate Jesus Christ is a moral exemplar of creaturely virtues such as humility because of his perfect human nature, and his exemplarity draws the practice of these virtues into intricate and necessary relation with God's very being. Moreover, the incarnation reveals that this interplay is inherent in the relation of these human virtues to divine virtue itself: the perfect form of humility is a type of divine mercy.

Although this chapter has not emphasized the issue of moral accountability important to earlier chapters, its exploration of Edwards's humility provides a foundation for recognizing that Edwards's view of moral formation (and consequently his vision of moral agency) differs from that of Aristotle. For Aristotle, virtues are human excellences, and humans become virtuous through habitual actions and practices constitutive of their nature's *telos*. On the surface, it may seem that we could speak of this sort of Edwardsean human virtue in similar ways: virtues such as humility are human excellences, and they are constitutive of a human *telos*. But for Edwards, even the created excellences are finally more proper to God than to humans, and it is therefore logical that humans cannot pursue them apart from God's assistance. In the next chapter, we will see that Edwards rejects Aristotle's view of moral formation in favor of an alternative model of accountability, just as we have seen that his view of created excellences has a final reference point in God.

5

Virtuous Repentance
Apprehending and Approving God's Moral Excellence

Chapters 3 and 4 both considered a type of human virtue with a direct relationship to divine virtue. True virtue in humans images and participates in divine love, and creaturely humility, at least as the incarnate Christ embodies this virtue, is an image or type of divine mercy. In this chapter I turn to virtuous repentance, one of a category of human virtues that God cannot be said to practice because these virtues presuppose sin. In contrast to both true virtue and humility, human repentance has no proper correlate in God's being. Virtuous repentance is constituted by regret for one's own sin and hatred for one's own evil, and God, as a morally perfect being, has no need to exercise either of these dispositions. Yet Edwards nonetheless designates repentance as a virtue in humans, and his account of this virtue reveals an additional dimension of the interplay between divine and human moral agency in the practice of human virtues.

This chapter begins with an examination of Edwards's account of repentance. Edwards's virtuous repentance is a disposition of the heart that is instilled in humans after their conversion, and, correlatively, after their possession of a spiritual sense (or taste).[1] As such, it is legitimate to describe this repentance as a corollary to true virtue in humans. The term "corollary" signifies a logical relation between repentance and true virtue: for Edwards, virtuous repentance follows from the love to God through which humans increase in love for the created universe as a whole, but this repentance is simultaneously not identical to true virtue. A comparison of Edwards's account of repentance to the Scottish philosopher Francis Hutcheson's virtue theory illuminates the broader significance of this category of human virtue for understanding Edwards's account of moral formation. Building on scholars who affirm a parallel between Edwards's spiritual sense and Hutcheson's "moral sense," I argue that Edwards's account of the relation between the spiritual sense and our cultivation of virtuous repentance is strikingly similar to the relation between the moral sense and the cultivation of virtue that Hutcheson proposes. This similarity is marked by the centrality of the concepts of "apprehension" and "approbation" for Edwards's and Hutcheson's moral systems. This comparison of Edwards to Hutcheson demonstrates that Edwards's position theologically enriches Hutcheson's account of moral formation, just as Edwards's understanding of the meaning of true virtue is a theological adaptation of Cambridge Platonism (as I argued in chapters 2 and 3). Edwards ultimately embraces an essentially Hutchesonian account of moral formation but transforms this account theologically by firmly rooting it in the context of Christian conversion and salvation. This theological framework is essential to understanding the meaning of Edwards's virtuous repentance.

Recognizing the Hutchesonian underpinnings of Edwards's view of moral formation reiterates Edwards's significance as a figure who offers a theologically viable alternative to Aristotle's account of the virtues' acquisition. Although Hutcheson considered his own thought to be somewhat consistent with that of Aristotle,[2] the ancient philosophers whose work most influenced Shaftesbury and Hutcheson were Cicero and the Roman Stoics,[3] and this influence is evident in Hutcheson's understanding of virtue's acquisition. We will see that Edwards intentionally and deliberately turns to a Hutchesonian position in order to articulate a view of moral formation distinct from Aristotelian habituation. Edwards's account of virtuous repentance thereby reveals an additional dimension of the model of moral accountability he offers to contemporary ethicists.

Edwards's Virtuous Repentance

As with the categories of human virtue discussed previously, Edwards most overtly speaks of repentance as a virtue in *A History of the Work of Redemption*. Edwards contends that certain human virtues presume sin in the agent, and that repentance is one of these virtues. God, even in the human nature of Christ, decidedly does not possess these virtues that imply sin or imperfection: "Indeed there are particular virtues that sinful man may have that were not in Christ, not from any want or defect in his virtue, but because his virtue was perfect and without defect. Such is the virtue of repentance and brokenness of heart for sin, and mortification. These virtues were not in Christ because he had no sin of his own to repent of. But all virtues that don't presuppose sin were in him."[4] Edwards's identification of repentance as a virtue may seem surprising. The term "repentance" often refers to an action rather than a state of one's character. Yet

Edwards speaks of repentance in two different ways. One sort of Edwardsean repentance is not strictly virtuous; it is an act that humans perform prior to conversion. Virtuous repentance, in contrast, is a disposition or character state that an agent attains subsequent to conversion and the possession of a spiritual sense. Virtuous repentance is a corollary of truly virtuous love: as we apprehend and love God, we come to see our sin for what it is, to feel distaste and regret for this sin, and to renounce our sin actively on the basis of our hatred for it. In order to explore Edwards's account of the virtue of repentance, then, it is helpful to begin by contrasting Edwards's two types of repentance. An overview of Edwards's virtuous repentance shows that conversion and the spiritual sense are essential conditions of its practice, a point that is central to understanding how Edwards's view of repentance relates to Hutcheson's virtue.

At points, Edwards describes a type of repentance that is not finally virtuous, although in some forms it may be meritorious. Edwards suggests that repentance for sin is an act that "natural men" can perform through motives connected primarily to self-love rather than to virtue. The Holy Spirit can awaken our consciences and make us aware of sin prior to conversion.[5] As this happens, the Spirit makes us aware of our guilt and of the punishment we risk receiving from God.[6] "Wicked men and devils" are capable of seeing all of God's perfections (such as his greatness, majesty, and power) except for his beauty (2:264), and this vision may lead them to repent for their sin because of fear. Edwards describes this sort of repentance as a "sorrow for sin" arising from "self-love," a regret that is practiced by "hypocrites" (2:253). Edwards simultaneously identifies a less hypocritical form of nonvirtuous repentance. He recognizes a type of natural beauty in God that can also lead humans, independently of saving grace, to repent in some form. There is, Edwards argues, "natural good" in Christ's incarnation and redemption, and our minds may repent of sin because we recognize this natural good without having developed a true awareness of divine things (2:277; see also 265). It would seem that repentance arising from a perception of natural good has more potential to be meritorious than repentance arising from self-love, but Edwards does not resolve this point fully. Instead, he characterizes all repentance practiced by "natural man" in a manner that is ultimately inconsistent with virtue, for all genuine virtue must arise from a love to God that can only be instilled in us through a spiritual sense that God graciously gives us. The repentance of which humans are naturally capable is akin to what Edwards calls "legal humiliation" later in *Religious Affections*: in this state, "a sense of the awful greatness, and natural perfections of God, and of the strictness of his law, convinces men that they are exceeding sinful, and guilty . . . but they don't see their own odiousness on the account of sin" (2:311). Natural humanity can experience repentance, but this repentance is not virtuous, and indeed Edwards is forthright in affirming that "legal humiliation has in it no spiritual good, nothing of the nature of true virtue" (2:312).

Edwards also describes a second sort of repentance that occurs subsequent to our possession of a spiritual sense, and it is this repentance that he ultimately deems virtuous. In *A History of the Work of Redemption*, Edwards suggests that virtuous repentance can best be understood as "brokenness of heart for sin,"[7] and this view of repentance is consistent with a disposition that Edwards ascribes to the regenerate in *Religious Affections*. Virtuous repentance occurs as we encounter God and are made aware of our sin in comparison to God's moral perfections. Sin no longer has dominion over someone who has converted, but this person still has the capacity to sin.[8] Yet after conversion, such sin in which an agent continues will cause her a grief it did not cause before. This grief occurs because she has received a spiritual sense that enables her to perceive God's moral goodness and to recognize her own comparative failures. The spiritual sense aids in a moral agent's practice of repentance by giving her a capacity to perceive the great gulf between God's moral excellences and her own moral inadequacies. It is this repentance and regret of sin that is truly virtuous, for implicit in it is a dispositional love to God coupled with an awareness of our complete dependence on God.

Because of its connection to divine love, it is legitimate to characterize virtuous repentance as a corollary of true virtue. As true virtue increases, so does virtuous repentance. Recognition of our own sinful state and appreciation of God's comparative beauty are, for Edwards, key to the sort of repentance that can be considered a virtue. If people deny their sin, it is a sign that their religious discoveries are false and have produced false affections in them, for true religious affections make our sins plain:

> The nature of many high religious affections, and great discoveries (as they are called) in many persons that I have been acquainted with, is to hide and cover over the corruption of their hearts, and to make it seem to them as if all their sin was gone, and to leave them without complaints of any hateful evil left in them (though it may be they cry out much of their past unworthiness); a sure and certain evidence that their discoveries (as they

call them) are darkness and not light. 'Tis darkness that hides men's pollution and deformity; but light let into the heart discovers it, searches it out in secret corners, and makes it plainly to appear; especially that penetrating, all-searching light of God's holiness and glory. (2:327)

Those who have truly experienced conversion will be aware of their continued sin and feel remorse for it, rather than allowing themselves to be deceived that they no longer sin. Edwards reiterates this point later in *Affections*, and he presents this repentance more clearly as a corollary of love to God. As we long for God, we will at the same time increasingly feel repentance for the sin we perceive in ourselves: "The more a true saint loves God with a gracious love, the more he desires to love him, and the more uneasy he is at his want of love to him: the more he hates sin, the more he desires to hate it, and laments that he has so much remaining love to it: the more he mourns for sin, the more he longs to mourn for sin: the more his heart is broke, the more he desires it should be broke: the more he thirsts and longs after God and holiness, the more he longs to long" (2:377). Virtuous repentance, then, occurs after conversion and increases after conversion, just as love to God does. As we love God increasingly, we hate sin, and we lament the sin that we perceive to be in ourselves. Moreover, we will see that the spiritual sense given to us at conversion makes repentance possible because this faculty has the capacity to see and love God. The mechanics through which we cultivate virtuous repentance are therefore best understood in the context of Edwards's view of conversion and the activity of the spiritual sense.

Hutcheson's View of Moral Formation

Before turning to Edwards's account of conversion, it is necessary to highlight certain elements of Hutcheson's moral thought. Although Edwards engages many of his philosophical contemporaries, Hutcheson is particularly important to Edwards's view of the workings of the spiritual sense. Hutcheson's account of moral formation is a helpful starting point for understanding Edwards's conception of the process by which virtuous repentance is brought about in the converted soul.

The Relation of Edwards to Hutcheson

Contemporary Edwards scholarship recognizes Edwards's familiarity with Hutcheson's thought. It is quite likely that Edwards read works by Samuel Clarke,

Shaftesbury, and Hutcheson in his study at Yale, where these British moral philosophers were part of the curriculum.[9] Edwards is known to have owned two major moral treatises that Hutcheson wrote in the 1720s,[10] and his writings refer to Shaftesbury explicitly as early as 1723 and to Hutcheson as early as 1738.[11] It is therefore plausible that Edwards's early exposure to Shaftesbury and Hutcheson led him to develop his notion of the spiritual sense in conversation with their ideas about taste, conscience, and the operations of sense in relation to virtue, if not with Hutcheson's fully developed moral sense theory.

Yet this argument is somewhat controversial. While Avihu Zakai believes that Edwards was well acquainted with Hutcheson's writings by 1738, so that they can be seen to influence even *Charity and Its Fruits*,[12] Norman Fiering offers an alternative account of Edwards's relation to Hutcheson's moral sense that remains influential among scholars. Fiering contends that Edwards did not read Hutcheson's *Inquiry* until after 1746 and therefore was "not yet fully acquainted with the benevolist school" when he put forth his account of the spiritual sense in the *Religious Affections*. He concedes that in this text Edwards does cite the entry on "taste" from an encyclopedia highly influenced by Hutcheson, but Fiering nevertheless hypothesizes that Edwards developed his spiritual sense independently of Hutcheson and was "amazed and dismayed" to discover that Hutcheson defended a natural moral sense so similar to the spiritual sense through which Edwards was seeking to uphold the necessity of special grace for human virtue.[13] Following Fiering, many scholars who link Hutcheson to Edwards focus on Edwards's *Two Dissertations*, both because they are written much later (and consequently after Edwards is certain to have read Hutcheson) and because they represent a more explicit engagement of Edwards with British moral philosophers.[14]

If Fiering's analysis is correct, it can at least be said that it is legitimate to affirm parallels between Edwards's spiritual sense and Hutcheson's moral sense. At the same time, Zakai's evidence suggests that it is not impossible that Edwards was aware of parallels to the benevolist school even while writing of the spiritual sense in *Religious Affections* and was more intentionally drawing from Hutcheson than Fiering assumes. Perhaps even more compelling evidence comes from *Religious Affections* itself, in which Edwards, in citing the encyclopedia article to which Fiering alludes, attributes the view of "taste" described in it, rather cryptically, to "a late great philosopher of our nation." Edwards goes on to draw an overt parallel between this "natural taste" and his own "divine taste" (2:282–83), a parallel that I discuss at greater length below. My own sympathies therefore lie with Zakai, but even Fiering's interpretation of Edwards's interaction with Shaftesbury and Hutcheson demonstrates the merit of comparing his thought to Hutcheson's when focusing on the moral capacities of the regenerate.

I will ultimately suggest that Hutcheson's understanding of the moral sense and the soul's cultivation of virtue are foundational to Edwards's view of the means whereby the converted soul comes to exercise the virtue of repentance. Whether Edwards intentionally transformed benevolist thought or simply developed his spiritual sense in concert with it, his account of the process through which we achieve the virtue of repentance functions as a version of Hutcheson's account of how we become virtuous. Edwards has theologically modified Hutcheson's view so that virtuous repentance (as a corollary of true virtue) is limited to those who have received the benefits of spiritual grace. But his consistency with Hutcheson can be seen both in his understanding of the moral faculty and in the place he gives to sensory knowledge in the cultivation of virtue.

Hutcheson on Sense, Reason, and the Cultivation of Virtue

Hutcheson is a Presbyterian pastor who shares with Edwards and the Cambridge Platonists a concern to refute Hobbes's voluntarist account of God. In order to challenge Hobbes's account of God's will as most fundamentally constituted and directed by its own power, Hutcheson defends God's benevolence and presents benevolence as the core of human virtue. He contends that we are naturally able to be virtuous because God has created us with a natural faculty that leads us toward benevolence. This faculty, which Hutcheson designates the "moral sense," is our primary source of moral knowledge and the faculty most central to our cultivation of virtue. Human reason, in turn, is more or less instrumental for our pursuit of virtue. By making reason secondary to the moral sense, Hutcheson presumes a certain kind of alignment between the moral sense and virtue; this alignment affects his understanding of moral formation and development. For Hutcheson, the key moral act is not a cognitive act of understanding. Instead, humans exercise virtue, and are formed in meritorious dispositions, as they apprehend and approve goodness and beauty. Although Edwards will depart from and challenge Hutcheson's presupposition that we can acquire virtue independently of conversion, Hutcheson's view of the moral sense and its acts of apprehension and approbation are nevertheless formative for Edwards's own understanding of the spiritual sense and its activities.

In order to understand Hutcheson's view, it is helpful to begin by recognizing that Hutcheson affirms the importance of sensory impressions as a foundation for knowledge. It logically follows from Hutcheson's elevation of sensory knowledge that good and evil reside in objects external to us: for Hutcheson, goodness or a lack of it is inherently present in material objects, independently of how we judge them or how they may benefit us. This interpretation of Hutcheson is at odds with some twentieth-century readings of his thought. In an influential article, William Frankena holds that Hutcheson's moral theory is noncognitivist, so that moral judgments are simply expressions of emotional reactions and statements of a particular type of pleasure.[15] Henning Jensen is critical of Frankena's particular reading of Hutcheson but accepts Frankena's essential view of Hutcheson as a noncognitivist.[16] More recently, however, Knud Haakonsen contends that Hutcheson's moral thought achieves a "basic coherence between moral realism and natural law"[17] such that Hutcheson does, in fact, present the moral sense as apprehending moral qualities that are objectively present in the natural order. Therefore, for Haakonsen, Hutcheson is a cognitivist:

> For Hutcheson, our putative moral judgements are in fact real judgements; ... the putative objects of such judgements are in fact real objects; and ... these objects are empirically ascertainable features of human nature. ... Moral perception is *not* a subjective affective experience; and moral judgements are thus not simply the expressions of such experiences. Whether we make moral judgements of our own behaviour or that of others, our moral perception and thus our moral judgement are explicitly *representative*, and thus either true or false. Further, moral judgements are emphatically of something quite distinct from the pleasures which moral behaviour may and, upon reflection, will occasion in agent as well as spectator.[18]

Though twentieth-century scholars differ in their accounts of Hutcheson's understanding of beauty (partly because Hutcheson himself is not entirely consistent), it is nevertheless clear that, at least at many points in his writing, Hutcheson explicitly argues that moral qualities reside in objects independently of our approval of them, so that our senses perceive and approve beauty that is actually present in objects. Hutcheson thereby expresses his intention to affirm that both physical beauty and moral beauty are objective qualities residing in the world. When we observe forms and recognize that they are beautiful, we are not ascribing beauty to them because they give us pleasure or somehow serve our interests; rather, their inherent beauty is the cause of the pleasure we feel upon seeing them: "we do not say that [an object] is beautiful because we reap some little pleasure in viewing it, but we are pleased in viewing it because it is antecedently beautiful." Our approval of beauty in objects is parallel to our approval of virtue in people: "when we admire the virtue of another, the whole excellence, or that quality which by nature we are determined to approve, is conceived to be in that other."[19] Hutcheson's argument that we approve of things because of their prior beauty applies to actions as well. He explains that we observe actions and recognize them as good not because they benefit us but because our senses accurately perceive the goodness that is evident in them.[20] For Hutcheson, then, goodness (be it beauty in objects or benevolence in actions) does not depend on human assessments of it but is inherently part of the created order, a point consistent with Edwards's own theology of creation.

Hutcheson moreover affirms an epistemological relationship between the truth present in the external world and our natural moral intuitions or preconceptions. He locates this natural intuition in a particular faculty of the human person, the moral sense. By positing the existence of this sense, Hutcheson is able to account for his empirical observation that all humans instinctively feel that virtue is good. Hutcheson suggests that our difficulty in explaining our natural moral inclinations is based in "our previous notions of a small number of senses."[21] Coupled with our recognition of the weakness of reason[22] and its inadequacy to lead us toward virtue,[23] any natural human inclinations to approve virtue must necessarily be grounded in our senses or feelings.[24] Since we can observe a natural human inclination toward virtue, this inclination must lie in a sense, and Hutcheson creates the moral sense to account for his recognition that we are somehow constructed to approve of virtuous acts, and, through our desire for self-approval, to pursue virtue ourselves. The moral sense, then, functions precisely as a sense. Its primary activity is to observe the world, to approve or disapprove of the things it observes, and to cause a person to feel pleasure or pain in response to these observations. The ability of the moral sense to perceive virtue is comparable to the natural tendency of our internal sense of beauty to perceive and approve order and harmony in the world.[25]

Hutcheson presents the moral sense as a natural part of our constitution and contends that God, in God's goodness,[26] has given us this sense so that we can pursue virtue. This pursuit takes place through our moral sense's apprehension (or perception) of virtue and its approbation (or approval) of virtue. Hutcheson says that our moral sense, which enables us to "perceive virtue or vice, in ourselves, or others,"[27] is part of our very nature,[28] rather than having been shaped by custom and education, and is present in all of us.[29] In endowing us with a moral sense, God has naturally equipped us for virtuous actions, which shows that he has not abandoned humankind and left us inherently self-interested and unable to be virtuous:

> [Hutcheson's] principle design is to shew that human nature was not left quite indifferent in the affair of virtue, to form to itself observations concerning the advantage or disadvantage of actions and accordingly to regulate its conduct. . . . The author of nature has much better furnished us for virtuous conduct than our moralists seem to imagine, by almost as quick and powerful instructions as we have for the preservation of our bodies. He has given us strong affections to be the springs of each virtuous action; and made virtue a lovely form, that we might easily distinguish it from its contrary, and be made happy by the pursuit of it.[30]

In creating us with a moral sense, God has constructed us so that we naturally approve of benevolent actions that tend toward our common good, the end he has ordained for humanity.[31] Hutcheson asks why people approve the public good, and he explains, "The reasons assigned are such as these, 'It is the end proposed by the Deity.' But why do we approve concurrence with the divine ends? This reason is given, 'He is our benefactor.' But then, for what *reason* do we approve concurrence with a benefactor? Here we must recur to a *sense*."[32] The moral sense, then, is the natural faculty that God has given us so that we might perceive goodness in acts of benevolence toward each other.

Not only does the moral sense enable us to perceive and approve benevolence, but Hutcheson stresses that its approbation of benevolence is necessary in order to move us to *perform* virtuous acts: in other words, approbation is central to Hutcheson's account of the moral formation through which we are enabled to act virtuously. Hutcheson maintains that the moral sense (both directly and indirectly—that is, through guiding other instincts and affections) is the faculty that moves the will. Jensen suggests that Hutcheson follows Shaftesbury in presenting moral judgments as intrinsically motivating; morality is "intensely practical, dynamic, and moving," so that our knowledge of it will lead us to act virtuously.[33] Hutcheson partly demonstrates this relationship between moral sense and will in his discussion of the desires that the moral sense produces in us. Our moral sense's apprehension and approbation of virtue produces in us a desire to be virtuous because we wish to approve our own actions and dispositions, and we know that we will approve them if they are virtuous. The moral sense "yields desires of virtue, and aversion to vice, according to the notions we have of the tendency of actions to the public advantage or detriment."[34] We come to desire benevolence because we seek self-approval, and this desire is independent of our selfish preconceptions of whether a benevolent action or disposition might benefit us.[35] A recognition that our moral sense's approval of virtue leads us to develop benevolent dispositions enables Hutcheson to claim that this sense actually guides us to be virtuous: "God has given us a *moral sense*, to direct our actions."[36]

Hutcheson explains that our moral sense provides "justifying reasons" for human acts, and our instincts or affections provide "exciting reasons."[37] Because Hutcheson conceives of exciting reasons as immediate motives for our actions, it might seem that our motives relate more to general instincts than to the moral sense itself. But the particular contrast that Hutcheson draws between exciting and justifying reasons demonstrates that his distinction between the two does not presume that the moral sense is deficient in its ability to move our wills to act. He cannot attribute *all* of our motives for action to the moral sense itself, because his conception of the moral sense as naturally inclined toward benevolence runs counter to his admission that we do not always act in a manner that the moral sense would approve.[38] Nevertheless, the moral sense functions to approve benevolent actions, and our desire for self-approval will lead us to resist those instincts that oppose benevolence; thus, even though the moral sense does not move us in all of our acts, it plays a significant role in enabling our acts that are virtuous by serving as a means through which we judge our moral activity.[39] Furthermore, in leading us to approve virtue, the moral sense works closely with the instincts that lead us to act virtuously so that we will know that acts are good or bad as we perform them. The moral sense's "approbation" provides us with a self-awareness that makes our pursuit of virtue authentic: "Having removed these false springs of virtuous actions [that is, concepts of virtuous actions as springing from self-love], let us next establish the true one, viz. some determination of our nature to study the good of others; or some instinct . . . which influences us to the love of others; even as the moral sense, above explained, determines us to approve the actions which flow from this love in ourselves or others."[40] Thus, even though it is properly "instincts" rather than the moral sense that immediately motivate acts of virtue, we can see that the moral sense's approbation of benevolence is necessary in order to reinforce virtuous dispositions in us.

In understanding sense to be the moral director of the will, Hutcheson presents "approbation" as a key moral act. Approbation is the will's response to external circumstances that our senses perceive. This approbation takes place as virtuous impressions present themselves to our minds and these impressions are perceived by the moral sense. We are conditioned not simply to perceive virtue and vice but more actively to "approve" virtue and "condemn" vice; these actions are a "determination of our minds." Virtue inspires particular sentiments in us, sentiments of "good-will" and "love" toward the agent who enacts virtue. We are driven by a "*natural determination* to approve and admire, or hate and dislike actions."[41] The activity of the moral sense, then, involves the response of our wills and affections to external objects that confront us. Approbation is a response to virtue that necessarily involves a human will's manifestation of expressions of approval.

Edwards's Account of the Cultivation of Repentance

The Hutchesonian picture of the workings of sense and reason is helpful for understanding Edwards's account of virtuous repentance, even though Edwards expressly challenges Hutcheson's claim that the pursuit of virtue is natural to us. For Edwards, not only are we by nature dependent upon God for the pursuit of virtue, but original sin also prevents our faculties from being able to seek virtue apart from God's gracious intervention. Nevertheless, Edwards's account of the movement of the elect toward virtue following their conversion has striking commonalities with Hutcheson's position. In conversion, Edwards explains, we are given a spiritual sense that functions as a "principle" that enables our natural faculties to incline toward virtue, as well as a "divine taste" that inclines us toward a meritorious approval of spiritual beauty. The activity of the spiritual sense (and the taste and dispositions that arise from it) parallels the activity of Hutcheson's moral sense, and, like this moral sense, presumes a view of sensory knowledge as related to an external moral order. Yet Edwards presents this activity in theological terms: we come to exercise virtuous repentance as our soul (with the aid of the spiritual sense) encounters, apprehends, and approves God's moral perfections.

To make this argument, I begin by considering Edwards's account of conversion and the spiritual sense, particularly noting his rejection of an Aristotelian account of how we cultivate virtue. In rejecting Aristotelian habituation, Edwards instead upholds Hutcheson's position. Having made this point, I turn more directly to Edwards's account of the cultivation of virtuous repentance. Edwards's understanding of how we come to exercise the virtue of repentance after conversion mirrors Hutcheson's view of how our natural faculties lead us toward virtue. We encounter a moral order external to us (in Edwards's system, we encounter God), and through this encounter we come to apprehend and approve God's moral beauty. In turn, our apprehension and approval lead us toward a virtuous response that is a corollary of this apprehension and approval: a hatred and distaste for our sin.

Conversion and the Spiritual Sense: The Beginnings of Virtuous Repentance

Although Hutcheson and Edwards speak of the cultivation of virtue in similar ways, Edwards sets his own view of virtue in a decidedly theological context, that of conversion. Conversion does not make humans immediately virtuous. Edwards distinguishes justification from sanctification and does not presume that the elect are sanctified immediately upon conversion. But at the moment of conversion, God instills in the elect a spiritual sense that gives them a capacity to pursue virtue. The spiritual sense is not equivalent to a fully virtuous disposition, nor is a human's progress toward virtue necessarily constant following her possession of a spiritual sense. Nevertheless, the spiritual sense is an essential starting point for the cultivation of virtue, apart from which persons cannot exercise true virtue or its corollary, virtuous repentance. Before considering how the cultivation of virtue following the possession of the spiritual sense mirrors Hutcheson's account of the cultivation of virtue, it is helpful to explore Edwards's notion of conversion more thoroughly.

Edwards often speaks of conversion as a process whereby humans are given a spiritual sense that reorients their faculties. Conversion, he explains in *Religious Affections*, is a "change in nature" effected by God (2:340). By defining conversion in this way, Edwards ensures that divine grace is central to its achievement, and, correlatively, to the virtue that the elect exercise following their conversion. Only God has the power to change a person's nature: "Such power as this is properly divine power, and is peculiar to the Spirit of the Lord: other power may make a great alteration in men's present frames and feelings; but 'tis the power of a Creator only that can change the nature, or give a new nature" (2:340). This change, however, does not result in the immediate and complete exercise of perfect virtue; instead, it gives an agent the capacity to pursue virtue. Edwards explains that the spiritual sense is a "new principle of nature" that regenerates the elect. The spiritual sense is a disposition or capacity that they are given upon conversion and that provides a foundation for their ability to pursue virtue. Humans lack this capacity apart from the particular intervention of God's special grace that takes place in conversion:

> This new spiritual sense, and the new dispositions that attend it, are no new faculties, but are new principles of nature. I use the word "principles," for want of a word of a more determinate signification. By a principle of nature in this place, I mean that foundation which is laid in nature, either old or new, for any particular manner or kind of exercise of the faculties of the soul; or a natural habit of foundation for action, giving a person ability and disposition to exert the faculties in exercises of such a certain kind; so that to exert the faculties in that kind of exercises, may be said to be his nature. So this new spiritual sense is not a new faculty of understanding, but it is a new foundation laid in the nature of the soul, for a new kind of exercises of the same faculty of understanding. So that new holy disposition of heart that attends this new senses, is not a new faculty of will, but a foundation laid in the nature of the soul, for a new kind of exercises of the same faculty of will. The Spirit of God, in all his operations upon the minds of natural men, only moves, impresses, assists, improves, or some way acts upon natural principles; but gives no new spiritual principles. (2:206)

Conversion, then, is an event that changes human nature such that natural faculties can be exercised in new ways. God gives the elect new "principles" or dispositions that allow them to work in ways that they could not work apart from the particular assistance of divine grace.[42] It is true that God imparts virtue to us in a sense, for God imparts God's own being. But Edwards's emphasis is upon the capacity God gives us to pursue virtue, the new principle that enables us to seek it.

Because the spiritual sense functions as a capacity or principle, it is clear that Edwards's view of conversion logically extends beyond an initial event, and encompasses human moral formation subsequent to an individual's possession of the spiritual sense. The saints are, in some sense, *formed* in holiness because the spiritual sense is a capacity rather than a fully realized state. For the most part, the elect must cultivate the spiritual sense after receiving it. Edwards recognizes that there is a "very imperfect degree, in which this sense is commonly given at first," and a "small degree of this glorious light [of God's illumination] that first dawns upon the soul" in conversion (2:275). Edwards conceives this moral formation as part of conversion as well. Conversion is not only an event to be anticipated by those who have not yet experienced it; it is also an experiential reality in which the saints take part over time, as they fully realize the reorientation of their faculties that is enabled by divine grace at the first moment of conversion. Roger Ward explains that Edwards speaks of conversion as both an occurrence to be anticipated and a more extended reality in which divine grace unifies human faculties and directs them toward the good: "Conversion works both ways for Edwards. First, conversion is what he speaks about to draw souls toward the 'good' we anticipate in God, and second, he speaks of conversion as an opening into the continuous discovery of the 'good' found in the experience of God. In both cases the divine effect of conversion and our realization of it are the same event, whereby God's influence is present in the human experience of a discovery that incorporates the faculties of understanding, willing, and desiring into a spiritual unity." Ward contends that the focus of *Religious Affections* is a consideration of the contours of conversion within the lives of the saints. Whereas Edwards's revival texts, such as "A Divine and Supernatural Light," seek to encourage conversion in souls who have not yet experienced it, *Religious Affections* examines the spiritual knowledge of conversion "as it appears within the living reality of the saints, as the dynamic principle that holds them to God." Ward suggests that *Religious Affections* describes conversion as a process of continued discovery: the twelve signs of true religious affections that Edwards offers in this text "bring to view the pivotal transitions of a soul in the discovery of its effective change of inclination toward God and the divine character of the object it seeks with its heart."[43] *Religious Affections* is therefore a helpful text for understanding Edwards's view of conversion as a change in one's being that is in one sense immediate but that, in another sense, is fully realized over time and must be continually realized in order to be authentic.

Edwards makes it clear that the change of nature God effects at conversion will be "abiding" if it is authentic.[44] Granted, Edwards does acknowledge that people will sin even following conversion; given his strong view of original sin, it would be difficult to say otherwise.[45] Yet Edwards is also clear that by presenting conversion as a change in nature, he is suggesting that conversion must be represented by a new state of one's being, for this is what nature is: "If there be a very great alteration visible in a person for a while; if it ben't abiding, but he afterwards returns, in a stated manner to be just as he used to be; it appears to be no change of nature. For nature is an abiding thing" (2:341). In referring to conversion as a change in nature, Edwards indicates that conversion necessarily involves a change in an agent's character subsequent to regeneration rather than simply referring to a single moment within an individual's spiritual journey.

This point is strengthened by Edwards's suggestion that grace works to convert the elect continually. The elect receive grace, and this grace sanctifies them over time, operating within them in a manner that increasingly conforms them to Christ: "The saints don't only drink the water of life, that flows from the original fountain; but this water becomes a fountain of water in them, springing up there, and flowing out of them. . . . Grace is compared to a seed implanted, that not only is in the ground, but has hold of it, has root there, and grows there, and is an abiding principle of life and nature there" (2:343). Grace, then, does not operate only at the first moment of conversion, but it continues to transform our natures.[46] On some level, Edwards views conversion as gradual, as a process of moral formation through which individuals are increasingly conformed to Christ.

Significantly, although Edwards's account of conversion includes the activity of the saints following their gracious possession of a spiritual sense, his understanding of the moral formation that takes place after conversion runs counter to Aristotle's view of moral formation. Along with Anri Morimoto, whose work I mentioned in chapter 1, William Danaher has recognized this point. Danaher argues that in contrast to such thinkers as Paul Lewis and James Gilman, who present Edwards as augmenting an Aristotelian view of virtue with a conception of the emotions as morally significant,[47] it is more proper to see Edwards's position as offering a completely different account of moral formation. Danaher acknowledges that Edwards employs some of the same "terms and concepts" of Aristotelian and Thomist views of virtue in that he describes virtue as a "dispositional state of character." But Edwards resists the idea that we can acquire virtues through moral education.[48] Edwards rejects Aristotelian habituation because he sees it as conflicting with his theological views that God enables virtue directly in an individual.[49] This rejection leads Edwards to affirm an alternative view of moral formation in both *Religious Affections* and the later treatise *Original Sin*.

Stephen Wilson presents Edwards's emphasis on constancy in moral dispositions as a sign that Edwards's virtue ethic has (to some degree) an Aristotelian orientation. In a sanctified person, Wilson explains, "virtuous affections outweigh selfish or cruel affections" and a "delight in God supersedes the delight in worldly things." For Wilson, these features of Edwardsean virtue demonstrate Edwards's essential continuity with Aristotle's account of habit.[50] Certainly Wilson is right to note Edwards's emphasis on constancy and even on repetition. *Original Sin* demonstrates that to see actions as indicative of one's nature requires constancy and repetition, showing indirectly that conversion cannot be a change in nature unless it is in some sense an extended state over time: "one act don't prove a fixed inclination; but . . . constant practice and pursuit does."[51] Yet a close look at *Original Sin* suggests that in defending constancy as part of our moral character after conversion, Edwards is aligning his view of moral formation not with Aristotle but with Hutcheson. Wilson is right to see constancy as a feature of Edwards's thought, but this constancy is not an indication of Edwards's Aristotelianism. Indeed, Edwards's defense of constancy as a sign of virtue in *Original Sin* appeals explicitly to Hutcheson rather than to Aristotle.

Immediately prior to a passage in which he lauds Hutcheson for making several points about moral good and evil that are "evidently agreeable to the nature of things, and the voice of human sense and reason" (3:224), Edwards affirms that it is agreeable to humanity's "common sense" to realize that actions are good when they proceed from virtuous dispositions:

> This is the general notion, not that principles derive their goodness from actions, but that actions derive their goodness from the principles whence they proceed; and so that the act of choosing that which is good, is no further virtuous than it proceeds from a good principle, or virtuous disposition of mind. Which supposes, that a virtuous disposition of mind may be before a virtuous act of choice. . . . If the choice be first, before the existence of a good disposition of heart, what signifies that choice? There can, according to our natural notions, be no virtue in a choice which proceeds from no virtuous principle. . . . And therefore a virtuous temper of mind may be before a good act of choice, as a tree may be before the fruit, and the fountain before the stream which proceeds from it. (3:224)

Having made this point, Edwards immediately cites Hutcheson's argument that virtues and vices are either affections or actions that are consequent on affections, and he uses this point as grounds for contending that virtuous dispositions and affections are prior to the actions that proceed from them (3:224–25). Through this argument, Edwards rejects an Aristotelian view of habituation in favor of a mode of thinking more typical among Edwards's immediate interlocutors. For

Edwards, as for Hutcheson, virtuous dispositions must be prior to virtuous actions; it is logically untenable for virtuous actions to *form* us in virtuous dispositions because our actions are not "virtuous" until *after* we possess a virtuous disposition from which they can proceed. Although conversion does allow for some degree of moral formation *subsequent* to the possession of a spiritual sense, Edwards contends that repeated acts do not form us in particular dispositions or establish "habits" in us; instead, a particular disposition *that already exists* will be made evident in the repeated performance of actions: "The very supposition of a *disposition* to right *action* being first obtained by repeated right action, is grossly inconsistent with itself: for it supposes a course of right action, *before* there is a disposition to perform any right action" (3:229). Prior to the Fall, for example, humans' love to God was not something cultivated through the repeated performance of loving actions; instead, humans were created with a disposition to love God from which actions expressing that love followed (3:229). In keeping with Edwards's logic in this argument, the true state of one's nature or dispositions will be made evident over time, through the actions one performs. Edwards decidedly rejects a notion of habit that implies that the performance of actions is what forms and shapes our dispositions.

Edwards's rejection of Aristotelian habituation is important because it underscores the distinctive account of moral formation that his position offers to contemporary Christian virtue ethics. Although Edwards resists the Aristotelian view that actions form us in dispositions and are the means through which we acquire virtue, he nonetheless develops an account of the virtues that allows for moral formation to take place subsequent to our possession of the spiritual sense. In both *Religious Affections* and *The Life of David Brainerd*, Edwards builds on Hutcheson's understanding of approbation as a virtuous activity of the moral sense. Like Hutcheson's position, Edwards's account of the spiritual sense's approbation suggests that humans pursue virtue as they encounter and engage the external world and approve the virtue in it. Yet Edwards theologically transforms Hutcheson's conception of the virtues' acquisition: the virtue that the elect encounter and approve is God's virtue, the only real moral excellence. God reveals the divine nature to those who possess a spiritual sense, and the spiritual sense engages in the moral exercise of perceiving and approving God's virtue.

Apprehension, Approbation, and Assent: The Spiritual Sense's Activity in Forming Virtuous Dispositions

Both *The Religious Affections* and *The Life of David Brainerd* suggest an underlying Hutchesonian framework in Edwards's conception of moral formation following conversion. Hutcheson's ideas of apprehension and approbation undergird Edwards's view of how the spiritual sense forms virtuous dispositions in the elect. Edwards embraces an account of moral formation that stands in contrast to Aristotelian habituation and that ensures God's centrality to our cultivation of virtue. At the initial moments of conversion, God reveals himself to us and our spiritual sense approves him, thereby ensuring that the "excellency of divine things" functions as "the foundation of all holy affections."[52] Our apprehension and approval of God's moral excellences gives rise to our truly virtuous dispositions, including both true virtue and its corollary, virtuous repentance.

Religious Affections identifies the apprehension and approbation of divine moral perfections as a central function of the spiritual sense. Through the spiritual sense, the elect apprehend the beauty of God, beauty that "arises from God's moral perfection" (2:273). Apprehension of God, and of genuine moral goodness and beauty, is the root of all real knowledge and all spiritual knowledge. Apart from seeing God and apprehending God's moral beauty, we are "ignorant of the whole spiritual world" (2:275). God alone is excellence and beauty, and if we do not see this, we are unable to see the source of any beauty that can be perceived in the world: "He that sees the beauty of holiness, or true moral good, sees the greatest and most important thing in the world, which is the fullness of all things, without which all the world is empty, no better than nothing, yea, worse than nothing. Unless this is seen, nothing is seen, that is worth the seeing: for there is no other true excellency or beauty. . . . This is the beauty of the Godhead, and the divinity of Divinity (if I may so speak), the good of the infinite Fountain of Good" (2:274). Apprehending God's moral goodness is thus in certain ways a prerequisite for truly virtuous activity, because this apprehension enables us to see God properly.

It is important to recognize that, for Edwards, it is not simply our apprehension of God, but more specifically our *approbation* of God, that is a morally significant activity. The spiritual sense does not simply see God; it actively approves God and loves God and, in doing so, gives its assent to God. Edwards explains that the spiritual sense is a "sense of the heart," meaning that it does not simply see God's excellence but takes joy in this excellence: "There is a distinction to be made between a mere notional understanding, wherein the mind only beholds things in the exercise of a speculative faculty; and the sense of the heart, wherein the mind don't only speculate and behold, but relishes and feels" (2:272). The sense of the heart affects both the will and the understanding, so that when we see God's moral beauty, our understanding perceives its excellence and our will simultaneously delights in it:

> Spiritual understanding consists primarily in a sense of heart of that spiritual beauty. I say, a sense of heart; for it is not speculation merely that is concerned in this kind of understanding: nor can there be a clear distinction made between the two faculties of understanding and will, as acting distinctly and separately, in this matter. When the mind is sensible of the sweet beauty and amiableness of a thing, that implies a sensibleness of sweetness and delight in the presence of the idea of it: and this sensibleness of the amiableness or delightfulness of beauty, carries in the very nature of it, the sense of the heart; or an effect and impression the soul is the subject of, as a substance possessed of taste, inclination, and will. (2:272)

In a manner similar to Hutcheson, for whom the moral sense approves and relishes the virtue it apprehends, Edwards presents the spiritual sense as approving God, as actively taking joy in the divine moral excellences.

Moreover, Edwards suggests that the spiritual sense instills in us a particular disposition or "taste" that tends to approve divine things, an argument that underscores the similarities between his account of moral formation and Hutcheson's position. I have not discussed Hutcheson's notion of moral taste explicitly because it is not sufficiently different from the moral sense to merit its own treatment in this context; "taste" is best understood as a term Hutcheson uses to show how the moral sense manifests itself practically. It functions as a way of speaking about the virtuous dispositions that we possess because of our moral sense, dispositions that incline us to apprehend and approve virtue.[53] As I noted earlier in this chapter, Fiering recognizes that *Religious Affections* cites an entry on "taste" in an encyclopedia that was heavily influenced by Hutcheson. Edwards develops his notion of spiritual sense in conjunction with a view of "divine taste" that is a clear parallel to the notion of natural taste in Hutcheson and Shaftesbury and that underscores the idea that approbation is, for Edwards as well as for Hutcheson, a key moral act.

Edwards on occasion speaks of both the "spiritual sense" and "divine taste" as performing essentially the same roles: both are ways of speaking about the Holy Spirit's establishment in us of a disposition that gives us a capacity to act virtuously by approving and assenting to God. When Edwards, in *Religious Affections*, employs the notion of "divine taste" to describe the Holy Spirit's guiding the behavior of the elect, he begins by affirming that, as philosophers have noted, humans have a natural taste that allows them to make judgments about justice and beauty in temporal things (2:282). He explicitly derives this notion of taste from an encyclopedia Hutcheson influenced; after citing this encyclopedia's entry on "taste," Edwards affirms a parallel ability in the elect to make proper moral judgments based on their tastes' apprehension of beauty. The Holy Spirit dwells in us and gives us the capacity to make sound moral judgments (presumably through our exercise of the spiritual sense, though Edwards is not explicit about this). Our spiritual sense gives us a disposition to apprehend moral actions and perceive their beauty so that we can judge them rightly:

> Now as there is such a kind of taste of the mind as this, which philosophers speak of, whereby persons are guided in their judgment of the natural beauty, gracefulness, propriety, nobleness and sublimity of speeches and actions, whereby they judge as it were by the glance of the eye, or by inward sensation, and the first impression of the object; so there is likewise such a thing as a divine taste, given and maintained by the Spirit of God, in the hearts of the saints, whereby they are in like manner led and guided in discerning and distinguishing the true spiritual and holy beauty of actions; and that more easily, readily, and accurately, as they have more or less of the Spirit of God dwelling in them. And thus the sons of God are led by the Spirit of God, in their behavior in the world. (2:283)

This gracious disposition gives us the capacity to know what actions are proper for us to perform: "A holy disposition and a spiritual taste, where grace is strong and lively, will enable a soul to determine what actions are right and becoming Christians, not only more speedily, but far more exactly, than the greatest abilities without it" (2:283). The Holy Spirit thereby leads us to discern good and evil when we encounter them.[54] Edwards thus describes moral judgments in the elect as following from their dispositions' response to the world they apprehend rather than as cultivated through repeated actions.

The nature of this knowledge, moreover, is such that it is necessarily connected to the will and to action. It is not simply that our divine taste leads us to see the good, but our apprehension of the good leads us to pursue moral behavior. Following Hutcheson, Edwards argues that moral perceptions are immediate, so that we can understand them without the assistance of our reason; we have "no need of a train of reasoning" (2:281). As something that functions independently of reason, the "spiritual understanding" we gain immediately from this taste is not merely a speculative knowledge of what is good but a "divine supernatural sense and relish of the heart" (2:285). Our apprehension of moral beauty involves our soul in an act of approbation and assent; we "incline" toward a morally beautiful object and "relish" it: "When a holy and amiable action is suggested to the thoughts of a holy soul; that soul, if in the lively exercise of its spiritual taste, at once sees a beauty in it, and so inclines to it, and closes with it. On the contrary, if an unworthy unholy action be suggested to it, its sanctified eye sees no beauty in it, and is not pleased with it; its sanctified taste relishes no sweetness in it" (2:281). Edwards's discussion of taste thereby demonstrates the ways in which Edwards's use of Hutcheson leads him toward an account of moral formation for which approbation and assent, rather than a habituative view of moral formation, are key.

Virtuous Repentance as a Disposition Enabled by the Spiritual Sense

The significance of approbation for Edwards's view of moral formation is particularly evident with regard to the cultivation of virtuous repentance. In order to practice this virtue, we must first see ourselves rightly and acknowledge our sin for what it is. We can only recognize our need to repent when we apprehend God's moral beauty. Upon encountering God's self-revelation, our spiritual sense and divine taste will approve and love God and, as a corollary to this love, will hate and regret the evil and sin that we see in ourselves. Edwards affirms in *Religious Affections* that approving God enables us to see "the true evil of sin: for he who sees the beauty of holiness, must necessarily see the hatefulness of sin, its contrary" (2:274). Apart from the spiritual sense that allows us to perceive "the beauty of holiness," we are "totally blind, deaf, and senseless"; our knowledge "is but the shadow of knowledge, or the form of knowledge" (2:274). Prior to our conversion, we may on occasion recognize and appreciate the "natural good" that the triune God possesses, but not the "spiritual beauty"[55] that enables us truly to repent. We may naturally feel an aversion to sin because of our approbation of this goodness (2:277). But true repentance follows from spiritual understanding, from the approbation of divine beauty that the spiritual sense of the elect performs.

Because repentance arises from our perception and approval of God, Edwards explains that grace functions to increase repentance. As our perception of God gives us joy, we increasingly recognize our own sin and understand its evil, as compared to God's goodness. Through experiencing and perceiving God's special grace, the elect are able to discern sin:

> True grace tends to promote convictions of conscience. Persons are wont to have convictions of conscience before they have any grace: and if afterwards they are truly converted, and have true repentance . . . this . . . has no tendency to put an end to convictions of sin, but to increase them. It don't stupefy a man's conscience; but makes it more sensible, more easily and thoroughly discerning the sinfulness of that which is sinful, and receiving a greater conviction of the heinous and dreadful nature of sin . . . and more convinced of his own sinfulness, and wickedness of his heart. (2:363)

Through the gracious operation of the spiritual sense, we come to recognize that sin opposes the "will and law and honor of God," and this recognition leads us to understand "the infinitely hateful nature of sin, and its dreadfulness upon that account" (2:363–64). After conversion we will tend to be increasingly "alarmed with the appearance of moral evil, or the evil of sin" (2:364). Repentance, then, follows from the apprehension and approbation of God, an act of which the spiritual sense of the elect is capable.

Edwards's narrative of David Brainerd's conversion, *The Life of David Brainerd*, likewise details the importance of apprehension and approbation for virtuous repentance. To some degree, Edwards presents approbation of God's moral goodness as a central part of the first moment of conversion itself; Brainerd is unable adequately to repent of his sins until he encounters God and, through his spiritual sense, approves God's moral excellences. Before his conversion, Brainerd is aware of his sinfulness to some degree, but he finds himself still secretly hoping to please God through performing religious duties.[56] He believes that he might be capable of somehow deserving Christ's mercy because of his own good works (7:106–8). In order to have true repentance and be redeemed, he needs to turn to God for his salvation rather than depend on his own abilities, but he nevertheless finds himself attempting to seek salvation through his own merits, in the hope that his awareness of his sin will alone lead him toward conversion: "When at any time I took a view of my convictions of my own sinfulness, and thought the degree of 'em to be considerable, I was wont to trust in my convictions: But this confidence, and the hopes that arose in me from it, or soon making some notable advances toward deliverance, would ease my mind, and I soon became more senseless and remiss" (7:112). In order for his soul to be converted, he needs to receive a disposition that will enable him fully to see his own sin for what it is, and to recognize that if he receives salvation, it will be purely through God's grace (7:114).

Brainerd is given this virtuous disposition, the disposition that enables him properly to repent, at the same moment when God reveals himself to him. Through this vision of God, Brainerd apprehends and approves the divine perfections. Prior to this moment, he explains, he had continued to cling to the hope of meeting the Law's demands by his own efforts (7:119). At the moment of his conversion, however, he is illuminated by a vision of the divine glory that captivates his soul. This vision reveals to Brainerd God's excellences and the beauty of God's perfect moral character, and it is through this vision, and the approving response of Brainerd's soul to the vision, that Brainerd is able truly to possess a disposition of virtuous repentance for his sins. God "brings him to" this sort of disposition, suggesting that the disposition is a spiritual disposition given by divine grace:

> I had no particular apprehension of any one person in the Trinity . . . but it appeared to be the divine glory that I then beheld. And my soul "rejoiced with joy unspeakable" to see such a God, such a glorious divine being; and I was inwardly pleased and satisfied, that he should be God over all forever and ever. My soul was so captivated and delighted with the excellency, loveliness, greatness, and other perfections of God, that I was even swallowed up in him. . . . Thus God, I trust, brought me to a hearty disposition to exalt him and set him on the throne, and principally and ultimately to aim at his honor and glory as King of the universe. (7:138–39)

Brainerd is able to acknowledge his own inability to be virtuous apart from God, and thereby to recognize his sin for what it is, only after apprehending God and having God's merits revealed to him. This vision is, for Brainerd, coupled with an approbation of God's moral character; Brainerd's soul rejoices in God's perfections and is captivated by them. Although Brainerd periodically struggles to retain this disposition, he is nevertheless able to come closest to maintaining it through subsequent reflections on God's glory, both through personal moments in which he apprehends God's excellences and through reflections on these excellences as he encounters them in scripture (7:143). Apprehension and approbation of the moral excellences and beauty of God enable Brainerd to move beyond attempts to achieve salvation through his own efforts toward a disposition that acknowledges his own sinful state and sees his own evil for what it is. This virtuous repentance is coupled with a continual turning toward God, both as the proper object of glory and as the arbiter of salvation. Brainerd's conversion underscores and exemplifies the apprehension and approbation of God's moral character that Edwards presents in *Religious Affections* as part of the virtuous life. Brainerd's recognition and approval of God's moral perfections is necessary in order for him to recognize his own sin and to repent of it. Conversion and the cultivation of virtue require and depend upon God's self-revelation, which leads our spiritual sense toward sentiments of approval and joy.

Repentance, the Spiritual Sense, and the Authenticity of Moral Agency: Revisiting the Issue of Moral Accountability

Before leaving the virtue of repentance, it is important to consider the precise sense in which our spiritual sense is "led" toward virtuous sentiments. Such consideration allows us to revisit an issue central to this text: the issue of moral agency and accountability in humans. The parallel between Edwards's spiritual sense and Hutcheson's moral sense underscores our need to examine the issue because both Edwards and Hutcheson emphasize the immediacy with which approbation occurs when the sense perceives moral good. For Edwards, affirming this immediacy is a means of upholding God's overwhelming moral beauty. Because God is beauty itself, it is logical that those who possess a spiritual sense would immediately apprehend and rejoice in this beauty, independently of cognitive reasoning and judgment. But if God bestows the spiritual sense upon the elect independently of their merit, and if possession of a spiritual sense immediately leads an agent toward a particular moral disposition, then in what sense can a virtuous act or disposition be authentically ascribed to an agent?

To understand Edwards's position, it is helpful to return to the contrast between Edwards and Aristotle. We have seen that Edwards's commitment to a particular view of divine providence and the necessity of grace leads him toward an account of virtue that is at odds with Aristotelian habituation. An Aristotelian perspective on virtue suggests that the repeated performance of actions can form us in virtue, a formation that some Christian thinkers have historically perceived as undermining the necessity of divine grace for human morality. Edwards himself is wary of the concept of habituation for this reason. His emphasis on divine activity in salvation underscores the theological claims that are important to his account of moral formation, and particularly to his account of the process by which we cultivate virtuous repentance.

Edwards contends that God "causes" our salvation, and it logically follows from this view that God causes conversion and its consequences, including the pursuit of repentance. In *A History of the Work of Redemption*, Edwards makes it clear not only that we need God's assistance to be virtuous but that it is precisely God's moral praiseworthiness that is crucial in this process: it is God's "righteousness" that causes salvation (9:115). Edwards uses this term to speak both of the righteousness embodied by the incarnate Christ and of the activity of God in individual humans' contemporary experiences of conversion. God's righteousness, for Edwards, is at work in the process of repentance and conversion. This righteousness is a means through which God restores life to human souls as they convert and are sanctified: "Man's soul was ruined by the fall, the image of God was ruined, man's nature corrupted and destroyed, and man became dead in sin. The design [God's design in redemption] was to restore the soul of man in conversion and to restore life to it, and the image of God in conversion and to carry on the restoration in sanctification, and to perfect it in glory" (9:124). This restoration, in turn, is made possible through the work of the righteous Jesus Christ; Edwards rebukes those who trust in their own righteousness when it is Christ's righteousness that accomplishes salvation and the restoration of souls to God (9:335). From the Fall until the end of the world, God continually makes possible the conversion of particular fallen souls and their movement toward the practice of holiness: "This effect [of conversion] that I here speak [of] is the application of redemption with respect to the souls of particular persons in converting, justifying, sanctifying, and glorifying of them. By these things the souls of particular persons are actually redeemed. . . . And in this sense the Work of Redemption is carried on in all ages from the fall of man to the end of the world" (9:120–21). Humans cannot practice the virtues through their own power, but God, precisely because of his righteousness, can bring about salvation and conversion. God's moral righteousness is therefore necessary for any virtue, such as repentance, that is intrinsically connected to conversion. It is fitting, then, that our apprehension of God's moral beauty is an immediate cause of our approbation of this beauty.

It cannot be denied that Edwards is interested in affirming God's exclusive goodness and sovereignty to such a degree that he would prefer to risk undermining human freedom rather than risk suggesting that humans might be able to pursue virtue independently of God. In *Religious Affections*, for example, he clearly affirms humans' dependence upon their creator: "'Tis very true that all grace and goodness in the hearts of the saints is entirely from God: and they are universally and immediately dependent on him for it" (2:342). And in emphasizing the immediacy of moral approbation, Edwards risks undermining human free will by leaving open the possibility that God's moral beauty compels a particular response in the individual who possesses a spiritual sense. To some degree, this possibility seems not to trouble Edwards, and indeed, at one point in *Religious Affections* he affirms that the Holy Spirit leads us in ways that do compel a particular response: "And as to a gracious leading of the Spirit, it consists in two things; partly in *instructing* a person in his duty by the Spirit (the 'spiritual instruction' that the Holy Spirit gives us through divine taste), and partly in powerfully *inducing* him to comply with that instruction" (2:281). This passage suggests that Edwards is comfortable with affirming that divine grace can move our wills in a manner that compromises human autonomy and that might therefore be seen as threatening to undermine human moral accountability.

At the same time, however, Edwards clearly wishes to speak of the Holy Spirit's leading of the dispositions of the elect as something over which we exercise some control, or, at the very least, as something in which our agency participates. Edwards is careful to explain that we are led by the Spirit because the Spirit has given us a particular disposition. The Holy Spirit leads us through dispositions that can properly be called our own, so that our actions can likewise be intelligibly called ours. In other words, our own converted soul, rather than the Holy Spirit, is finally what leads our activities. The Holy Spirit is involved only by giving us the capacity to see a virtuous course of action more clearly than we would otherwise be able to do: "A holy disposition and spiritual taste, where grace is strong and lively, will enable a soul to determine what actions are right and becoming Christians, not only more speedily, but far more exactly, than the greatest abilities without it" (2:283). Here Edwards seems to suggest that it is the human soul, and human faculties, that determine a person's course of action rather than the immediate work of the Spirit; the Spirit gives us spiritual faculties that "teach and guide a man in his behavior" just as natural faculties do (2:283–84). Although the Spirit leads our hearts, our hearts themselves are active in determining what is beautiful and what we should love: "Thus a holy person, is led by the Spirit, as he is instructed and led by his holy taste, and disposition of heart; whereby, in the lively exercise of grace, he easily distinguishes good and evil, and knows at once, what is a suitable amiable behavior toward God and toward man . . . and judges what is right, as it were spontaneously, and of himself, without a particular deduction, by any other arguments than the beauty that is seen, and goodness that is tasted" (2:282). For Edwards, then, the Spirit is working in our hearts, but humans nonetheless judge the actions and dispositions that we should pursue "of ourselves" through the beauty we perceive.

Edwards makes this point even more explicitly as part of his discussion of conversion as a "change of nature." He suggests that conceiving conversion in this way is intended, in part, to guard against a vision of human virtue as something that divine grace compels the elect to perform independently of the consent of their own faculties. When the Holy Spirit imparts grace to the soul, God is said to live in us, but he does not effectively take a human moral agent's place. Instead, God instills in that agent the capacity to overcome the bonds of original sin. Christ is the source of all exercises of grace, but Edwards remains adamant that Christ does not violently compel the will to go against its own nature to perform them: "All the exercises of grace are entirely from Christ: but those exercises are not from Christ, as something that is alive, moves and stirs something that is without life, and yet remains without life; but as having life communicated to it; so as through Christ's power, to have inherent in itself, a vital nature. In the soul where Christ savingly is, there he lives. He don't only live without it, so as violently to actuate it; but he lives in it, so that that also is alive" (2:342). By presenting conversion as a change in nature, then, Edwards seeks to give logical coherence to the idea that converted humans' virtuous actions are something to which they are morally accountable even as divine grace enables these actions.

Recent scholarship on Thomas Aquinas's account of the gifts of the Holy Spirit offers insight into what is at stake in conceiving the indwelling of the Holy Spirit as central to a virtue ethic, as Edwards does. Thomas O'Meara's 1997 article "Virtues in the Theology of Thomas Aquinas" is critical of the "Thomism" offered by many virtue ethicists in the latter part of the twentieth century because, O'Meara explains, these positions fail to address the distinctions Aquinas draws among acquired virtues, infused virtues, and the gifts of the Holy Spirit. According to O'Meara, contemporary scholars such as MacIntyre and Hauerwas tend to characterize Aquinas's position as a modified Aristotelianism without examining adequately the theological concepts of grace and the Holy Spirit that are central to his thought. O'Meara points out that Aquinas does not see acquired virtues (those virtues that he derives from Aristotle, and that persons can achieve through natural processes of habituation) as virtues in an absolute sense.[57] In the *Summa theologiae*, Aquinas contends that "only infused virtues are complete and deserve to be called virtues absolutely,"[58] a claim that Edwards likewise affirms (as we will see in chapter 6). In discussing the infused virtues, however, Aquinas differentiates them not only from acquired virtues but also from what he calls the "gifts of the Holy Spirit." Both the infused virtues and the gifts of the Spirit are given to us through acts of God's grace,[59] but whereas the infused virtues are perfections of those virtues whose norms are derived from our natures, the gifts of the Spirit are special qualities that we exercise as the Holy Spirit dwells within us.

Something very like this Thomistic distinction is present in Edwards's thought as well. I explain in chapter 6 that there are, in fact, Edwardsean infused virtues, forms of certain natural attributes (such as justice and love to one's family) that have been perfected by divine grace. Yet Edwards distinguishes these infused virtues from true virtue and also from the qualities of humility and repentance that function as corollaries of true virtue. This distinction suggests that Edwards's understandings of love, humility, and repentance are parallel not to Aquinas's infused virtues but to the gifts of the Holy Spirit. Significantly, one of Aquinas's gifts of the Holy Spirit is the gift of "understanding," a gift that illuminates and cleanses our minds so that we truly see God's goodness and beauty as well as our own sinfulness.[60] Aquinas thus designates a quality parallel to Edwardsean repentance as a gift of the Holy Spirit.

The relation of Edwards's virtues to the gifts of the Holy Spirit suggests that non-Aristotelian descriptions of moral formation can plausibly lead us toward an authentic picture of moral accountability. According to Edwards's view of moral formation, the Holy Spirit dwells within us and guides our behavior without compelling our actions or undermining our agency. Divine and human agency are intimately connected in the pursuit of these virtues; by emphasizing the dwelling of the Holy Spirit in our hearts, Edwards aligns our pursuit of virtue with the activity of God within us. To be fair, this notion of the relation between divine and human agency is not something that Edwards resolves perfectly. Edwards's desire to affirm divine sovereignty and the exclusivity of divine goodness makes him wish to leave room for the possibility that the Holy Spirit may induce us to perform moral actions.[61] At the same time, however, Edwards's emphasis upon the ways in which humans remain accountable for their actions even when God's Spirit dwells within them indicates that he implicitly understands the moral activity of those in whom the Spirit dwells as something in which these agents authentically participate, an act of joyfully consenting to God's presence in our hearts and to the dispositions in which God seeks to form us.

VIRTUOUS REPENTANCE

Edwards's discussion of virtuous repentance reveals another dimension of his theory of the human virtues. Whereas love and humility correspond to virtues in the divine being, repentance is a virtue that God logically cannot possess. Yet repentance is a corollary of true virtue. As we love God, we will logically increase in our dispositional hatred of sin and our regret that sin is at work in our own lives.

This consideration of Edwards's virtuous repentance is also important because it underscores the differences of Edwards's virtue theory from Aristotelian views of habituation. Hutcheson's moral sense theory informs Edwards's understanding of moral formation generally, and Hutcheson's influence is particularly evident in Edwards's account of the exercise of virtuous repentance, because approbation of God's moral excellence is so central to its practice. Edwards's virtuous repentance is something that humans can pursue only after their possession of a spiritual sense that allows them properly to see God's moral beauty and their own comparative sin.

In chapters 3, 4, and 5 we have seen that love, humility, and repentance are all virtuous dispositions that God enables in the elect through the gift of a spiritual sense. This spiritual sense, in turn, is the means through which we realize the character traits proper to creatures who have been created and redeemed by God. God is virtue and goodness itself, and is greater than all other beings. It is therefore fitting that we love and glorify God, that we practice humility by recognizing our own limitations in comparison with God's goodness, and that we exercise repentance by hating our sin. In loving God, we give ourselves up to him and trust that this being who is Love, by his very nature, will order all things for good. We develop virtuous dispositions that are suited to embracing our positions within this providential plan, within the universe that has been rationally ordered to glorify God, and, in glorifying God, to glorify virtue itself.

6

Justice and Partial Loves
The Natural Goodness of Incomplete Virtues

In addition to the attributes that he identifies explicitly as virtues, Edwards characterizes two additional sorts of qualities as in some sense meritorious. The first of these is justice; the second is a set of natural loves that are private or partial, directed toward a subset of creation rather than toward God and the totality of God's created universe. Edwards resists calling the pursuit of these qualities "virtuous" because their achievement does not require the intervention of God's special grace; humans can pursue these qualities by cultivating their natural faculties. But Edwards does address these attributes at some length in the *Two Dissertations*, and examining this discussion and contextualizing it in relation to his historical predecessors gives us a more complete picture of Edwards's account of the human virtues than would a more limited focus on those qualities that are unequivocally truly virtuous. Edwards characterizes justice and partial loves as expressions of "natural goodness" that possess a "secondary" beauty. This beauty images and reflects the beauty of true virtue and is present in the world because of God's providential ordering of creation.

Because justice and partial loves take part in a beauty that is typologically related to the beauty of true virtue, it might seem appropriate to describe them as secondary virtues. They are complementary to true virtue and share many of its qualities. However, because Edwards distinguishes them decisively from true virtue, they cannot be considered virtues in the same manner that the other human virtues are. Unlike the other human virtues, justice and partial loves are attainable (at least in theory) independently of conversion; original sin disrupts humans' abilities to pursue natural goodness, but its pursuit is not impossible. And yet because justice and partial loves take part in a beauty that reflects true virtue's goodness, it would be insufficient to suggest that they are merely Augustinian "splendid vices": Edwards is clear that they possess both a "negative moral goodness" and a more positive goodness. For Edwards, these attributes are emanations of God's goodness and beauty that coincide, to a limited but nonetheless important degree, with the moral goodness of true virtue and its corollaries. Because of this coincidence, it is fitting to think of justice and private loves as incomplete human virtues. These incomplete virtues possess a small measure of goodness, demonstrated in their partial congruence with true virtue or benevolence. They reflect and image the goodness of true virtue in a limited sense, and are themselves "good" as communications and expressions of God's goodness. Moreover, they have the capacity to become sanctified, suggesting that these incomplete virtues' latent natural goodness gives them an inherent potential to be made truly virtuous.

In developing this account of justice and partial loves, Edwards draws upon understandings of divine providence and the rationalism of the created order that reinforce the historical arguments of the preceding chapters. In chapters 2 and 3 I argued that whereas Schneewind sees modern voluntarism as the only logical means through which Enlightenment thinkers could defend God's necessity for morality, Edwards's ethics represents an alternative that Schneewind has overlooked. Edwards's accounts of true virtue in God and humans integrate features of modern voluntarism with claims characteristic of modern thinkers who seek to oppose voluntarism. His position is therefore a fusion of modern voluntarism with rationalist claims that tempers the possible problematic tendencies of each approach to ethics. This chapter, in turn, demonstrates that Edwards's theology of creation combines central elements of John Calvin's thought, which is generally considered voluntarist, with the ideas of the British rationalist Samuel Clarke, a successor to the Cambridge Platonists who developed his own position largely as a challenge to Hobbes's voluntarism. As a position that integrates Reformed natural law theory with a sort of rationalism that affirms some goodness in the created order even after the Fall, Edwards's theology of creation is consequently neither strictly voluntarist nor strictly "antivoluntarist" in Schneewind's sense. Edwards is able to maintain and defend God's goodness without sacrificing God's centrality for the human moral enterprise.

In order to develop these claims, this chapter begins with a general explanation of the accounts of justice and partial loves that Edwards puts forth in the *Two Dissertations*. His discussion of these attributes is best understood in the context of his theology of creation. Particular arguments tied to Calvin's natural law theory and the rationalism of Clarke influence Edwards's cosmology; I highlight these ideas and then turn to Edwards's own writings to explain how his work builds on and develops these earlier traditions in theologically significant ways. I conclude by returning to Edwards's view of justice and partial loves and contend that Edwards's theology of creation helps to show how these naturally good attributes function as incomplete human virtues.

Edwards's Understanding of Justice and Partial Loves

A central thesis of *The Nature of True Virtue* is that there is no genuine virtue in any disposition or action that can be pursued independently of intervening divine grace. Edwards explicitly argues that no act is truly virtuous unless it arises from a love to God and, correlatively, from a general love directed toward all of God's creation, an impartial love such as that which the Stoics make central to virtue.[1] At the same time, Edwards does argue that we can perceive a certain type of beauty in God's creation: essentially, material and immaterial objects are beautiful when they are proportionate. *True Virtue* discusses, at some length, the attributes of justice and private loves and suggests that these natural qualities possess a form of this beauty. Edwards presents both just dispositions and actions and the dispositions and actions affiliated with private loves as inferior to true virtue, but the relation of these qualities to true virtue is more complicated than it would initially appear. Consistently with a Neoplatonist framework, Edwards contends that both justice and private loves exhibit a beauty through which they stand in a typological relation to true virtue. Alone, they do not suffice for true virtue. At the same time, Edwards affirms that persons who possess a spiritual sense and a truly virtuous disposition will approve justice and private loves. There is a type of continuity between these qualities and true virtue, even as there is simultaneously tension in this relationship.

Edwards's View of Justice

In *The Nature of True Virtue*, Edwards develops a complex understanding of justice that is tied to both beauty and love. He first describes justice as a type of proportion or equality, developing this argument in the context of a broader conversation about the nature of "secondary" beauty and its relation to true virtue, or benevolence. He explains that benevolence, consisting as it does in the consent and union of spiritual minds to God, is more beautiful than anything else in the universe: because benevolence is the "proper and peculiar beauty of spiritual and moral beings," it may fittingly "be called the highest, and first, or primary beauty that is to be found among things that exist."² At the same time, he recognizes an "inferior, secondary beauty" that images this primary beauty, a claim that is undergirded by his theology of creation. Secondary beauty, Edwards explains, is present in the material universe and is akin to uniformity or proportion. It is also at work in mathematical principles (we perceive beauty in the symmetry of a geometric figure), art (we perceive beauty in "the figures on a piece of chintz or brocade"), design (we perceive beauty in a recognition that a thing is structured in a manner appropriate to its use or purpose), and music (we perceive beauty in the harmony of notes) (8:561–66). Edwards affirms that this beauty is an "analogy" of spiritual beauty, an "image" of the beauty of true virtue:

> The reason, or at least one reason, why God has made this kind of mutual consent and agreement of things beautiful and grateful to those intelligent beings that perceive it probably is that there is in it some image of the true, spiritual original beauty, which has been spoken of. . . . The other is an image of this, because by that uniformity diverse things become as it were one, as it is in this cordial union [that takes place in benevolence]. And it pleases God to observe analogy in his works, as is manifest in fact in innumerable instances; and especially to establish inferior things in an analogy to superior. . . . And so he has constituted the external world in an analogy to things in the spiritual world, in numberless instances. (8:564)

We can approve beauty without perceiving the analogy (8:573), in part because God has constructed us to approve it. Nevertheless, the true nature of this beauty consists in its analogy to the beauty of benevolence.

Justice, Edwards goes on to suggest, is a beauty of this type as well. Secondary beauty can be observed clearly in "things immaterial" as well as in material things; Edwards gives social order and the operation of human wisdom as examples of this beauty of proportion in material things (8:568). This beauty is likewise present in justice: "So there is a beauty in the virtue called *justice*, which consists in the agreement of different things that have relation to one another, in nature, manner, and measure: and therefore is the very same sort of beauty with that uniformity and proportion which is observable in those external and material things that are esteemed beautiful" (8:569). Edwards's description of justice can be understood in terms of proportion and equality of exchange. It is just that when we do good, good will be done to us, and when we do evil, we receive evil.

Edwards identifies a type of beauty in justice connected to the harmony and order we perceive in it:

> There is a natural agreement and adaptedness of things that have relation one to another, and an harmonious corresponding of one thing to another: that he which from his will *does* evil to others should *receive* evil from the will of others, or from the will of him or them whose business it is to take care of the injured, and to act in their behalf: and that he should suffer evil in *proportion* to the evil of his doings. Things are in natural regularity and mutual agreement, not in a metaphorical but in a literal sense, when he whose heart opposes the general system should have the hearts of that system, or the heart of the Head and Ruler of the system, against him: and that in consequence, he should receive evil in proportion to the evil tendency of the opposition of his heart. (8:569)

By justice, then, persons receive what they deserve. For Edwards, there is a proportionality and logic undergirding this principle, and we naturally approve justice because of this proportionality.

Having defined justice first in terms of proportion and order, Edwards affirms that these concepts are not sufficient for understanding the true nature of justice. Justice is morally meritorious and beautiful not simply because it is proportionate but more essentially because, in its most perfect form, it is complementary to benevolence. A certain kind of alignment between perfect justice and benevolence is made evident in Edwards's observation that persons who are truly virtuous will delight in justice. Justice is beautiful because it somehow coincides with and expresses the benevolence that is true virtue itself: "*just* affections and acts have a *beauty* in them distinct from, and superior to, the uniformity and equality there is in them: for which, he that has a truly virtuous temper, relishes and delights in them. And that is the expression and manifestation there is in them of benevolence to Being in general." Just and benevolent affections and actions give rise to complementary effects: Edwards identifies both a "tendency of general benevolence to produce justice" and a "tendency of justice to produce effects agreeable to general benevolence"; these tendencies are the reason that justice is "pleasing to a virtuous mind." Edwards affirms that there is "something in the tendency and consequences of justice that is agreeable to general benevolence," because justice can, in many ways, promote the "general good" and thereby glorify God (8:572).

Benevolence, in turn, tends to increase justice by acting in accordance with the principle of proportion at work in the operations of justice. Justice lies in the approval of desert, and benevolence (as the love of Being in general) will tend to produce complacence (8:548), or a love for particular beings as they deserve to be loved, "in proportion to the degree of existence" (8:546) and "virtue" (8:571) that each possesses. When we are truly virtuous, we love others to a degree proportionate to their virtue. Through this argument Edwards logically ensures that those who are truly virtuous will love God above all: "'Tis true that benevolence to Being in general, when a person hath it, will naturally incline him to justice, or proportion in the exercises of it. He that loves Being, simply considered, will naturally (as was observed before), other things being equal, love particular beings in a proportion compounded of the degree of being and the degree of virtue, or benevolence to being, which they have. And that is to love beings in proportion to their dignity" (8:571). True justice, then, follows from benevolence and is aligned with it, so that benevolence can be seen as operating according to its principles. This alignment is the source of justice's moral beauty.

Edwards underscores his contention that proportion is insufficient for understanding the full beauty of justice or the perfect beauty of benevolence when he argues that proportionate actions follow from benevolence rather than giving rise to it. Not only does this point allow Edwards to affirm benevolence as a disposition that is achieved by the supernatural intervention of grace rather than by natural habituation, but it also enables him to draw a distinction between a justice that has been sanctified by benevolence and a natural justice acquired through repeated actions. I return to this distinction in the final section of this chapter. Edwards is clear that benevolence cannot be produced by proportionate justice and is morally superior to it. In contrast to complacence, benevolence "doth not necessarily presuppose beauty in its object" (8:543) and therefore cannot be captured by the notion of proportionate relations. Edwards therefore explains that proportionate actions may follow from benevolence but cannot be said to lead to it: "After benevolence to Being in general exists, the proportion which is observed in objects may be the cause of the proportion of benevolence to those objects: but no proportion is the cause or ground of the existence of such a thing as benevolence to Being. The tendency of objects to excite that degree of benevolence which is proportionate to the degree of being, etc. is the *consequence* of the existence of benevolence; and not the ground of it" (8:571). In making this point, Edwards guards against any argument that acquired justice can lead to benevolence; true virtue, he affirms, requires the direct intervention of divine grace. Nevertheless, this argument at the same time allows for a type of consistency between benevolence and justice, such that benevolence will tend toward justice and will approve justice. The beauty of perfect justice lies in its agreement with benevolence (8:571), which Edwards defines both in terms of its analogy to the beauty of benevolence and in terms of benevolence's tendencies to promote justice.

In addition to its relation to benevolence, another feature of justice that suggests that it has the capacity to surpass the simple natural beauty of proportion is its coincidence with divine law: Edwards affirms an "agreement of *justice* to the will and command of God" (8:572). The natural conscience, our faculty that approves justice, concurs with God's law after it has been "enlightened" (8:594). Significantly, however, Edwards contends that our conscience can naturally apprehend and approve the justice of divine activity, particularly that of God's condemnation of sinners, even independently of a particular moment of being enlightened (8:595, 597). Edwards suggests that the divine law with which justice coincides encompasses a set of duties that God places upon us in connection to our status as his creatures, and he does not indicate that original sin completely impedes our pursuit of these duties. For Edwards, we are subject to duties, and these duties are part of justice: "most of the duties incumbent upon us, if well considered, will be found to partake of the nature of justice" (8:569) We owe duties to God in connection to our relation to God as "Creator, Preserver, and Benefactor," duties to Christ in response to what he has accomplished for us in terms of redemption, and duties to humans with whom we stand in relation—parents, children, spouses, friends, and neighbors (8:569). In each of these sets of duties, there is a quality of proportion and logic that demonstrates how justice is commensurate with them.[3] Edwards's justice, then, can be said to possess some degree of moral goodness and beauty because of its alignment with benevolence. It coincides with the divine law that God has placed upon us as God's creatures, and that our natural conscience has some capacity to recognize even independently of God's intervening grace.

Edwards's View of Private Loves

In addition to justice, a second category of incomplete virtues that Edwards discusses at length is encompassed in various instances of private loves, or actions and dispositions of love that are exercised in relation to a particular person or persons. Edwards introduces these concepts as part of an analysis of the viability of sentimentalist accounts of the virtuous character of natural affections. In contrast to an Aristotelian position that would tend to associate virtue with friendship,[4] Edwards contends that private natural affections can be seen, for the most part, as arising from self-love and therefore as lacking the nature of true virtue. Diana Fritz Cates argues that one can read Aristotle's view of friendship and family relationships as providing settings in which moral agents learn how to exercise virtuous compassion for persons outside these immediate relationships.[5] Edwards does not deny that such broader loves may be cultivated within more immediate relationships, but he is adamant that these loves lack the nature of true virtue because their origin is ultimately in love of self rather than love to God. In *The Nature of True Virtue* Edwards defines the self-love that gives rise to love of family and friends as "a man's regard to his confined *private self*, or love to himself with respect to his *private interest*" (8:577). Yet, strikingly, Edwards does not link all expressions of this self-love to sin's distortion of our natures but to their original formation and natural proclivities, an argument that I will show is largely consistent with Calvin's view of the natural law. At the same time, Edwards acknowledges that sin has distorted human nature so that this nature is subject to pride. The dispositions that are effects of divine creation coexist alongside dispositions that are effects of original sin.

For Edwards, the "laws of nature" are such that our love for ourselves will cause us to love those who love us. "God has constituted our nature" so that self-love will lead us to be pleased with others' approval of us and displeased with their disapproval (8:577–78): "Pleasures and uneasinesses of this kind are doubtless as much owing to an immediate determination of the mind by a fixed law of our nature as any of the pleasures and pains of external sense. . . . 'Tis evidently mere self-love that appears in this disposition. It is easy to see that a man's love to himself will make him love love to himself, and hate hatred to himself. And as God has constituted our nature, self-love is exercised in no one disposition more than in this" (8:578).

We are constructed, then, so that through self-love we come to love those who love us: "a man's love to those that love him is no more than a certain expression or effect of self-love" (8:579). Because private loves are the natural effect of self-love, they contain no more virtue than self-love itself does.[6] Yet they remain an expression of self-love, again because this is how God has structured the laws of nature: "'tis not at all strange that the Author of nature, who observes order, uniformity, and harmony in establishing its laws, should so order that it should be natural for self-love to . . . cause our heart to extend itself in one manner toward inanimate things which gratify self-love without sense or will, and in another manner towards beings which we look upon as having understanding and will, like ourselves, and in exerting those faculties in our favor and promoting our interest from love to us" (8:581). Edwards extends this claim that private loves derive from self-love not only to love for friends but also to other private natural loves. It is self-love that leads us to love our children, for example (8:584). Private loves, then, have their origin not in a natural faculty such as a moral sense but in self-love.

However, it need not follow from this position that natural loves must be considered selfish or vicious, as if they were effects of distorted postlapsarian pride rather than of our created instincts for self-love. Granted, Edwards argues that the various sorts of natural loves are not of the nature of true virtue, nor can they be said to lead to true virtue (just as justice does not lead to benevolence). Yet they are natural consequences of the way that God has constructed us, and Edwards therefore could not argue that they lack moral goodness completely without undermining God's character. Edwards identifies multiple private loves that are natural expressions of the construction of our nature. These include love to one's family (8:601), mutual affection between the sexes (8:603–4), pity for others' distress (8:605–7), and gratitude (8:610). Indeed, Edwards even affirms that it is possible to practice a qualified type of benevolence naturally, a type of benevolence that is not truly virtuous because it does not involve love to God or to the *whole* of the universe: apart from grace, a person can "come to have benevolent affections limited to a party that is very large, or to the country or nation in general of which they are a part, or the public community they belong to." These loves "don't arise from a principle of virtue," nor do they "have a tendency to produce" virtue (8:602). Yet they do arise from a natural instinct given by God for humankind's preservation (8:607), and, as such, they are consistent with the workings of providence.

It should be noted that certain forms of self-love *are* vicious. Particular manifestations of self-love follow from the postlapsarian distortion of our wills rather than from the instincts with which we were created. If this were not the case, then my argument that Edwardsean partial loves have some degree of moral goodness might raise questions about whether Edwards is subject to the concerns I raised in chapter 3 regarding the Cambridge Platonist position. I suggested there that the Cambridge Platonists' emphasis upon the natural capacities of humans to pursue virtue at times tends toward latitudinarianism. Because they minimize (and in many cases reject outright) the traditional Calvinist doctrine of original sin, the Cambridge Platonists can be seen as contributing to the strand of early modern moral discourse that effectively (though unintentionally) renders God superfluous to human morality. I argued that Edwards guards against this tendency by integrating Cambridge Platonism with a more standard Puritan account of original sin. But the consequences of Edwards's view of original sin, as I outlined them in chapter 3, are that Edwards sees the possession of a spiritual sense as a necessary foundation for the pursuit of virtue. If Edwards were indeed to make too strong a case that we have natural capacities for goodness, this could open him to a charge of Pelagianism.

But Edwards guards against this risk, even in the *Two Dissertations*, by acknowledging that pride has distorted our natures since the Fall. In *True Virtue* Edwards says that a distorted self-love (which he calls "pride" elsewhere in this text and in other works) is the origin of our sinful actions and dispositions, just as properly ordered self-love is the origin of our partial loves: "All sin has its source from selfishness, or from self-love, not subordinate to regard to Being in general" (8:614). Sin runs counter not only to the activity of the spiritual sense but also to the exercises of the natural conscience and moral sense.[7] Sin distorts self-love so that it becomes selfishness, a belief that "self" is "all"; Edwards explains that humanity can readily be habituated into this belief. "Pride and sensuality" likewise diminish "natural affections, and natural pity" (8:614–15). Thus, in saying that our natural instincts toward self-love can give rise to partial loves and that partial loves have some degree of moral beauty, Edwards does not effectively exclude God from the natural pursuit of these naturally good qualities; God can never become superfluous as long as original sin affects humans so greatly.

Nevertheless, with regard to those natural loves that do coincide with and extend from the instincts with which we were created (even the prelapsarian instincts of self-love), Edwards affirms a sort of coincidence between these natural loves and true virtue that shows how these natural loves can be seen as in some sense good, and as contributing to the purposes for which we were created. Just as Edwards indicates some goodness in justice by recognizing that even its most limited form images true virtue's beauty, so he affirms some measure of goodness in these natural loves by suggesting that they possess qualities that are part of true virtue's "general nature," the nature of love. Truly virtuous love is expressed in both benevolence and complacence, and private loves partake in both of these elements of true virtue; these private affections "have something that *belongs to the general nature* of virtue. The general nature of true virtue is love. It is expressed both in love of benevolence and complacence; but primarily in benevolence to persons and beings, and consequently and secondarily in complacence in virtue, as has been shown. There is something of the general nature of virtue in those natural affections and principles [of private loves] . . . in both those respects" (8:609).

These natural affections cohere with benevolence to some degree, although they differ from it in origin and scope. Like justice, certain loves share the tendencies and effects of benevolence. Pity for persons in distress "has partly the same influence and effect with benevolence"; specifically, benevolence and pity both "cause persons to be uneasy when the objects of it [love] are in distress, and to desire their relief." Other loves, Edwards explains, "have truly a sort of benevolence in them," and they differ from true virtue only because the objects of these loves are limited and private (8:609). This is often true with regard to affection between the sexes, gratitude, and love between parents and children; each coheres with benevolence and complacence (8:610). The deficiency of these loves lies not in their nature but in the narrowness of their focus.[8] Private loves share the nature of benevolence, but they lack true virtue because they do not recognize God as the head of all Being or direct themselves toward the general good (8:611). These loves are therefore partly constitutive of our good.

Reason, Nature, and Providence: The Intellectual Background of Edwards's Theology of Creation

A consideration of Edwards's theology of creation provides a broader context for understanding his contention that justice and partial loves are forms of natural goodness that possess a secondary beauty. In *The End for Which God Created the World*, Edwards delineates the accounts of creation and providence that show how justice and partial loves can be naturally good even as they are insufficient for true virtue. This theology of creation, in turn, is best characterized as a fusion of elements of Calvinist natural law theory with claims central to the British rationalist tradition represented in Samuel Clarke. Edwards's account of creation is shaped by Calvin's view of divine providence and by Clarke's affirmation of the inherent rationality of the universe, although Edwards also departs from both Calvin and Clarke in significant ways. I therefore turn to the views of these thinkers before examining Edwards's understanding of creation in greater depth.

Calvin's Natural Law

Although Edwards's theology of creation is not an exact restatement of Calvin's, two features of Calvin's natural law theory particularly demonstrate how Edwards develops his account of the created order in continuity with the traditional Reformed understanding of natural law. Calvin conceives the cosmos as naturally ordered toward God, and as providentially directed so that it is drawn toward God's goodness. Edwards's position in *The End for Which God Created the World* is for the most part consistent with this contention. Edwards also follows Calvin in affirming the importance of the human conscience. At the same time, he differs from Calvin in his view of precisely how God sustains creation, which suggests that Edwards and Calvin likewise differ in their understandings of the effects of original sin on the cosmos. For Calvin, divine providence functions to restrain a cosmos that, because of original sin, would otherwise tend toward chaos. Edwards, in contrast, emphasizes the rationality of creation in a manner that suggests that original sin affects the human will but not the created order; divine providence therefore does not restrain chaos but instead complements the orders of creation.

Susan Schreiner's *The Theater of His Glory: Nature and the Natural Order in the Thought of John Calvin* offers a helpful overview of Calvin's account of creation. Schreiner argues that Calvin essentially stands in continuity with "orthodox" Christian thought, in affirming that God brought "orders of creation" into being *ex nihilo*. Orthodox Christianity, as Schreiner characterizes it, affirms that both the cosmos and the human person are intrinsically ordered by God in their creation, and God's providence sustains and guides them in a manner that complements the ordering that he gives them when they initially come into being.[9] An examination of Calvin's own texts corroborates Schreiner's argument. In the *Institutes of the Christian Religion*, Calvin explicitly recognizes the continuity of this view of creation with the Christian tradition as a whole:

> Wherefore, in order that we may apprehend with true faith what it is necessary to know concerning God, it is of importance to attend to the history of the creation, as briefly recorded by Moses and afterwards more copiously illustrated by pious writers, most especially by Basil and Ambrose. From this history we learn that God, by the power of his Word and his Spirit, created the heavens and the earth out of nothing; that thereafter

he produced things inanimate and animate of every kind, arranging an innumerable variety of objects in admirable order, giving each kind its proper nature, office, place, and station.[10]

Calvin suggests that God created all things "in wisdom" and established order in creation when it first came into being: "So far as the order of nature is concerned, we know that it has been Divinely established, and fixed from the beginning." God rejoices in his created works[11] because they reflect the order that God has established for them.

Not only is creation arranged in an orderly manner, but Calvin more specifically stresses that creation is ordered in a manner that glorifies God, a claim central to Edwards as well. Creation is a worthy subject because meditating on its wonders will lead us to give glory to God. Calvin describes creation as a mirror in which we can see God's perfections:

> Still there can be no doubt that the Lord would have us constantly occupied with such holy meditation, in order that, while we contemplate the immense treasures of wisdom and goodness exhibited in the creatures as in so many mirrors, we may not only run our eye over them with a hasty, and, as it were, evanescent glance, but dwell long upon them, seriously and faithfully turn them in our minds, and every now and then bring them to recollection. . . . Let the reader understand that he has a genuine apprehension of the character of God as the Creator of the world; first, if he attends to the general rule, never thoughtlessly or obliviously to overlook the glorious perfections which God displays in his creatures; and, secondly, if he makes a self application of what he sees, so as to fix it deeply on his heart. The former is exemplified when we consider how great the Architect must be who framed and ordered the multitude of the starry host so admirably, that it is impossible to imagine a more glorious sight . . . and at the same time so regulating the inequality of days as to prevent every thing like confusion. The former course is, moreover, exemplified when we attend to his power in sustaining the vast mass, and guiding the swift revolutions of the heavenly bodies, &c. These few examples sufficiently explain what is meant by recognizing the divine perfections in the creation of the world.[12]

Calvin thereby affirms both that God's creation of the world is ordered and that this order reflects God's own perfections. The very structures that God instills in creation direct it toward the good, a point that is largely consistent with Edwards's theology in *End* as well as with the broader Augustinian tradition.

Calvin's account of the natural conscience can likewise be seen as foundational to Edwards's understanding of the human person. Schreiner suggests that Calvin preserves certain elements of the medieval natural law tradition as well as of Cicero's natural law theory. Calvin contends that the "'seeds' of law and conceptions of justice and equity have been implanted in all human minds so that we recognize the need for law and justice without a teacher or legislator."[13] These medieval and Ciceronian claims are particularly evident in Calvin's view of the conscience. In his *Commentary on Romans*, Calvin argues that some measure of the knowledge of good and evil is imprinted on our hearts. We cannot choose to act in a manner that is good, but we can recognize good actions and approve them. Therefore, Paul recognizes that in the Gentiles,

> there is imprinted on their hearts a discrimination and judgment by which they distinguish between what is just and unjust, between what is honest and dishonest. He means not that it was so engraven on their will, that they sought and diligently pursued it, but that they were so mastered by the power of truth, that they could not disapprove of it. Without reason then is the power of the will deduced from this passage, as though Paul had said, that the keeping of the law is within our power; for he speaks not of the power to fulfill the law, but of the knowledge of it. Nor is the word *heart* to be taken for the seat of the affections, but only for the understanding.[14]

Apart from God's special grace, we lack a complete knowledge of the law, but our conscience nevertheless possesses the seeds of this knowledge by common grace: "Nor can we conclude from this passage, that there is in men a *full* knowledge of the law, but that there are only some seeds of what is right implanted in their nature."[15] Moreover, Calvin is explicit in affirming that these natural capacities are present in spite of the Fall. God has given us a natural faculty—to which Calvin sometimes refers as "common sense," the "dictates of nature," or "nature"—that effectively gives us insight into the natural law, even after the Fall.[16] Calvin's *Commentaries* demonstrate this view of conscience as continuing to possess a "seed of religion" even after the corruption of original sin affects it: "The chief parts of the light which remain in our corrupt natures are two: first, everyone has a certain seed of religion implanted in him; and secondly, every man's conscience is capable of distinguishing good from evil."[17] Calvin accepts the idea of conscience as having the capacity naturally to recognize good and evil and affirms that human corruption does not destroy its essential abilities.

At the same time, Calvin stresses the limits of the conscience's abilities as well, underscoring humanity's need for divine grace and for the particular revelation of God in the scriptures. In the *Commentaries* Calvin explains that the good and evil that the conscience is capable of discerning are only shadows in comparison to what Christ offers, and that the conscience cannot naturally guide us to Christ: "In short, natural reason can never guide men to Christ. Even though prudence teaches men to regulate their lives, and though they are born capable of the arts and sciences, the whole thing vanishes and leaves nothing behind."[18] The written Mosaic law is essential for morality because sin hampers our abilities to pursue the right motives (that is, love to God and neighbor,[19] motives identical to those that Edwards sees as truly virtuous). The law of Moses makes clear the law of which our natural conscience possesses only a seed and presents in a written form the information that original sin obscures our knowing fully:

> The very things contained in the two tables are, in a manner, dictated to us by that internal law, which, as has been already said, is in a manner written and stamped on every heart. For conscience, instead of allowing us to stifle our perceptions, and sleep on without interruption, acts as an inward witness and monitor, reminds us of what we owe to God, points out the distinction between good and evil, and thereby convicts us of departure from duty. But man, being immured in the darkness of error, is scarcely able, by means of that natural law, to form any tolerable idea of the worship which is acceptable to God. At all events, he is very far from forming any correct knowledge of it. In addition to this, he is so swollen with arrogance and ambition, and so blinded with self-love, that he is unable to survey, and, as it were, descend into himself, that he may so learn to humble and abase himself, and confess his misery. Therefore, as a necessary remedy, both for our dullness and our contumacy, the Lord has given us his written Law, which, by its sure attestations, removes the obscurity of the law of nature, and also, by shaking off our lethargy, makes a more lively and permanent impression on our minds.[20]

Calvin recognizes that original sin has not obscured our ability to know virtue entirely, but he does affirm that its effects are severe, and it is largely because of these effects that God's particular revelation in the scriptures is so necessary in order to ensure that we act morally. Conscience is a means through which we perceive God's desires for our behavior, but its perceptions and abilities are limited.

Calvin develops these accounts of the created orders and the natural conscience as part of a broader understanding of the workings of divine providence. This account is instructive because it coincides with Edwards in part, but it also runs counter to the theology of creation that Edwards develops in *End* in ways that point to differences between Edwards's and Calvin's views of sin. Edwards, like Calvin, will embrace the idea that the orders of creation are providentially ordered and sustained such that God is intimately involved in them: Calvin affirms, "Nor is it only by a general Providence that the Lord maintains the world which He has created, but He arranges and regulates every part of it, and more especially, by his protection, he keeps and guards believers whom he has received under his care and guardianship."[21] At the same time, Calvin emphasizes a particular understanding of the "ordering" work of divine providence that differs from Edwards, indicating that Calvin and Edwards have differing conceptions of God's activity in relation to the world. Schreiner contends that for Calvin, the cosmos no longer contains inherent order after the Fall, and God's providence functions largely to contain and restrain the world and prevent it from falling into chaos. The postlapsarian created order is inherently unstable, so that nature would cease to exist, or disintegrate into chaos, without the constant intercession of God's hand. Calvin does not wish to deny the integrity of the nature God created, but he does suggest that divine providence must restrain creation rather than simply sustaining and preserving it; he sees the natural world as in some sense "held in check by God."[22] Calvin's "Commentary on Psalm 145" underscores Schreiner's point. In this text Calvin acknowledges that even though God has ordered the world in its creation, the Fall often prevents the world from acting in accordance with what has been ordered: "The fair order which subsisted in it by God's original appointment often fails since the Fall through our sins."[23] Similarly, in "Commentary on Psalm 96," Calvin explains that although God has established orders in creation, after the fall these orders are unstable apart from God's immediate involvement with them: "Still we are to remember that so long as un-godliness has possession of the minds of men, the world, plunged as it is in darkness, must be considered as thrown into a state of confusion, and of horrible disorder and misrule; for there can be no stability apart from God."[24] For Calvin, then, the providence of God functions to restrain a world that might otherwise descend into chaos, rather than simply to guide a world intimately in accordance with the orders present in creation.

Calvin's views of natural law and conscience can be seen to influence Edwards's theology of creation, as can the general claim that God sustains creation providentially in accordance with the orders that he has instilled in it. Yet his affirmation that creation is at risk to descend into chaos apart from God's providential hand represents a difference in emphasis. There is one feature of Edwards's thought—his notion of "continuous creation," the idea that God recreates the world at each moment and is thereby its immediate cause[25]—that does seem consistent with Calvin's perspective, but, for the most part, it appears that Calvin and Edwards ultimately differ in their views of sin: Edwards is more concerned to emphasize the ways in which sin has negatively affected the human will, whereas Calvin has a broader view of sin's effects, such that he sees sin as distorting creation itself rather than simply disrupting humans' abilities in relation to it. Though Edwards writes in the Calvinist tradition, he emphasizes the world's rationality and order to a greater degree than Calvin does, an emphasis that is not fundamentally opposed to Calvin but that nevertheless aligns Edwards more fully with such thinkers as the Cambridge Platonists and their successors. In speaking of the reasonableness of the universe's construction, Edwards employs terminology and lines of argument that are strikingly similar to the position of the British rationalist Samuel Clarke, who wrote after the Cambridge Platonists and was influenced by them.

Clarke and the Rationalism of the Created Universe

Clarke upholds the rational nature of the created universe as a means of challenging Hobbesian voluntarism and skepticism. He explicitly affirms that his view of the moral order is set up as a critical response to Hobbes's argument that there is no natural difference between good and evil and, correlatively, that these moral categories depend solely on the constitution of laws.[26] It is as a challenge to Hobbes, then, that Clarke contends that good and evil are founded in the nature of things, independently of the divine will, and that the universe is fundamentally rational. As we saw in chapters 2 and 3, Edwards is likewise concerned to combat Hobbesian materialism and moral skepticism, and this concern leads him to draw from the thought of British moralists who uphold God's goodness in order to counter Hobbes's voluntarism. Therefore, although Edwards shares Calvin's desire to affirm the necessity of God's revelation and law and upholds a view of original sin that leads him to reject the notion that humans are capable of acting in accordance with the laws rationally established in the universe, his account of creation itself can be seen to have much in common with the views of Clarke. Edwards's understanding of original sin leads him toward a limited view of human abilities to act in accordance with the universe's inherently rational structure, but he nevertheless defends a type of reasonableness in the universe's operations, a rationality that is instilled in it through divine providence and that original sin has not destroyed. Edwards's similarities to Clarke suggest that the function of divine providence in Edwards's thought is to sustain the universe in accordance with the orders established at creation rather than to restrain its tendencies toward chaos.

We will see that the language that Clarke uses to develop the argument that good and evil are founded in the nature of things is echoed in Edwards. Clarke contends that God establishes morality through acting in accordance with "eternal fitnesses" (which Clarke sometimes refers to as the natural law). Clarke explains that there are eternal "relations" among concepts that serve as standards by which a given action can be deemed reasonable and that are the source of moral obligation. Clarke's affirmation of these relations is significant, in turn, because he goes on to contend that the divine will necessarily abides by them. God's will, Clarke explains, is constructed in a manner such that it will necessarily choose to act in accordance with goodness and justice and to conform to the eternal standards set by these relations. It is "fitting" for both God and creatures to act in accordance with the eternal standards of morality. God and creatures share the duty of acting in a "fit" manner independently of any additional law decreed by God's will, and this duty is derived from eternal moral relations rather than from God's will or positive law:

> The same necessary and eternal *different relations,* that different things bear one to another; and the same consequent *fitness* or *unfitness* of the application of different things or different relations one to another; with regard to which, the will of God always and necessarily *does* determine itself, to choose to act only what is agreeable to justice, equity, goodness, and truth, in order to the welfare of the whole universe; *ought* likewise constantly to determine the wills of all subordinate rational beings, to govern all their actions by the same rules. . . . That is; these eternal and necessary differences of things make it *fit and reasonable* for creatures so to act; they cause it to be their *duty,* or lay an *obligation* upon them, so to do; even separate

from the consideration of these rules being the *positive will* or *command of God*. (1:192)

Certainly God's law conforms to these eternal standards and is not at odds with them, but we are bound to the standards even prior to God's establishment of the law: "as this law of nature is infinitely superior to all authority of *men*, and independent upon it; so its obligation, primarily and originally, is antecedent also even to *this* consideration, of its being the positive will and command of *God* himself" (1:213).

Clarke does not wish to suggest that these eternal standards constrain God's will—he notes that God "chooses" to act in accordance with these fitnesses—and, strikingly, he appears to attempt to appease modern voluntarists by suggesting that God (though bound to moral standards) exercises his will arbitrarily in some matters, most notably when he brings creatures into being.[27] Nevertheless, eternal fitnesses and standards abide in the created world itself, and it is they, independently of God's will, that are morally obligating. God's goodness consists in his abiding perfectly by these standards. Clarke explains that just as there are eternal laws of mathematics,

> so in moral matters, there are certain necessary and unalterable respects or relations of things, which have not their original from arbitrary and positive constitution, but are of eternal necessity in their own nature. . . . When things are created, and so long as it pleases God to continue them in their being; their *proportions*, which are *abstractly* of eternal necessity, are also in the *things themselves* absolutely unalterable. Hence God himself, though he has no superior, from whose will to receive any law of his actions; yet disdains not to observe the rule of equity and goodness, as the law of all his actions in the government of the world. . . . The rules of this eternal law, are the true foundation and measure of his dominion over his creatures. (1:213)

God, for Clarke, acts in accordance with what is fit, and our moral obligation is derived from the same eternal standards and fitnesses that give rise to divine law. Functionally, God does not create the law, but his law coincides with it, and in following it he serves as an exemplar of perfect moral behavior to humans. God has no superior, but God recognizes that it is right to direct his actions through the abstract eternal rules of justice and goodness, and we ought to do the same.[28]

Divine providence wills the good of the universe because it is "fitting" for this to be the case: "It is a thing manifestly fitter in itself, that the all-powerful governor of the world, should do always what is best in the whole, and what tends most to the universal good of the whole creation; than that he should make the whole continually miserable" (1:193). Humans, Clarke goes on to explain, should follow God by willing the good of the universe and of all the persons in it.[29] The concepts of eternal truths and fitnesses are central to Clarke's understanding of the functioning of the universe and also to his account of God's interactions with the created order.

Although Edwards coincides with Clarke in employing the language of "fitness" to describe God's actions in creating the world and establishing moral categories, he departs from Clarke in one sense that is important to mention, because this departure guards Edwards against some of the pitfalls Schneewind associates with "antivoluntarist" positions such as Clarke's. Clarke characterizes the eternal fitnesses in a manner that emphasizes their independence from God. Whereas Edwards presents moral rectitude as a standard internal to God's essence,[30] Clarke emphasizes the independence of moral standards from God's will to so great a degree that he presents these standards as more or less external to God's being. Clarke does understand God to possess "infinite knowledge, wisdom, and power," but the "eternal rules of infinite goodness, justice, and truth" are not intrinsic to the divine nature (1:199). It is God's wisdom, rather than the internal nature of these moral standards, that leads God to act in accord with the natural law and right reason. God "constantly directs all his own actions by the eternal rule of justice and goodness" (1:213). Yet these rules are not part of God's own being, a claim that causes problems for any attempt a pure Clarkean might make to contend that morality is necessarily theological. If eternal moral laws stand independent of God, then it would seem to follow that God is inessential for morality. Edwards's departure from Clarke on this point demonstrates his concern to avoid conceiving morality as possible independently of God. At the same time, like the Cambridge Platonists, Clarke represents a tradition whose merit Edwards clearly recognizes as a counter to Hobbesian materialism, even as Edwards seeks to guard against some of its conclusions.

In addition to appealing to the language of "fitness" to discuss the moral ordering God establishes in the world, Clarke develops a view of human reason that is worth noting for our discussion of Edwards, because Norman Fiering has suggested that Edwards's view of the natural conscience is heavily influenced by Clarke's rationalist understanding of humans' created moral capacities.[31] Clarke explains that God has given us a faculty of reason through which we can perceive the objective moral categories of good and evil: if humans sin, they act "contrary to that understanding, reason, and judgement, which God has implanted in their natures on purpose to enable them to discern the difference between good and evil" (1:201). Moreover, Clarke indicates that this knowledge is sufficient for informing us of our moral obligations; he links this point both to Paul's description of the law of God written on the hearts of the Gentiles in Romans 2:14–15 and to Plato's suggestion that even a young child will intuitively be able to speak about moral relations in a manner that recognizes their similarity to mathematical axioms (1:203). Our conscience recognizes that we should act in accordance with the eternal standards of justice and goodness that it knows to be meritorious, which makes it all the more lamentable when we fail to follow this rule:

> Further, it appears from the abstract and absolute reason and nature of things, that all rational creatures ought, that is, are obliged to take care that their wills and actions be constantly determined and governed by the eternal rule of right and equity.... So no man, who either has patience and opportunities to examine and consider things himself, or has the means of being taught and instructed in any tolerable manner by others, concerning the necessary relations and dependencies of things; can avoid giving his assent to the fitness and reasonableness of his governing all his actions by the law or rule before mentioned, even though his practice, through the prevalence of brutish lusts, be most absurdly contradictory to that assent. That is to say: by the reason of his mind, he cannot but be compelled to own and acknowledge, that there is really such an obligation indispensably incumbent upon him; even at the same time that in the actions of his life he is endeavouring to throw it off and despise it. (1:201–2)

Our natural reason, Clarke contends, is capable of knowing right and wrong, and we are obligated to act morally because we understand what it means to do so. Clarke does not deny that we are subject to sin, but he suggests that we are capable of learning the nature of moral good and evil through our reason, and that this knowledge, in turn, obligates us to choose to do the good. He acknowledges that people such as Hobbes deny that all persons have the capacity to know what is objectively morally good, and he concedes that vicious education may make the acquisition of this knowledge more difficult (1:204), but he points to our positive and negative judgments of others' behavior as evidence of the moral nature of our reason (1:205–7).

Though Edwards's descriptions of the world's rationality build on a discourse represented well by Clarke, Edwards differs from Clarke in a manner similar to his differences from the Cambridge Platonists that I discussed in chapter 3: Edwards's view of original sin and his commitment to our need for special grace make him more cautious about the workings of natural reason than Clarke ultimately is. Clarke recognizes that people are sometimes corrupt, and that natural reason obligates us to morality but does not necessarily lead to moral behavior, a claim that Edwards would certainly accept. But Clarke goes one step further: he presumes that people are capable of being taught how to behave virtuously, a claim that Edwards would very much oppose (as we see in his critiques of Aristotelian habituation). As long as people's understandings are neither "very imperfect, [n]or very much depraved," Clarke believes that their natural reason can perceive moral good and evil.[32] Furthermore, Clarke affirms that (again with the exception of severe cases of problematically ordered faculties) this understanding directs our wills, just as God's understanding of the moral order directs his will;[33] Edwards would reject this claim as well. Clarke ultimately believes that our natural reason's grasp of morality can lead us sufficiently to act morally, a view that runs counter to Edwards's understanding of original sin.

Clarke's suggestion that our natural reason can teach us benevolence underscores his differences from Edwards. I noted above that Edwards argues that neither justice nor private loves lead to true virtue. Edwards affirms differences in scope between justice and benevolence consistent with the claims of modern natural lawyers, although he gives moral priority to benevolence rather than to justice. Clarke, in contrast, defines virtue in terms of "universal justice" as well as benevolence, and he implies that both can ultimately be acquired naturally. Clarke conceives benevolence as "not only the doing barely of what is just and right, in our dealings with every man; but also a constant endeavouring to promote in general, to the utmost of our power, the welfare and happiness of all men" (1:209). Though he does not emphasize love to God as a component of virtue in the way that Edwards does, Clarke points to God's activity as evidence that it is moral to uphold and seek the good of the whole.[34] As with the case of other obligations and duties in which God serves as exemplar, Clarke suggests that our reason can naturally know that we should follow this divine model of universal love. This universal love is accessible to the natural reason, and its performance is something in which we can engage solely through having our knowledge and affections rightly formed. Benevolence is the most effective activity through which we can do the good for others that we naturally recognize as our obligation to do:

> To which end [that is, doing good to others] universal love and benevolence is as plainly the most direct, certain, and effectual means; as in mathematics the flowing of a point, is, to produce a line; or in arithmetic, the addition of numbers, to produce a sum. . . . Of all which, the mind of man is so naturally sensible, that, except in such men whose affections are prodigiously corrupted by most unnatural and habitual vicious practices, there is no duty whatsoever, the performance whereof affords a man so ample pleasure and satisfaction, and fills his mind with so comfortable a sense, of his having done the greatest good he was capable to do, of his having best answered the ends of his creation, and nearliest imitated the perfections of his creator . . . as the performance of this one duty, of universal love and benevolence, naturally affords. (1:209–10)

Clarke thus affirms that we can naturally pursue benevolence, and indeed he goes on to suggest (drawing from Cicero) that "self-love" rightly ordered can ultimately lead to benevolence (1:210–11), a claim that Edwards specifically rejects in his argument that private loves cannot be a means through which we come to practice truly virtuous benevolence. Clarke's account of the workings of natural reason and its ability to direct our wills and move us to pursue benevolence are thus positions that Edwards rejects.

As with Calvin, then, Clarke offers a view of the natural order that can be seen as influencing Edwards, particularly in his notion that the construction of the world is established by God's actions, which take place in accordance with what is "fit." At the same time, Edwards rejects certain elements of Clarke's position more overtly than Calvin's. His emphases in his account of providence differ from those of Calvin, but he explicitly and adamantly rejects Clarke's contention that our natural reason can lead us to pursue benevolence. Characterizing Edwards's theology as a fusion of Calvinist natural law with British rationalism helps us to take these departures into account, even as we appreciate Edwards's engagement with the intellectual conversations that clearly informed his thought.

Edwards's Theology of Creation

Recognizing the Calvinist and rationalist influences upon Edwards highlights key theological concerns that shape his view of creation and undergird his account of the incomplete virtues. *The End for Which God Created the World* offers a description of the created world that provides grounds for understanding these natural human attributes as morally beautiful and as part of the means through which creation glorifies God, and several passages in *True Virtue* suggest that both these incomplete virtues and our faculties for approving them can best be understood in the context of this broader Edwardsean account of creation. An examination of Edwards's theology of creation in *End* demonstrates how Edwards's theological commitments give rise to the claim that justice and partial loves are in many ways consistent with true virtue, even as Edwards ultimately treats our motives for pursuing them as suspect because they lack the influence of intervening divine grace. In *End*, Edwards characterizes the created world as ordered toward God's glory, a characterization that gives ontological support to his claims in *True Virtue* that true virtue in some ways coincides with justice and partial loves. Edwards conceives the created order as a setting in which the existence of natural goodness is both plausible and evident, even though this goodness coexists with original sin and its effects.

The Created World as Ordered to God's Glory and Goodness

Fiering argues that there is an "inherent rationalism" in Edwards's universe such that God governs creation through his wisdom.[35] And indeed, Edwards's *End for Which God Created the World* consistently emphasizes the reasonableness of God's method of structuring the world. Particular features of this cosmology reflect Edwards's indebtedness both to Calvin's natural law theory and Clarke's rationalism, which further supports my argument in earlier chapters that Edwards's position is a fusion of elements of modern voluntarism and modern intellectualism. Edwards's account of creation demonstrates that he is shaped by Calvin's natural law theory, and Calvin is generally understood as a central representative of modern theological voluntarism. But Edwards's development of Calvin's natural law theory reveals that he was also deeply influenced by Clarke, who is opposed to voluntarism. I revisit the question of Edwards's voluntarism in the next section, but I note it here in order to highlight the ways in which Edwards's position represents a striking integration of two arguments that a historian of modern moral thought might assume to be radically at odds with each other. The influence of Clarke and Calvin upon Edwards's account of the rational nature of creation is evident both in his argument that God, in creating, acts in accordance with fitnesses and in his view of the universe as providentially ordered toward the good.

Like Clarke, Edwards defends God's goodness and the goodness God imparts to the created order by appealing to the language of fitness. Edwards argues that God, as a morally perfect being, acts according to what is "fit," and this fitness is evident in God's creation of the world. At the same time, whereas Clarke's opposition to voluntarism leads him to characterize eternal moral fitnesses such that they could stand independent of God, Edwards is careful to contend that these fitnesses are both internal to God's being and constitutive of it, a contention that preserves God's centrality for the establishment and determination of goodness in the world. For Edwards, the "moral rectitude" of God's heart disposes him "to everything that is fit, suitable and amiable in itself."[36] God's moral goodness leads him to act consistently with the standard of fitness, and in emphasizing God's inclination to cohere to this standard, Edwards suggests that God can be said to act in accordance with fitnesses as much as if they were not internal to his very being: "It is most certainly proper for God to act according to the greatest *fitness*, in his proceedings; and he knows what the greatest *fitness* is, as much as if perfect rectitude were a distinct person to direct him" (8:425). But, in contrast to Clarke, Edwards makes it clear that this moral rectitude is *not* finally external to God's being, and this point is underscored in his explanation of why love to God is the highest and most perfect form of virtue. As a being guided toward fitness by his own rectitude, God will act in a manner that coheres with the nature of things and esteem greatest the being who possesses more goodness and being than any other, that is, God himself. Thus moral fitness, as Edwards understands it, consists chiefly in loving God above all else. Love to God is the primary virtuous motive because God, as moral rectitude and goodness itself, is the being most worthy of love:

> The moral rectitude of God's heart must consist in a proper and due respect of his heart to things that are objects of moral respect: that is, to intelligent beings capable of moral actions and relations. And therefore it must chiefly consist in giving due respect to that Being to whom most is due; yes, infinitely most, and in effect all. For God is infinitely and most worthy of regard. The worthiness of others is as nothing to his. . . . To him belongs the whole of the respect that any moral agent, either God or any intelligent being, is capable of. . . . Therefore if moral rectitude of heart consists in paying the respect or regard of the heart which is due, or which fitness and suitableness requires, fitness requires infinitely the greatest regard to be paid to God; and the denying supreme regard here would be a

conduct infinitely the most unfit. Therefore a proper regard to this Being is what the fitness of regard does infinitely most consist in. (8:422)

God's "holiness consists" in his moral affections that tend to glorify objects that are most worthy of glory (8:422). It necessarily follows from God's moral goodness that God will ensure his own glory through his activity; in doing so, he does not act selfishly but instead celebrates the very essence of goodness, virtue, and beauty.

Edwards's affirmation of the fitness of God's actions provides a foundation for further arguments that explain how it is that goodness is present in the natural world. Having established that God acts according to his internal moral fitnesses, Edwards affirms that creation is a means through which God does what is fitting by fulfilling his disposition to glorify himself. God's power, goodness, justice, and wisdom are perfect, and a perfect attribute will be exercised in every way possible. Creation is one mode of these attributes' exercise, a vehicle through which they are given full expression: "It seems a thing in itself fit, proper, and desirable that the glorious attributes of God, which consist in a sufficiency to certain acts and effects, should be exerted in the production of such effects as might manifest the infinite power, wisdom, righteousness, goodness, etc., which are in God. If the world had not been created, these attributes never would have had any exercise" (8:428–29). Edwards characterizes the world here as so closely connected to God's moral attributes that he risks suggesting that God depends upon the world in order to achieve the highest possible degree of goodness. He clearly affirms in God the possession of dispositions or capacities to produce particular effects. God's moral qualities are "attributes which consist in a sufficiency for correspondent effects" (8:429). The created world, in turn, is one locus in which these sufficiencies are realized.

This feature of Edwards's position has led to some contemporary discussions of whether Edwards successfully preserves divine aseity, the notion that God is sufficient for God's own existence. Sang Hyun Lee's widely influential work *The Philosophical Theology of Jonathan Edwards* characterizes Edwards's understanding of creation as an actualization or fulfillment of dispositions that are constitutive of God's being. For Lee, Edwards develops a "dispositional ontology" that fuses emanation with teleology; in drawing these concepts together, Edwards is able to retain the Neoplatonist understanding of creation as emanation while simultaneously ensuring that creation is purposive and intentional, in contrast to such thinkers as Plotinus and Spinoza.³⁷ Yet while Lee's position is intended to characterize Edwards as preserving divine intentionality, his argument ultimately presents Edwards as potentially compromising God's aseity in a manner that risks implicitly conceiving God as depending on his creatures. Stephen Holmes argues that Lee ties Edwards to a type of process theology that conceives God's generation of the world as not effectively distinct from the Father's generation of the Son. The consequence of Lee's reading of Edwards, according to Holmes, is that God (in Christ) and the created world are not sufficiently distinguished.³⁸ Though Lee does in fact affirm God's aseity, Holmes is right to note these potential difficulties in Edwards's view of creation as Lee characterizes it: Lee is clear that it is the same divine disposition, the "original disposition" operating *ad intra* and *ad extra*, that is at work in God's internal life and in God's creation of the world, and he conceives Edwards's God as ever increasing, even as God is in certain senses fully actual and fully existent.³⁹ Holmes may not fully appreciate Lee's desire to ensure God's aseity and his commitment to a view of creation as an intentional activity, but the concerns he raises about Lee's position are legitimate. Recent scholars, moreover, have largely accepted Lee's reading of Edwards.⁴⁰ It must therefore be acknowledged that Edwards sometimes speaks of creation as the fulfillment of God's dispositions.

While Edwards does articulate his position in a manner that makes his view of God's nature a legitimate point of contention among scholars, a close look at this particular discussion of these divine sufficiencies demonstrates that Edwards's intention here is not to establish a relation between God and creation such that God depends on creation to fulfill his needs, but instead to affirm that God's goodness will necessarily mean that God's created world is good. He defends the goodness of the created world as a means of praising God. Creation is a means through which God exercises his morally excellent attributes; it logically follows that the object of their exercise will likewise be morally excellent:

> But then if the attributes which consist in a sufficiency for correspondent effects are in themselves excellent, the exercises of them must likewise be excellent. If it be an excellent thing that there should be a sufficiency for a certain kind of action or operation, the excellency of such a sufficiency must consist in its relation to this kind of operation or effect; but that could not be, unless the operation itself were excellent. . . . As God therefore esteems these attributes themselves [that is, his own moral excellences] valuable, and delights in them, so 'tis natural to suppose that he delights

in their proper exercise and expression. For the same reason that he esteems his own sufficiency wisely to contrive and dispose effects, he also will esteem the wise contrivance and disposal itself [that is, the object effected, or the world]. And for the same reason as he delights in his own disposition to do justly, and to dispose of things according to truth and just proportion, so he must delight in such a righteous disposal itself.[41]

Edwards's central concern is not to redefine God's being such that it depends upon the creation of the world, but simply to affirm the world's goodness (an affirmation that lays a foundation for conceiving justice and partial loves as complementary to true virtue). For Edwards, the created world is an expression of the dispositions of a morally perfect being, an object constructed by God as a communication of goodness and a means of celebrating and glorifying goodness. It follows that God must have ordered this world in a way that is good.

The idea that the natural world is ordered toward goodness is underscored by Edwards's view of the world not only as designed to glorify God but also as a vehicle through which God makes his goodness known to others. Just as Calvin affirms that our recognition of the goodness of God's works will lead us to glorify God, so does Edwards contend that it is fitting for divine virtue to be revealed (and thereby made known) through creation: "It seems to be a thing in itself fit and desirable, that the glorious perfections of God should be known, and the operations and expressions of them seen by other beings than himself" (8:430–31). The fitness of the revelation of God's morality follows from the fitness of the moral disposition's exercise: "If it be fit that God's power and wisdom, etc., should be exercised and expressed in some effects, and not lie eternally dormant, then it seems proper that these exercises should appear, and not be totally hidden and unknown" (8:431). Edwards explains that God knows his own moral goodness whether he sees its effects or not; therefore, if it is fitting for God's dispositions to be exercised, this fitness must arise from the fitness of their being known by creatures. It is good that God's creatures know his goodness, that "God's glory should be known by a glorious society of created beings" (8:431). From this argument it logically follows that God would construct the world in a manner that allows creatures to see his goodness in its operations.

Edwards makes the case for the goodness of the created world even more explicit by suggesting that God communicates his "fullness" to creatures. Edwards explains that he uses the term "fullness" to signify God's "natural and moral goodness" (8:433n5) and that God has a disposition to share this goodness that leads him to impart it to creatures. Consistent with Neoplatonism, Edwards characterizes God's communication of goodness to creatures as a diffusion such that God is characterized almost as an overflowing goodness. The disposition that moves creation, the "diffusive disposition that excited God to give creatures existence" (8:434), is a disposition of "fullness" or goodness. God's goodness is moved to diffuse itself, and it is this diffusion of goodness that takes place in the act of creation: creation arises from "a disposition in the fullness of the divine to flow out and diffuse itself" (8:435). Divine fullness is part of God's very being, God's nature, and it is this moral fullness that is the origin of creatures' existence. Edwards speaks of God's general benevolence as a "good disposition in his nature to communicate of his own fullness in general; as his knowledge, his holiness, and happiness; and to give creatures existence in order to it" (8:439). The communication of "good" to creatures is the thing most pleasing to God (8:503). God thus creates in a manner that is reasonable and fitting, and God's acts of creation impart goodness to God's creatures.

The Plausibility of Natural Goodness in a World Affected by Sin: Revisiting Issues of Voluntarism and Human Agency

Although Edwards does not conceive justice and private loves as truly virtuous, his theology of creation describes a world in which natural goodness can be present even as human sin limits its pursuit. Because Edwards maintains that God providentially orders the world toward the good, it follows that morality is a category that in some sense coincides with the natural world, as I noted in chapter 2. Furthermore, for Edwards, this coincidence remains present in the cosmos even after the Fall. Whereas Calvin perceives the postlapsarian world to incline toward chaos apart from God's restraining grace, Edwards underscores the point that moral good is a category that is both reasonable and part of the "nature of things"; his argument echoes Clarke's contention that morality is grounded upon reason. Both this claim and Edwards's related argument that God imparts goodness to creatures are important for my broader point that Edwards allows some room for incomplete virtues that can be pursued independently of grace, even though he is careful to make it clear that these dispositions fall short of true virtue.

Edwards's affirmation of a type of rationality and goodness in the postlapsarian world provides a vehicle for revisiting questions about Edwards's conception of moral accountability. As I observed in chapter 3, Edwards's argument that true virtue and the spiritual sense are distributed through God's will might initially appear to signify a type of voluntarism at work in his view of morality such that God arbitrarily decides who may be moral. Moreover, chapter 5 identifies marked similarities between Edwards's spiritual sense, by which we are enabled to pursue virtue, and Hutcheson's moral sense. Hutcheson's moral sense, in turn, raised concerns about voluntarism and accountability for subsequent thinkers such as Richard Price, a rationalist successor of Clarke. Price argues that Hutcheson's moral sense theory is essentially voluntarist because it allows the constitution of morality to be arbitrary. According to Price, Hutcheson's moral sense is an arbitrary principle placed in us by the mere pleasure of God. Price is concerned that Hutcheson perceives the moral order as arising from within us rather than being from nature itself. Price believes that this position leads to a view of morality as an arbitrary category based on the vagaries of human subjects. He is adamant that in order to guard against the arbitrariness implicit in Hutcheson's moral sense, we must affirm that right and wrong are in the nature of things. They are real characteristics of actions, and not something in our own minds. Furthermore, he suggests, we must affirm that there are eternal moral distinctions if we are to speak of moral attributes in God.[42]

Price wrote his *Review of the Principal Questions of Morals* in 1758, the year of Edwards's death, so Edwards would not have been aware of his specific argument.[43] Nevertheless, Edwards's argument in the final chapter of *The Nature of True Virtue* makes some effort to guard against these potential concerns that rationalists might raise against sentimentalism. My challenge to contemporary noncognitivist readings of Hutcheson in chapter 5 demonstrates the plausibility of contesting Price's interpretation of Hutcheson by arguing that Hutcheson's position is compatible with a view that morality is in the "nature of things." Edwards is even more explicit than Hutcheson in guarding against the notion that morality is arbitrary or detached from nature. In aligning himself with Hutcheson's perception of morality as necessarily related to sentiment and beauty, Edwards clarifies this position by explicitly denying that virtue and virtuous sentiments are constructs unrelated to the natural order. This argument is significant because it demonstrates continuity between Edwards's understanding of true virtue and the structure and ordering of the cosmos. This continuity, in turn, shows how natural human attributes that cohere in the "nature of things" (in keeping with God's design for them) can be considered incomplete forms of true virtue. In defending this argument, Edwards lays the foundation for a view of the moral life that allows room for humans to pursue a (limited) set of "good" dispositions independently of special grace.

Even though true virtue is connected to human sentiment, Edwards contends that it is "founded in the reason and nature of things." He explains that it is proper to link virtue with beauty and sentiment insofar as virtue represents a quality that can be perceived "immediately" (by those who possess a spiritual sense) rather than through a process of "argumentation" (8:619). He agrees with those thinkers who associate virtue with sentiment, insofar as this connection functions as a way of recognizing that "they who see the beauty there is in true virtue, don't perceive it by argumentation on its connections and consequences, but by the frame of their own minds, or a certain spiritual sense given them of God, whereby they immediately perceive pleasure in the presence of an idea of true virtue in their minds" (8:620). But he distances himself from any suggestion that the construction of the spiritual sense is an arbitrary act of God, and that God might just as easily have created morality to stand at odds with the natural order: "But if thereby is meant that the frame of mind, or inward sense given them by God, whereby the mind is disposed to delight in the idea or view of true virtue, is given arbitrarily, so that if he had pleased he might have given a contrary sense and determination of mind, which would have agreed as well with the necessary nature of things, this I think is not true" (8:620).

The question of whether the construction of the spiritual sense is arbitrary becomes a central focus of *True Virtue*'s final chapter: "Therefore now the question is, whether God in giving this temper to a created mind, whereby it unites our loves to Being in general, acts so arbitrarily that there is nothing in the necessary nature of things to hinder but that a contrary temper might have agreed or consisted as well with that nature of things, as this?" (8:620). A second, related focus is whether human use of the terms "good" and "evil" is "arbitrary, without respect to any common sentiment at all, conformed to the nature of things" (8:624). Edwards's discussion of both of these questions demonstrates his interest in affirming the congruence of true virtue with "the nature of things" and hence with the structure of the created world.

In contending that morality (and, correlatively, the spiritual sense) stand in keeping with objective standards, Edwards makes claims that echo Clarke's position and that build on *End*'s argument that God's creation of the natural world is fitting. The structures of the moral order are aligned with external standards of fitness, and indeed, Edwards affirms, God's very being coheres to these standards. Edwards contends that the idea that virtue is constitutive of God's being is, in fact, necessarily true: a truly virtuous disposition is "by absolute necessity his [God's] own temper and nature" (8:621). Insofar as truly virtuous love consists in "agreement or consent of being to Being" (8:620), God logically must agree with himself and cannot be divided: "God himself is in effect Being in general; and without all doubt it is in itself necessary (and impossible it should be otherwise) that God should agree with himself, be united to himself, or love himself." True virtue is therefore God's "necessary nature" (8:621). Echoing Clarke and the British rationalist tradition, Edwards suggests that God conforms to an objective view of moral goodness, although he departs from these rationalists by locating this standard in God's own being.

Just as God's being is consistent with an eternal standard of moral goodness, so does human true virtue consist in our alignment with a goodness present in "the nature of things." Edwards makes clear that the spiritual sense is a cognitive faculty, acquiring knowledge of moral standards that are actually present in the world and external to the human agent. He explains that the scriptures speak of our moral faculty as "understanding" to signify that this faculty's constitution agrees with the general structure of the universe: "These things may help us to understand why that spiritual and divine sense, by which those that are truly virtuous and holy perceive the excellence of true virtue, is in the sacred Scriptures called by the name of light, knowledge, understanding, etc. If this divine sense were a thing arbitrarily given, without any foundation in the nature of things, it would not properly be called by such names" (8:622). In making this point, Edwards seeks to show that moral good and evil are not relative to the beliefs of a human agent who perceives and pursues them but instead are external to all human agents: "For, if there were no correspondence or agreement in such a sense with the nature of things, any more than there would have been in a diverse or contrary sense, the idea we obtain by this spiritual sense could in no respect be said to be a knowledge or perception of anything besides what was in our own minds. For this idea would be no representation of anything without" (8:622). Humans mistakenly differ in their use of the terms good and evil, but these differences signify humans' tendencies to err, rather than indicating that morality itself is subjective: "Mankind in general seem to suppose some general standard or foundation in nature for a universal consistence in the use of the terms whereby they express moral good and evil; which none can depart from but through error and mistake" (8:627). As in God, then, moral good and evil in humans are not arbitrary categories but instead cohere in the nature of things.

Although these claims relate to the nature of true virtue rather than to justice and partial loves, they have implications for how we understand these incomplete virtues as well. The human ability to practice true virtue requires the intervention of God's special grace, but God has created the world in such a way that true virtue is not at odds with it but is its fulfillment. Though I made this point in chapter 3, I reiterate it here because the idea that there is some degree of continuity in nature between true virtue, on one hand, and justice and private loves, on the other, is essential if we are to recognize the logic of characterizing these natural qualities as genuinely "good" dispositions that reflect (in a limited sense) the beauty of true virtue. If morality were disconnected from the natural order, then natural traits could not be said to partake of it in any degree, but the coherence of true virtue to Edwards's view of creation suggests that the created world is a setting in which the existence of natural, incomplete virtues is plausible.

At the same time, as I noted in relation to the idea of partial loves, sin can distort and disorder self-love so that it is not expanded and expressed in attributes that partake in natural goodness. I have argued that Edwards departs from Calvin's view of original sin by affirming a sort of rationalism at work even in the postlapsarian universe. Yet he does not embrace Clarke's rationalism so fully that he perceives true virtue, or benevolence, as something we can acquire naturally. By building on rationalism only in part, Edwards is able to avoid one concern Schneewind raises with regard to "antivoluntarist" positions such as Clarke's: Schneewind suggests that rationalists such as Clarke affirm the eternal nature of moral laws, and the independence of these laws from God's will, to such a degree that they unintentionally render God superfluous for human morality. Like Clarke, Edwards affirms eternal moral standards, but he simultaneously recognizes some degree of human inability to pursue the moral life (both by following these eternal laws and by cultivating virtue) independently of God's assistance. Original sin has obscured the proper workings of our will and conscience, although it is possible that our conscience may be schooled. I develop this point more fully in the next section, where I contend that Edwards understands the natural conscience (when properly exercised) to oppose sin. But it is not only Edwards's view of original sin that guards against Schneewind's concern; it is also his more general emphasis upon God's sovereignty. Edwards's reiterated affirmation of the dependence of creatures upon God, coupled with his theology of creation in *End*, suggests that Edwards sees God's grace as necessarily operative even in the pursuit of meritorious attributes that we may achieve independently of his intervening salvific grace.

Edwards's theology of creation, then, affirms the goodness and rationality of the created world such that natural goodness can exist in the world in spite of original sin. In contrast to Calvin, who sees the world as disordered and tending toward chaos after the Fall, Edwards upholds a rationality at work in it. Sin affects the human will by disordering it so that we tend, apart from grace, to love ourselves disproportionately and thereby to compromise our ability to practice true virtue and to pursue justice and partial loves. But Edwards depicts the natural conscience and natural affections in a manner that suggests that through the assistance of providence, these faculties can pursue a meritorious natural goodness even independently of God's intervening grace and the work of the spiritual sense.

The Pursuit of Justice and Partial Loves

In describing Edwards's view of justice and natural affections, I have shown that these qualities possess some portion of the beauty and character of true virtue, even though they cannot properly be called true virtue. I now explore more precisely the natural goodness of these attributes. It is helpful first to explain Edwards's understanding of our natural human faculties, so as to consider the sense in which postlapsarian humans can be said to pursue good actions and dispositions. Edwards's view of natural conscience and natural affections suggests that the justice and partial loves that created faculties can pursue are "good" insofar as they contribute to our natural flourishing. The habitual pursuit of justice and private loves constitutes dispositions that to some extent resemble true virtue. To be sure, these dispositions are not finally truly virtuous because their scope is too narrow to partake in true virtue and because, unlike true virtue, they do not involve a self-aware and intentional love to God. Yet these dispositions are naturally good to a degree that surpasses the goodness of splendid vices. It is appropriate to describe these qualities as incomplete virtues because they authentically point toward and take part in a love that typologically images true virtue. Although Edwards himself does not employ the term "incomplete virtues," he offers three arguments that implicitly support such a reading of justice and partial loves. First, he presents these qualities as having a "negative moral goodness." Second, he suggests that these qualities can be said to *oppose* sin in some sense. Third, he contends that the pursuit of these qualities complements and coincides with true virtue in important ways.

Natural Conscience and the Natural Affections as Constructed Through Divine Providence

Edwards's view of sin is such that humans are unable to pursue the true virtue for which we were created apart from the special intervention of God's grace. Yet Edwards does allow that divine providence has instilled certain faculties in us, both a conscience and natural affections, that enable us to approve and pursue justice and partial loves. Just as these attributes fail to be truly virtuous in Edwards's terms, so do their corresponding natural faculties lack the spiritual and divine character of the spiritual sense associated with true virtue. They are distinct from the spiritual sense in primarily two ways: first, they can be said ultimately to originate in self-love rather than love to God, and therefore lack the nature of true virtue;[44] second, they may approve of truly virtuous dispositions in God and humans, but this approval lacks a sense of "delight" and a recognition of the full beauty of spiritual things (8:595–96). But, when rightly exercised, they are not amoral either. Like Calvin, Edwards affirms that God has providentially given us these particular instincts and faculties as means of ordering society and preserving humankind: we possess them "by the wise constitution of the great Governor of the world" (8:612). In fact, we will see that when we use these faculties properly to develop the character traits that they were established to encourage, we are pursuing naturally good dispositions, dispositions whereby we make ourselves amenable to the providence of God.

Edwards's accounts of the natural conscience and the private affections are instructive for recognizing precisely how God has ordered these natural faculties providentially. Edwards understands the natural conscience to have essentially two functions: first, it helps us to recognize the proportionate beauty of justice; second, it leads us to seek to be consistent with ourselves. While these functions are inferior to the activity of a truly virtuous disposition, our natural conscience nevertheless leads us to approve and seek the justice of which (as noted above) a truly virtuous disposition approves. Our conscience functions as a "sense of *desert*," leading us to apprehend "that secondary kind of beauty that lies in uniformity and proportion," the beauty of justice (8:581–82). While justice does not consist entirely in this secondary beauty, the fact that our natural conscience approves it will lead us to seek its pursuit because our conscience has the ability to empathize with others. Through the operations of conscience, we can put ourselves in another person's place and feel empathy toward her: "men in thinking of others do as it were put themselves in their place, they do it naturally, or rather habitually, instantaneously and without set purpose" (8:592). This substitution, coupled with our sense of desert, leads us to be uneasy when we do not act justly toward others (8:589). The natural conscience moves us to desire to be consistent with ourselves and to act toward those with whom we empathize in a manner appropriate to our sense of desert. Through the operation of natural conscience, then, we are led to treat others justly, in a manner of which our conscience would approve: "Natural conscience consists in . . . the disposition to approve or disapprove the moral treatment which passes between us and others, from a determination of the mind to be easy, or uneasy, in a consciousness of our being consistent or inconsistent with ourselves. Hereby we have a disposition to approve our own treatment of another, when we are conscious to ourselves that we treat him so as we should expect to be treated by him, were he in our case and we in his" (8:592). Our natural conscience therefore leads us to act justly and in a manner of which truly virtuous dispositions approve. Its motives for doing so arise from self-love, insofar as we are uneasy when we are not consistent with ourselves (8:589), and this motive is inferior to a truly virtuous motive. But this view of the workings of the natural conscience can be seen as part of a broader account of providence according to which God has created the world so that self-love leads us toward broader social concerns and affections.

Edwards underscores this suggestion that natural conscience leads us to pursue justice in his recognition of a concurrence between natural conscience and the law of God, as well as between natural conscience and true virtue to some degree. The equality and proportion of which natural conscience approves are present in moral good and evil, so that the conscience can naturally approve moral good without understanding it fully. Consequently, natural conscience and a truly virtuous disposition will tend to coincide in the objects that they approve.[45] Benevolence also leads us to put ourselves in others' places (8:594). Natural conscience, when exercised perfectly, coincides with the spiritual sense in terms of the sentiments and actions it approves and can therefore be said to coincide with God's law in some sense.[46] The natural conscience leads us to repent of sin, although not to exercise truly virtuous repentance, because our consciences recognize that it is just to yield to God and that vice deserves punishment. Likewise, a properly formed natural conscience approves benevolence. The difference between the conscience and the spiritual sense lies in the source of approval: conscience does not see and love the true spiritual beauty of benevolence even though it approves benevolence for its natural beauty and proportion (8:595), and its disapproval of sin is less severe than the complete hatred of sin that Edwards deems necessary for truly virtuous repentance (8:597), as I noted in chapter 5. But rightly formed conscience nevertheless agrees fully with the spiritual sense's approval of particular objects, although its motives are different: a completely formed conscience "agrees with the latter [true virtue] fully and exactly, as to the object approved, though not as to the ground and reason of approving. It approves all virtue and condemns all vice" (8:612–13). God has given us natural conscience to help us judge and pursue actions consistent with what he would pursue, even though our motives are not fully virtuous: "natural conscience is implanted in all mankind, there to be as it were in God's stead, and to be an internal judge or rule to all, whereby to distinguish right and wrong" (8:595).

God has likewise given us natural affections that providentially lead us toward actions that the spiritual sense would approve. As in the case of the natural conscience, many of these natural affections have their origin in self-love and therefore fall short of true virtue. Edwards's account of private affections is related to his understanding of providence—that is, God has providentially ordered our self-loves so that they lead us to exercise love for other humans, as well as to exercise pity and gratitude. Moreover, Edwards also allows that some private affections may arise from natural instincts. Just as God has given us a natural conscience, so has he given us instinctual "kind affections." In a manner consistent with Calvin's emphasis on providence as central to the idea of natural law, Edwards identifies "laws of nature" through which God providentially gives us these instinctual affections in order to encourage humanity's preservation and flourishing in the created world: "There are various dispositions and inclinations natural to men, which depend on particular laws of nature determining their minds to certain affections and actions toward particular objects; which laws seem to be established chiefly for the preservation of mankind, though not only for this, but also for their comfortably subsisting in the world. Which dispositions may be called 'instincts.'" Edwards here presents an account of the natural law according to which our natures are instinctively ordered to particular affections, including private loves, or "affections of the mind which mankind naturally exercise toward some of their fellow creatures or in some cases toward men in general" (8:600).

Edwards's discussion of our natural instincts demonstrates that he conceives natural law to function providentially and that self-love is key to this function. I observed above that Edwards does acknowledge a type of self-love that follows from sin and that can be characterized as a wrongful ordering of our affections, so that we prioritize love for ourselves above love to God (8:614). But he simultaneously recognizes a certain sort of self-love as providentially ordered by God. This sort of self-love directs us toward actions and dispositions that have natural goodness. Edwards maintains that God creates us with an instinct for self-love, and this instinct so immediately gives rise to private loves that it can almost be said that these are instinctive as well: with regard to the love of parents for children, Edwards affirms,

> But if any think that natural affection is more properly to be referred to a particular instinct of nature, than to self-love, as its cause, I shall not think it a point worthy of any controversy or dispute. In my opinion, both are true; viz. that natural affection is owing to natural instinct and also that it arises from self-love. It may be said to arise from instinct, as it depends on a law of nature. But yet it may be truly reckoned as an affection arising from self-love; because, though it arises from a law of nature, yet that is such a law as according to the order and harmony everywhere observed among the laws of nature, is connected with, and follows from self-love: as was shown before. (8:601)

In making this point, Edwards reveals that his view of self-love is a central part of his understanding of natural law. God has providentially created our natures so that self-love gives rise to other natural affections, and these are "instinctive" insofar as they arise from the very construction of our natures. As divine providence instills in us a natural conscience, so does it instill in us instincts for self-love that guide us toward natural dispositions that promote private loves. These natural faculties function providentially to encourage our preservation and also to encourage us to live in love with other creatures.

Justice and Private Loves as Incomplete Virtues

Our natural faculties direct us toward attributes that benefit us, then, though they are not truly virtuous. But are these qualities virtues in some lesser sense? On one hand, this appears not to be the case. Edwards suggests that virtues and vices are qualities that deserve "praise" or "blame" (8:626–27). And the natural qualities of justice and private loves are not strictly praiseworthy, in Edwards's terms, because only God is truly praiseworthy. Moreover, justice and private loves arise from our instincts, so that even if we could be praised for them, they in some sense lack true merit because they are merely dispositions that we are conditioned to exercise. Yet, on the other hand, Edwards conceives of these natural dispositions as dispositions that humans should seek. Moreover, many people are so mired in sin that they do not pursue them, and Edwards finds a rejection of these natural moral qualities to be problematic. It is therefore appropriate to understand Edwards's justice and private loves as expressions of natural goodness that constitute incomplete virtues. These qualities are naturally good because God has constructed us to pursue them as part of his providential design for the universe. Our cultivation of these attributes providentially tends toward our flourishing, preservation, and moral improvement. Edwards describes and upholds these attributes' goodness in three different ways: through the language of "negative moral goodness," by suggesting that these qualities oppose sin, and by affirming that these attributes can be "sanctified" or perfected. These arguments point toward the (imperfectly) virtuous character of justice and partial loves.[47]

Edwards contends in *The Nature of True Virtue* that justice and private loves involve a sort of goodness inferior to the goodness of true virtue, and he calls this quality "negative moral goodness." Negative moral goodness guards against sin; apart from it, persons would be wicked: "They [natural affections] have this negative moral goodness, because a being without them would be an evidence of a much greater moral evil." If the natural conscience, the faculty that approves justice, and the instincts that guide our natural affections are not working properly, this is a sign that sin is at work in our lives and shaping our actions. Sin is opposed not only to true virtue but also to "the dictates of that moral sense which is in natural conscience" (8:614). When we habitually sin, our conscience is clouded and unable to make proper judgments that recognize a logical connection between sin and punishment. Sin will likewise damage the capacities of the natural affections. Though these affections lack the nature of true virtue, they are not equivalent to sin or vice, because sin would diminish them:

> So with respect to natural *gratitude*, though there may be no virtue merely in loving them that love us, yet the contrary may be an evidence of a greater degree of depravity, as it may argue a higher degree of selfishness,

so that a man is come to look upon himself as *all*, and others as nothing, and so their respect and kindness as nothing. Thus an increase of pride diminishes gratitude. So does sensuality, or the increase of sensual appetites . . . tend by degrees to make the mind insensible to anything else; and those appetites take up the whole soul. . . . In like manner natural affection, and natural pity, though not of the nature of virtue, yet may be diminished greatly by the increase of those two principles of pride and sensuality. (8:615)

Sin and the natural affections are at odds, then, in that the increase of one depletes the other. A properly formed conscience and natural affections are signs that sin is not excessively functioning in a person's life and therefore signify a type of qualified natural goodness. They are not signs that we are pursuing our final and most central end of loving God, but they nevertheless are means through which we guard against sin.

At several points Edwards indicates that in appealing to the term "negative moral goodness" he does not simply intend to argue that the pursuit of justice and private loves is consistent with an absence or lack of sin. Instead, more strongly, he wishes to affirm that these attributes can be said to *oppose* sin. Justice and the natural affections can tend toward the general good of creation. In this tendency, they coincide with benevolence: "The present state of the world is so ordered and constituted by the wisdom and goodness of its supreme Ruler, that these natural principles for the most part tend to the good of the world of mankind. So do natural pity, gratitude, parental affection, etc. Herein they agree with the tendency of general benevolence, which seeks and tends to the general good" (8:616).

Moreover, Edwards explicitly acknowledges that in promoting justice and partial loves, the natural conscience and affections function "to restrain vice, and prevent many acts of wickedness. . . . Natural conscience tends to restrain sin in general, in the present state of the world." These functions of the natural faculties demonstrate God's providential activity: the natural affections and conscience accomplish these things because God has mercifully constructed the world in this way. Certainly Edwards affirms that the restraint of vice does not signify that these qualities are of the nature of true virtue, for God mercifully orders that many qualities, even self-love, that are not true virtue function to increase good and guard against vice (8:616). Yet in resisting sin and exercising these faculties as they were intended to be exercised, humans can be said to cultivate dispositions and actions that coincide with God's providence and thereby to pursue the natural goodness evident in these incomplete virtues.

A conception of these qualities as incomplete virtues is underscored by Edwards's affirmation that there are sanctified or infused forms of each of these attributes, and that these sanctified forms are truly virtuous. When speaking of natural affections and justice, Edwards argues that "there are affections of the *same denomination* [as these natural qualities] which are truly virtuous" (8:616). Although these natural qualities are not truly virtuous, they share true virtue's "denomination" in some degree, so that they are capable of being sanctified or perfected. Benevolence leads us to exercise pity that is consistent with natural pity but superior to it in that this "truly virtuous *pity* or compassion to others under affliction or misery from general benevolence" (8:616) functions to "excite compassion in cases that are overlooked by natural instinct." In turn, a virtuous gratitude "is one that arises from benevolence in addition to self-love." A "virtuous love of justice" arises from a true virtue that inclines us to wish that "every particular being should have such a share of benevolence as is proportioned to its dignity, consisting in the degree of its being and the degree of its virtue." The conscience itself is sanctified, as are familiar affections when "their operations [are] mixed with the influence of virtuous benevolence" and ordered by this benevolence (8:617). True virtue, then, sanctifies and completes these natural qualities without changing their "denominations." It is therefore fitting to recognize these qualities as incomplete virtues, attributes that possess a form of goodness that is inferior to true virtue but that is capable of being sanctified. Justice and private loves tend toward true virtue's effects, and, when perfected by love, they are able to partake fully of its nature.

Moral Agency, Accountability, and the Incomplete Virtues

Although Edwards affirms that virtue requires the intervention of divine grace and the gift of a spiritual sense, his theology nevertheless allows a positive role for the natural human attributes of justice and partial loves such that these attributes function as incomplete virtues. In part, Edwards stands in keeping with a broader Augustinian and Reformed view that suggests that the goodness of these attributes lies in God's providential direction of them to positive ends. But Edwards also suggests that these qualities possess a type of "natural goodness" consistent with his view of creation. These qualities are not truly virtuous, but they can be said to image true virtue in an incomplete sense, for although they are not salvific, they share true virtue's "denomination" and have the capacity to be perfected so that they may partake more fully in its nature.

I have argued that Edwards's account of moral formation is not finally Aristotelian because he is concerned to avoid any suggestion that habituation can lead to salvation. Edwards's contention that justice and partial loves lack the nature of true virtue underscores this point. These qualities, unlike the virtues I discuss in chapters 2, 3, and 4, can be cultivated through the right exercise of our natural faculties. At the same time, we see here that Edwards's ethic provides a place for recognizing that the pursuit of these qualities is good, and that their goodness reflects (in some measure) the goodness of true virtue.

Edwards's affirmation of the merit in pursuing such qualities further demonstrates his concern to allow for human moral agency within a moral vision that emphasizes the receptive character of human virtues. Although Edwards sometimes describes creatures' dependence upon God in a manner that risks compromising human freedom, these passages are softened when one reads them alongside *End*. In *End*, Edwards affirms that natural goodness is in the world because it has emanated from God's own goodness. God desired to diffuse his "fullness of good *ad extra*" (8:433), outside himself; as God created the world, God therefore infused it with this goodness (8:433–34). The creatures' own fullness is "as it were comprehended in God" (8:440–41), and as creatures live into this fullness, they come to be increasingly like God and to participate more fully in divine being (8:458–60). God "communicates good" to the creature when she is created (8:460), and creatures depend upon God for this communication. God is intimately involved in the life of the creature and in her pursuit of the good, but this involvement is mediated through the created order rather than accomplished in a manner that compromises the freedom of a human agent. If read in isolation from other texts, *End* could be interpreted as a forerunner of Deism, such that God is involved in our moral pursuits only through having provided us with particular moral faculties, faculties that we can naturally cultivate through our own devices to pursue good behavior. But Edwards's emphasis upon God's immediate involvement with creatures suggests that this reading is inconsistent with his intentions.

Having recognized Edwards's willingness to articulate positions that may (if viewed in isolation from each other) tend toward compromising human freedom or compromising the intimacy of divine agency, it is possible to understand the Edwardsean relation between divine and human activity as one that takes into account key features of both his understanding of creation and his view of divine activity. For Edwards, God is intimately and particularly involved with our moral activity, and one way in which this involvement takes place is through the gracious assistance of providence at work in the natural world. For Edwards, God is immediately present to creatures at every moment. Yet this presence need not undermine our freedom: it is mediated through the goodness that has been more generally infused into creation, and into each created individual. Thus Edwards maintains that God communicates his fullness to the world and to creatures through creation. Although original sin has distorted our wills, it has not destroyed the order and goodness evident in the world (as it has done for Calvin) or rendered this order entirely inaccessible to humans. The created world is a setting in which natural goodness can occur, and God's gracious providence sustains our natural faculties and is at work as we pursue this goodness.

Conclusion

*Virtues, Accountability, and Dependence:
Edwards's Significance for Contemporary Christian Ethics*

Edwards's ethic of receptive human virtues represents a compelling vision of the human moral life as fundamentally rooted in and dependent upon God. On one level, Edwardsean virtues are qualities proper to God's being, but in *A History of the Work of Redemption*, Edwards expands this conception of virtue to accommodate multiple dimensions of human moral experience, including human nature's finitude and sinfulness. In his implicit and explicit recognition of these features of human existence, Edwards develops an ethic that stands out in singular fashion from other accounts of ethics in the historical Christian tradition, and that speaks uniquely to many concerns of contemporary Christian ethicists working to recover traditions of the virtues.

For Edwards, we acquire the virtues by receiving them. True virtue and its corollaries are received through the direct intervention of God's converting grace, which bestows a spiritual sense upon the regenerate. The incomplete virtues are likewise received; we receive these virtues as God emanates his goodness to the created order and instills in us the natural capacities to pursue limited forms of this goodness, forms that image the more perfect goodness of true virtue. In one sense, we depend utterly on God for the practice of virtue. And yet, at the same time, Edwards's ethic provides conceptual tools for understanding how human agents can be morally accountable for their actions even when their pursuit of virtue is not entirely of their control. Edwards himself seems concerned to defend this claim at points. And from the standpoint of contemporary ethics, this is a claim worth defending.

Many Enlightenment thinkers optimistically emphasized human independence, human autonomy, and the idea that we can make or form ourselves and establish our own destinies. But the two world wars and the Holocaust sparked a twentieth-century recognition that not all events are within our control, and that part of the moral life requires figuring out ways to address the circumstances we are given through the best means possible. Alasdair MacIntyre's *Dependent Rational Animals: Why Human Beings Need the Virtues* suggests that the natural course of human life makes us all aware of the limitations of self-determination: at the beginning of our lives we are dependent upon others, and at the end of our lives, as our health fails, we depend upon others again. Society privileges those who appear independent, and persons with medical conditions that necessitate dependence often feel ashamed. MacIntyre's text, however, reminds us that dependence on others is part of the human condition. Dependence on others is not something that applies merely to a select group of unfortunates; instead, it is so integral to the human condition that all of us, at some point in our lives, experience it and are haunted by the awareness of our own vulnerability. If we do not take finitude and limitation seriously as a constitutive part of human nature, we run the risk of excluding many groups of persons from the human community: children, many of the elderly, persons who are ill, and many persons with disabilities.

To combat society's tendency to associate "autonomy" with the ideal human condition, MacIntyre develops an intriguing notion of "virtues of acknowledged dependence." The postulation of such virtues allows MacIntyre to defend the idea that dependence and vulnerability are compatible with moral merit.[1] He suggests that one can derive such virtue from a recognition of the parallels between humans and animals, a recognition that he ties to both Aristotle and Aquinas.[2] But Aristotelian habituation fails to go far enough in acknowledging and accounting for the dependent state of human creatures. This Aristotelian view of moral formation presumes, on some level, that our repeated practice of moral activities controls our dispositions. Even though Aristotle recognizes that something like luck is at work in moral formation, it is nonetheless the case that the very notion of habituation seems to provide a deceptively simple formula for achieving moral dispositions, a formula that implies that virtue is something we choose to pursue by following particular practices, and that our own activity is finally what shapes us into moral agents. I have noted that many historical Christian thinkers have challenged Aristotle's habituation on theological grounds, arguing that his position fails to take seriously the place of God's grace in the moral life. But the notion of habituation is troubling even without these theological concerns. This view of moral formation fails to consider adequately the frailty and vulnerability of humans, and to recognize the possibilities for moral beauty even in the midst of frailty and dependence.

CONCLUSION

I myself am not of the Reformed tradition, and I do not completely share Edwards's understanding of salvation and predestination. But whether or not we accept these specific ideas in Edwards, we can find his ethic persuasive and useful for contemporary reflection on divine grace and the moral life. Edwards's ethic is grounded in an account of humanity as simultaneously utterly dependent on God and nonetheless capable of (and accountable for) the pursuit of moral beauty. Humans, for Edwards, depend entirely upon God's sovereign and loving will, and in some ways they are unable to control the events surrounding them. But in the midst of situations that cannot be controlled, humans are responsible for developing moral responses to their circumstances and pursuing dispositions that are beautiful and good. It is not the case that circumstances of dependence make us unable to be moral. For Edwards, we pursue the virtues from within the specific circumstances of particular human experiences. And although only God *is* beauty and holiness in a pure and final sense, Edwards recognizes an array of human moral qualities that participate in this beauty. Through the activity of God, these qualities are accessible to us even in the midst of the limitations characteristic of human existence.

Edwards's balance of divine determinism with human responsibility distinguishes his virtue ethic from other views of ethics in the history of Christian thought. While many theologians affirm God's sovereignty over creation, Edwards radicalizes this affirmation in a manner that may appear to compromise humans' authorship of their own actions, and yet he simultaneously manages to preserve and defend the notion of human responsibility by redefining its meaning. Edwards's conception of moral accountability expands and enriches the efforts of contemporary virtue ethicists to conceive human beings not merely as autonomous wills. For Edwards, humans are vulnerable and fragile creatures. Recognizing and embracing this vulnerability is essential to the enterprise of moral growth, the acquisition of receptive human virtues. Ultimately, accepting this condition of dependence is a means of empowerment, for in recognizing our limits, we open ourselves to God's activity in our lives.

Notes

CHAPTER I

1. Jean Porter and Rosalind Hursthouse delineate these features of virtue in helpful ways. See Rosalind Hursthouse, *On Virtue Ethics* (Oxford: Oxford University Press, 1999), 11–12; and Jean Porter, *The Recovery of Virtue* (Louisville, Ky.: Westminster John Knox Press, 1990), especially 102–10.

2. Roland Delattre, "The Theological Ethics of Jonathan Edwards: An Homage to Paul Ramsey," *Journal of Religious Ethics* 19, no. 2 (1991): 71–102; William C. Spohn, "Sovereign Beauty: Jonathan Edwards and the Nature of True Virtue," *Theological Studies* 42 (1981): 394–421.

3. Paul Ramsey, "Editor's Introduction," in *Ethical Writings*, vol. 8 of *The Works of Jonathan Edwards* (New Haven: Yale University Press, 1957–), 12–27 (hereafter cited as *Works*).

4. William J. Danaher, *The Trinitarian Ethics of Jonathan Edwards* (Louisville, Ky.: Westminster John Knox Press, 2004).

5. Danaher observes that Edwards places "communion with God at the center of the moral life." Ibid., 8.

6. Robert M. Adams, *Finite and Infinite Goods: A Framework for Ethics* (New York: Oxford University Press, 1999), 14, 28–31.

7. Many scholars suggest that it would be shortsighted to see Thomas Aquinas as merely reiterating Aristotle's thought. See, for example, Thomas O'Meara, "Virtues in the Theology of Thomas Aquinas," *Theological Studies* 58 (1997): 254–85; and Jean Porter, "The Subversion of Virtue: Acquired and Infused Virtues in the Summa theologiae," *Annual of the Society of Christian Ethics* (1992): 19–41. Nonetheless, Aquinas's debts to Aristotle are commonly acknowledged, and his analysis of the virtues therefore differs from Edwards's in noteworthy ways. For example, chapter 4 discusses the differences between Aquinas's and Edwards's accounts of pride and humility.

8. Alasdair MacIntyre, *After Virtue: A Study in Moral Theory*, 2d ed. (Notre Dame: University of Notre Dame Press, 1984), 57–59, quotation on 186.

9. Ibid., 233.

10. MacIntyre contrasts Austen with Benjamin Franklin in order to show the positive features of her virtue concept (ibid., 181–87) and suggests that such novels as *Pride and Prejudice* and *Mansfield Park* serve as positive articulations of the premodern virtue tradition in a modern social setting. It should be noted, however, that while MacIntyre describes Austen as a "Christian writer," the virtues that she upholds in her novels, in contrast to the theological virtues of Edwards, are examples not of Christian virtue but of "modern republicanism"; that is, she seeks to preserve something like the ancient tradition of the virtues in modern society (ibid., 239–43).

11. Jeffrey Stout challenges MacIntyre's characterization of Austen as the last great representative of the virtue tradition by suggesting that this claim is true only if we adopt an Aristotelian account of the virtues. See Stout, *Democracy and Tradition* (Princeton: Princeton University Press, 2004), 133.

12. William Sparkes Morris's *The Young Jonathan Edwards: A Reconstruction* (Brooklyn: Carlson, 1991) offers a plausible account of the sources influencing Edwards's views of humanity's and creation's *telos*. Morris argues that the distinctions Edwards draws between "ultimate end" and "chief end" in *The End for Which God Created the World* echo the arguments of Burgerdicius, a philosopher whose conceptions of being and the universe were "largely Aristotelian" (86–90). Morris's argument suggests the

presence of "Aristotelian logic" in Edwards's thought, particularly in the early *Miscellanies* (102), and the idea that humans have a particular end is central to this logic. But Edwards's points of departure from Aristotle's ethics, particularly in his conception of moral formation, are decisive. The most significant departure relates to the acquisition of virtue, and a consideration of the "receptive" character of Edwards's virtues highlights and explores the implications of this departure.

13. Jerome B. Schneewind, "The Misfortunes of Virtue," *Ethics* 101, no. 1 (1990): 42–63.

14. Aristotle presumes "a society in which there was a recognized class of superior citizens, whose judgments on moral issues would be accepted without question." Ibid., 62. Subsequent citations of this work are given parenthetically.

15. Aristotle, *Nicomachean Ethics*, in *The Basic Works of Aristotle*, ed. and trans. Richard McKeon (New York: Random House, 1941), book 2, chapter 1, pp. 952–53, and book 2, chapter 4, p. 956.

16. Anri Morimoto, *Jonathan Edwards and the Catholic Vision of Salvation* (University Park: Pennsylvania State University Press, 1995), 41.

17. For Luther, "the most vital enemy of the righteousness of God is not the 'godless sinner' but the 'righteous' who think in terms of progress or movement" from moral action to salvation; these Christians erroneously think *"ad modum Aristotelis"* (Gerhard O. Forde, "The Exodus from Virtue to Grace: Justification by Faith Today," *Interpretation* 34, no. 1 [1980]: 37). Luther's *Lectures on Romans* argues that Christians should think in terms of moving not from "vice to virtue" but from "virtue to the grace of Christ," so that we rely on Christ's virtue rather than seeking salvation through our own merits. See Martin Luther, *Lectures on Romans*, trans. and ed. W. Pauck (Philadelphia: Westminster Press, 1961), 4.

18. Norman Fiering, *Moral Philosophy at Seventeenth-Century Harvard: A Discipline in Transition* (Chapel Hill: University of North Carolina Press, 1984), 23.

19. Keith Sprunger, "Ames, Ramus, and the Method of Puritan Theology," *Harvard Theological Review* 59, no. 2 (1966): 137–38. See also Fiering, *Moral Philosophy at Seventeenth-Century Harvard*, 23.

20. Fiering, *Moral Philosophy at Seventeenth-Century Harvard*, 24.

21. William Ames, *The Marrow of Theology*, 3d ed, trans. John E. Eusden (Boston: United Church Press, 1968; reprint, Grand Rapids: Baker, 1997), 2.2.18.

22. Mark Noll, *America's God: From Jonathan Edwards to Abraham Lincoln* (New York: Oxford University Press, 2002), 96.

23. Ames, *Marrow of Theology*, 2.2.15–16, 2.2.7.

24. For a helpful extended discussion of Ames's view of habit, see Fiering, *Moral Philosophy at Seventeenth-Century Harvard*, 93–94; and Norman Fiering, "Benjamin Franklin and the Way to Virtue," *American Quarterly* 30, no. 2 (1978): 204–5.

25. Noll, *America's God*, 96–97.

26. Gilbert Meilaender, *The Theory and Practice of Virtue* (Notre Dame: University of Notre Dame Press, 1984), 13.

27. Stanley Hauerwas and Charles Pinches, *Christians Among the Virtues: Theological Conversations with Ancient and Modern Ethics* (Notre Dame: University of Notre Dame Press, 1997), xiii, 3–16, 20–30.

28. The final section of Hauerwas and Pinches's work addresses "distinctively Christian" virtues. Hauerwas and Pinches do discuss Aristotle in this section, particularly in their account of courage as a Christian virtue, and to a more limited degree in their view of obedience, but their separate discussions of Aristotle and the New Testament underscore the ways in which Aristotelianism has posed challenges to Christian virtue ethics, even as it makes positive contributions as well (most notably in its account of friendship, which Hauerwas and Pinches address in their third chapter).

29. Stanley Hauerwas is the most obvious example of such a thinker, but see also Nancey Murphy, Brad J. Kallenberg, and Mark Thiessen Nation, eds., *Virtues and Practices in the Christian Tradition: Christian Ethics After MacIntyre* (Notre Dame: University of Notre Dame Press, 2003).

30. Porter, "Subversion of Virtue."

31. MacIntyre, *After Virtue*, 184.

32. Ibid., 182.

33. Alasdair MacIntyre, *Whose Justice? Which Rationality?* (Notre Dame: University of Notre Dame Press, 1988). See especially chapters 10 and 11.

34. Chapter 5 addresses Edwards's relation to Hutcheson in greater depth.

35. In addition to discussing Edwards's teleological logic, Morris argues that an Aristotelian metaphysics is evident in Edwards's thought (*Young Jonathan Edwards*, 103–28). In *Virtue Reformed: Rereading Jonathan Edwards's Ethics* (Leiden: Brill, 2005), Stephen A. Wilson also emphasizes Edwards's consistency with Aristotelian categories mediated through such philosophers as Nicolas Malebranche.

36. Wilson, *Virtue Reformed*, 196.

37. George Marsden, *Jonathan Edwards: A Life* (New Haven: Yale University Press, 2003), 466–67.

38. Norman Fiering, *Jonathan Edwards's Moral Thought and Its British Context* (Chapel Hill: University of North Carolina Press, 1981).

CHAPTER 2

1. For further discussion, see John P. Langan, "Augustine on the Unity and Interconnection of the Virtues," *Harvard Theological Review* 72 (1979): 81–95; and Eric Gregory, *Politics and the Order of Love: An Augustinian Ethic of Democratic Citizenship* (Chicago: University of Chicago Press, 2008), 263–66.

2. Theodore Beiser suggests that although the Cambridge Platonists never explicitly identify Calvinism as the root of the atheism they stringently critique, they describe this atheism in a manner that makes it consistent with Calvinist theology. See Beiser, *The Sovereignty of Reason: The Defense of Rationality in the Early English Enlightenment* (Princeton: Princeton University Press, 1996), 148, 163. Indeed, the Cambridge Platonists do criticize predestination and original sin forthrightly; these criticisms support Beiser's contention. Wilson likewise argues that Cudworth's criticism of these conceptions, particularly in settings in which he preached against them to Puritan audiences, suggests that he is offering "a critique of the Calvinist program more globally." Wilson, *Virtue Reformed*, 119.

3. Beiser, *Sovereignty of Reason*, 169–71.

4. G. A. J. Rogers, "The Other-Worldly Philosophers and the Real World: The Cambridge Platonists, Theology, and Politics," in *The Cambridge Platonists in Philosophical Context: Politics, Metaphysics, and Religion*, ed. G. A. J. Rogers, J. M. Vienne, and Y. C. Zarka (Dordrecht: Kluwer, 1997), 7.

5. Jerome B. Schneewind, "Voluntarism and the Foundation of Ethics," *Proceedings and Addresses of the American Philosophical Association* 70 (1996): 25–26.

6. Jerome B. Schneewind, *The Invention of Autonomy: A History of Modern Moral Philosophy* (Cambridge: Cambridge University Press, 1998), 31, 36, 99–100, 83.

7. Jennifer A. Herdt, "Affective Perfectionism: Community with God Without Common Measure," in *New Essays on the History of Autonomy: A Collection Honoring J. B. Schneewind*, ed. Natalie Brender and Larry Krasnoff (Cambridge: Cambridge University Press, 2004), 33.

8. See Stephen Darwall, *The British Moralists and the Internal "Ought": 1640–1740* (Cambridge: Cambridge University Press, 1995), 20–21.

9. J. A. Passmore suggests that Cudworth was such a great influence on Shaftesbury that Shaftesbury himself could be considered a Cambridge Platonist of sorts. See Passmore, *Ralph Cudworth* (Cambridge: Cambridge University Press, 1951), 90ff.

10. Marsden notes the strong influence of Cambridge Platonist Henry More's thought on New England thinkers, including Edwards (*Jonathan Edwards: A Life*, 72), and Stephen Wilson suggests that Edwards "uses" (while adapting) Cambridge Platonist concepts (*Virtue Reformed*, 121).

11. Marsden, *Jonathan Edwards: A Life*, 73–74.

12. Schneewind presents the Cambridge Platonists as the first "antivoluntarists." "Voluntarism and the Foundation of Ethics," 27.

NOTES TO PAGES 25–30

13. Ibid., 33, 27. Jennifer Herdt, however, has recently contested Schneewind's notion of a "shared moral community" as constitutive of modern antivoluntarist positions. "Affective Perfectionism," 30–32.

14. C. A. Patrides, "The High and Aiery Hills of Platonisme: An Introduction to the Cambridge Platonists," in *The Cambridge Platonists*, ed. C. A. Patrides (Cambridge: Harvard University Press, 1970), 22.

15. In "The Importance of Shaftesbury," *Journal of English Literary History* 20 (1953), Ernest Tuveson suggests that a "basic Christian pattern" underlies the thought of the Cambridge Platonists (270). Jennifer Herdt likewise argues that Whichcote's view of divine love provides him with a foundation for a doctrine of God that preserves divine transcendence. See Herdt, "Divine Compassion and the Mystification of Power: The Latitudinarian Divines in the Secularization of Moral Thought," *Annual of the Society of Christian Ethics* 21 (2001): 253–73. Wilson, too, defends the theology of the Cambridge Platonists, arguing that the Cambridge Platonists do insist on the "Holy Spirit's ineluctable presence in true morality" (*Virtue Reformed*, 117), that they affirm the incarnation as "necessary as a metaphysical backdrop for individual regeneration," and that they defend the claim that "some personal encounter with Jesus in the Word was required for moral generation" (120).

16. Beiser suggests that the Cambridge Platonists treat reason, rather than scripture or tradition, as the final arbiter of faith, and thereby risk rendering revelation effectively superfluous (*Sovereignty of Reason*, 176–77). He also indicates that the Cambridge Platonists do not succeed in arguing for the necessity of grace and of Christ's atonement within their system (164). James Deotis Roberts similarly argues that Whichcote risks presenting a Pelagian account of human nature. See Roberts, *From Puritanism to Platonism in Seventeenth-Century England* (The Hague: Martinus Nijhoff, 1968), 98–99.

17. Ralph Cudworth, "A Sermon Preached Before the House of Commons," in Patrides, *Cambridge Platonists*, 101–2.

18. Ibid., 113.

19. John Smith, "The Excellency and Nobleness of True Religion," in ibid., 160.

20. Patrides, "High and Aiery Hills of Platonisme," 36.

21. See Jennifer A. Herdt, "Cudworth, Autonomy, and the Love of God: Transcending Enlightenment (and Anti-Enlightenment) Christian Ethics," *Annual of the Society of Christian Ethics* 19 (1999): 48.

22. Patrides, "High and Aiery Hills of Platonisme," 36.

23. Cudworth, "Sermon Preached Before the House of Commons," 94, 93, 95, 117.

24. Smith, "Excellency and Nobleness of True Religion," 170.

25. John Smith, "The True Way or Method of Attaining to Divine Knowledge," in Patrides, *Cambridge Platonists*, 143.

26. Henry More, "The Purification of a Christian Man's Soul," in ibid., 212.

27. For further discussion of this distinction, see David B. Burrell, "Creation or Emanation: Two Paradigms of Reason," in *God and Creation: An Ecumenical Symposium*, ed. David B. Burrell and Bernard McGinn (Notre Dame: University of Notre Dame Press, 1990), 27–37.

28. Marsden, *Jonathan Edwards: A Life*, 4 (see also 76 and 439), 435–36.

29. Edwards, "God's Excellencies," in *Works*, 10:416, 423, 426.

30. Ibid., 10:420–21.

31. Ibid.

32. Edwards, "God Amongst His People," in *Works*, 19:462; "The Terms of Prayer," in *Works*, 19:780; *The Life of David Brainerd*, in *Works*, 7:780.

33. Edwards, *The End for Which God Created the World*, in *Works*, 8:424, 433–34; see also 440. Whether this emanation is best understood in Neoplatonic terms or in connection with a more scriptural revelation is a point of debate among scholars. The most accepted interpretation is that of Sang Hyun Lee, who in his *Philosophical Theology of Jonathan Edwards* (Princeton: Princeton University Press, 1988) presents an account of Edwardsean habit that depicts emanation in terms closer to those of Neoplatonism. Stephen Holmes, however, has recently offered a critique of Lee's argument that

contends that Lee's depiction of Edwards erroneously threatens God's aseity. See Holmes, "Does Jonathan Edwards Use a Dispositional Ontology? A Response to Sang Hyun Lee," in *Jonathan Edwards: Philosophical Theologian*, ed. Paul Helm and Oliver Crisp (Aldershot, UK: Ashgate, 2003).

34. *End for Which God Created the World*, 8:439 (see also 458).
35. Spohn, "Sovereign Beauty," 395, 399, 412–14.
36. Ramsey, "Editor's Introduction," 36–37, 20–21.
37. Stephen R. Holmes, *God of Grace and God of Glory* (Edinburgh: T & T Clark, 2000), 54ff.
38. Amy Plantinga Pauw, *The Supreme Harmony of All: The Trinitarian Theology of Jonathan Edwards* (Grand Rapids: William B. Eerdmans, 2002), 6–8, 13–14.
39. Edwards, *Charity and Its Fruits*, in *Works*, 8:132; *Discourse on the Trinity*, in *Works*, 21:123.
40. Pauw, *Supreme Harmony of All*, 6.
41. Pauw identifies this alignment as "the scholastic and Puritan consensus regarding the identity of all of God's attributes with God." Ibid., 72.
42. My earlier analysis of "God's Excellencies" suggests that Pauw here neglects a third perfection that Edwards aligns with God's being—that of excellence. This point, however, does not compromise the merit of Pauw's argument, and indeed it can be seen to complement it. At points, Edwards identifies "excellency" with "holiness"; in *The Religious Affections*, for example, he argues that genuine moral excellence "is holiness. Therefore holiness comprehends all the true moral excellency of intelligent beings: there is no other true virtue, but real holiness" (*Religious Affections*, in *Works*, 2:255). This connection between excellence and holiness suggests that excellence, like love, has an essential relation to the Holy Spirit. The "beauty" of God's essence is somewhat different, but at the very least it seems inextricably connected to the eternal harmony among the persons of the Trinity (see Pauw, *Supreme Harmony of All*, 85) and is in this sense essentially a Trinitarian concept as well.
43. Pauw, *Supreme Harmony of All*, 72.
44. *Discourse on the Trinity*, 21:113, 121.
45. "Terms of Prayer," 9:780.
46. Edwards, *The Distinguishing Marks of a Work of the Spirit of God*, in *Works*, 4:255–56.
47. *Discourse on the Trinity*, 21:123, 130, 136, 142, 144, 141.
48. *Charity and Its Fruits*, 8:373.
49. Michael J. McClymond, "Sinners in the Hands of a Virtuous God: Ethics and Divinity in Jonathan Edwards's End of Creation," *Zeitschrift für neuere Theologiegeschichte* 2 (1995): 21–22.
50. *Treatise on Original Sin*, in *Works*, 3:110.
51. Edwards, "The Torments of Hell Are Exceeding Great," in *Works*, 14:319. In a more troubling passage earlier in this sermon, Edwards explains that God's damnation of the reprobate reveals not his justice but his anger: "As God appointed the blessedness of the saints to show forth the exceeding greatness of his mercy and love, so the damnation of the wicked is to show the exceeding dreadfulness of his anger" (14:306–7). Edwards moves quickly, however, to focus on justice rather than anger, and this remains a more dominant theme: "From the deserts of wicked men, I argue thus: the least sin deserves eternal destruction" (14:309).
52. Edwards, "The Justice of God in the Damnation of Sinners," in *Works*, 19:341.
53. Ibid., 19:355.
54. Edwards, "Impending Judgment Averted Only by Reformation," in *Works*, 14:217, 223.
55. Ibid., 14:221.
56. Oliver Crisp, *Jonathan Edwards and the Metaphysics of Sin* (London: Ashgate, 2005), 13–14.
57. Edwards, *Miscellany 704*, in *Works*, 18:317.
58. Crisp, *Edwards and the Metaphysics of Sin*, 14, 18, 21, 54–78.
59. *Treatise on Original Sin*, 3:393–94.
60. Edwards's development of this claim is somewhat Humean: we cannot find actions meritorious unless we can legitimately presume that a virtuous act arises from a virtuous motive.
61. Edwards, *Freedom of the Will*, in *Works*, 1:153.

62. Ibid., 1:152–56, quotation on 155.
63. Ibid., 1:168; see also 156–72.

CHAPTER 3

1. Edwards, *The Nature of True Virtue*, in *Works*, 8:541. Hereafter cited parenthetically.
2. "This being a matter of the highest importance, I shall say something further to make it plain that love to God is most essential to true virtue; and that no benevolence whatsoever to other beings can be of the nature of true virtue, without it" (8:554).
3. Whichcote, "The Use of Reason in Matters of Religion," in Patrides, *Cambridge Platonists*, 43.
4. "So that in whatsoever miscarriages Men do fall, in all these they do go against their Light, and *hold the Truth in Unrighteousness*." Ibid., 49.
5. Ibid., 48.
6. "Hell arises *out of a Man's Self:* And Hell's Fewel is *the Guilt of a Man's Conscience* . . . both Hell, and Heaven, have their foundation *within* Men." Ibid., 46.
7. "There is something in every Man, upon which we may work, to which we may apply; to wit, *the Light of Reason and Conscience*; to which the Difference of Good and Evil may be made to appear." Ibid., 51.
8. As I demonstrate below, Edwards rejects, to some degree, the notion that we may know the content of goodness and virtue through our natural faculties.
9. See Patrides, "High and Aiery Hills of Platonisme," 39.
10. Whichcote, "Use of Reason," 45.
11. Patrides, "High and Aiery Hills of Platonisme," 38–39.
12. Whichcote, "Use of Reason," 49.
13. More, "An Hymn upon the Resurrection of Christ," in *Philosophical Poems of Henry More, Comprising Psychozoia and Minor Poems*, ed. Geoffrey Bullough (Manchester: Manchester University Press, 1931), 167–68.
14. Henry More, "Preface to *Philosophical Poems*," xxv, quoted in Patrides, "High and Aiery Hills of Platonisme," 38.
15. Ibid., 38.
16. Wilson characterizes George Turnbull in a manner similar to the way in which I characterize More (see *Virtue Reformed*, 123ff.). This depiction of Turnbull is insightful; Turnbull, too, was known to be an influence upon Edwards. I seek to complement rather than correct Wilson's insight by presenting More as a mediatory figure.
17. Roland Delattre suggests that Edwards's ethics involves the participation of creatures (after their renewal in Christ) in the life of God. See Delattre, "Theological Ethics of Edwards," 74.
18. Ibid., 88ff.
19. *End for Which God Created the World*, 8:441–43. Hereafter cited parenthetically.
20. Anthony Ashley Cooper Shaftesbury, *An Inquiry Concerning Virtue, or Merit* (1699), in *The British Moralists, 1650–1800*, ed. D. D. Raphael, 2 vols. (Oxford: Clarendon Press, 1969), 1:177, 169–72.
21. Joseph Butler, *Fifteen Sermons*, in Raphael, *British Moralists*, 1:367.
22. Julia Annas, *The Morality of Happiness* (Oxford: Oxford University Press, 1993), 38, 43–46.
23. Ibid., 175–77.
24. Michael Gass, "Eudaimonism and Theology in Stoic Accounts of Virtue," *Journal of the History of Ideas* 61, no. 1 (2000): 20–21, 23, 24, 29–32, 33–35. John Cooper similarly emphasizes the consistency of the Roman Stoics with earlier Stoa, which implies the presence of eudaimonism in Roman Stoic thought. He argues that the key moral task, for both early Stoics and Roman Stoics, is to develop a mental orientation such that we welcome gladly whatever circumstances nature places upon us, recognizing that nature is benevolent and that we, as a part of the universe, will benefit from the events caused by benevolent nature. Cooper, "Eudaimonism, the Appeal to Nature, and 'Moral Duty' in

Stoicism," in *Aristotle, Kant, and the Stoics,* ed. Stephen Engstrom and Jennifer Whiting (Cambridge: Cambridge University Press, 1996), 273–74.

25. *End for Which God Created the World,* 8:442.

26. See editor's preface in volume 10 of *Works,* 294.

27. Edwards, "Christian Happiness," in *Works,* 10:297.

28. Ibid., 10:303–4.

29. "Should we not think him a prince of ordinary clemency, he a master of extraordinary goodness, he a father of great tenderness, who never [commanded] anything of his subjects, his servants, or his children, but what was for their good and advantage? But God is such a king, such a lord, such a father to us." Ibid., 10:304.

30. Edwards, "The Pleasantness of Religion," in *Works,* 14:103–4.

31. Samuel Clarke, *A Discourse Concerning the Unchangeable Obligations of Natural Religion, and the Truth and Certainty of the Christian Revelation* (1706, 7th ed. 1728), in Raphael, *British Moralists,* 1:215–16.

32. Delattre, "Theological Ethics of Edwards," 86–87, 93–94, 98.

33. Wilson has noted that the Cambridge Platonists' view of sanctification lacks this recognition that sanctification and justification are linked, a recognition that would ordinarily be associated with Reformed thought. Wilson, *Virtue Reformed,* 117–18.

34. Holmes, *God of Grace and God of Glory,* 225.

35. Edwards contends that in humans there is an "innate sinful depravity of the heart." *Treatise on Original Sin,* 3:107. Hereafter cited parenthetically.

36. Edwards, "All God's Methods Are Most Reasonable," in *Works,* 14:161–97.

37. Edwards, "All That Natural Men Do Is Wrong," in *Works,* 19:519.

38. Edwards equates Christian love with charity; he notes that in the New Testament "charity" generally signifies love to humans but sometimes love to God. *Charity and Its Fruits,* 8:129–30. Hereafter cited parenthetically.

39. "If it be, all that is distinguishing and saving in true Christianity may be summarily comprehended in love, then hence Christians may try their experience whether it be real Christian experience. If it is so, they have love in them; it works by love, or issues in love" (8:145).

40. *Nature of True Virtue,* 8:594ff.

41. Bernard Williams, "Moral Luck," in *Moral Luck,* ed. Daniel Statman (Albany: State University of New York Press, 1993).

42. See, for example, John Bowlin, *Contingency and Fortune in Aquinas's Ethics* (Cambridge: Cambridge University Press, 1999).

CHAPTER 4

1. Edwards, "The Excellency of Christ," in *Works,* 19:567–68.

2. George Marsden contends that redemption is central to understanding Edwards's view of God's design for the world (*Jonathan Edwards: A Life,* 482), and Stephen Holmes argues that the work of redemption is the framework through which all other aspects of Edwards's theology can best be understood (*God of Grace and God of Glory,* 115–16). In Edwards's posthumously published collection of sermons *A History of the Work of Redemption,* Edwards calls redemption God's greatest work (*Works,* 9:512) and suggests at one point that the world was created so that it could be the site in which the "glorious work" of redemption is accomplished (9:524).

3. *Work of Redemption,* 9:304–5. Edwards suggests that the entire incarnation, the events of the incarnate Christ's life on earth, has the purpose of purchasing our salvation (9:295), a claim that stands in keeping with Calvin and the broader tradition of Reformed theology. Holmes observes that Edwards presents the entire life of Christ, rather than solely the atonement, as redemptive (*God of Grace and God of Glory,* 142–43), and the *Work of Redemption* likewise makes it clear that salvation does not lie

exclusively in the work of the atonement but also in the virtues and obedience that Christ displayed while incarnate.

4. *Work of Redemption*, 9:305, 309, 320.
5. Edwards reiterates this understanding of Christ's virtue as redemptive in his sermon "Like Rain upon Mown Grass" (*Works*, 22:309) and in his *Treatise on Original Sin* (3:200).
6. "Excellency of Christ," 19:590.
7. *Treatise on Original Sin*, 3:199.
8. Ibid.
9. *Religious Affections*, 2:284.
10. Ibid., 2:258–59.
11. *Work of Redemption*, 9:320. Hereafter cited parenthetically.
12. Edwards, "The Sorrows of the Bereaved Spread Before Jesus," in *Works*, 22:467.
13. "Excellency of Christ," 19:565.
14. *Distinguishing Marks*, 4:258.
15. "Excellency of Christ," 19:569. *Distinguishing Marks* reiterates the humility in Christ's character and practice: "The love that appeared in the Lamb of God was not only a love to friends, but to enemies, and attended with a meek and humble spirit" (4:258).
16. "Excellency of Christ," 19:568.
17. See also *Life of David Brainerd*, 7:91.
18. *Religious Affections*, 2:347.
19. "Excellency of Christ," 19:567.
20. *Distinguishing Marks*, 4:258.
21. Edwards, "Keeping the Presence of God," in *Works*, 22:531.
22. Edwards, "Continuing God's Presence," in *Works*, 19:413–14.
23. Edwards, "Mary's Remarkable Act," in *Works*, 22:397.
24. Edwards, *Some Thoughts Concerning the Revival*, in *Works*, 4:414. Hereafter cited parenthetically.
25. *End for Which God Created the World*, 8:456.
26. Against those who presume that this idea seems to present God as selfish, Edwards says that an alternative position "will contradict a former objection against God's taking pleasure in communications of himself, viz. that inasmuch as God is perfectly independent and self-sufficient, therefore all his happiness and pleasure consists in the enjoyment of himself" (8:457). This point is important because scholars have raised questions about whether Edwards's account of emanation in *End* sufficiently distinguishes God from creatures and thereby preserves a Christian understanding of creation as an intentional act rather than a Neoplatonist view of emanation through which God's goodness and being necessarily flow into creation. See McClymond, "Sinners in the Hands of a Virtuous God."
27. *End for Which God Created the World*, 8:456.
28. Edwards challenges those who insist that "God's own glory was not an ultimate end of his creation of the world" (8:457).
29. "That which this [any] person looks upon as his interest may interfere with or oppose the general good. Hence private interest may be regarded and pursued in opposition to the public. But this can't be with respect to the Supreme Being, the Author and Head of the whole system: on whom all absolutely depend" (8:452).
30. "Excellency of Christ," 19:567–68.
31. "The proper trial and evidence of humility is stooping or complying with those acts or circumstances when called to it that are very low and contain great abasement." *Work of Redemption*, 9:322. Hereafter cited parenthetically.
32. *Some Thoughts Concerning the Revival*, 4:418.
33. *Religious Affections*, 2:334–35.
34. Peter Brown, "The Saint as Exemplar in Late Antiquity," in *Saints and Virtues*, ed. John Stratton Hawley (Berkeley and Los Angeles: University of California Press, 1987), 5–8.

35. Gerald Schlabach, "Augustine's Hermeneutic of Humility: An Alternative to Moral Imperialism and Moral Relativism," *Journal of Religious Ethics* 22 (2002): 304–5, 316.

36. Albert Verwilghen, "Jesus Christ: Source of Christian Humility," in *Augustine and the Bible*, ed. and trans. Pamela Bright (Notre Dame: University of Notre Dame Press, 1999), 302–3, 309–10.

37. Augustine, *Tractates on the Gospel of John*, trans. John Gibb and James Innes, in *Nicene and Post-Nicene Fathers*, 1st ser., ed. Philip Schaff, 14 vols. (Buffalo: Christian Literature Publishing, 1886–89; reprint, Edinburgh: T & T Clark, 1986–89), 7:284.

38. "For by no other path was it possible for us to return but by humility, who fell by pride, according as it was said to our first creation, 'Taste, and ye shall be as gods.'" Augustine, *Of Faith and the Creed*, trans. S. D. F. Salmond, in ibid., 3:324.

39. Ibid., 3:325.

40. "Of this humility, therefore, that is to say, of the way by which it was needful for us to return, our Restorer Himself has deemed it meet to exhibit an example in His own person." Ibid., 3:324.

41. Verwilghen, "Jesus Christ: Source of Christian Humility," 304.

42. Thomas Aquinas, *Summa theologiae*, 2d rev. ed., 1920, trans. Fathers of the English Dominican Province, http://www.newadvent.org/summa/index.html, II.II.Q143.

43. Ibid., Q162, A1–2.

44. Mary M. Keys, "Aquinas and the Challenge of Aristotelian Magnanimity," *History of Political Thought* 14, no. 1 (2003): 39, 42–44.

45. Aquinas, *Summa theologiae* II.II.Q129, A1–3.

46. Ibid., Q129, A3, Q161, A1.

47. Ibid., Q161, A1.

48. Daniel J. Harrington and James F. Keenan, *Jesus and Virtue Ethics: Building Bridges Between New Testament Studies and Moral Theology* (Chicago: Sheed and Ward, 2002).

49. Aquinas, *Summa theologiae* II.II.Q133, A2.

50. Ibid., Q133 A1–A2.

51. Augustine, *On the Trinity*, trans. Arthur West Haddan, in *Nicene and Post-Nicene Fathers*, 3:176.

52. Ibid.

53. Augustine, *On the Morals of the Catholic Church*, trans. Richard Stothert, in ibid., 4:53.

54. *Work of Redemption*, 9:320–23.

55. *Distinguishing Marks*, 4:258.

56. *Religious Affections*, 2:350. Hereafter cited parenthetically.

57. Hauerwas and Pinches are critical of such indifference and link it to Stoicism, in which they perceive a type of "fatalism" to be at work. *Christians Among the Virtues*, 175; see also 216n29.

58. "Excellency of Christ," 19:568.

59. Edwards, "The Sweet Harmony of Christ," in *Works*, 19:443.

60. "Excellency of Christ," 19:569.

61. Ibid., 19:590.

62. Edwards, "The Free and Voluntary Suffering and Death of Christ," in *Works*, 14:497.

63. Ibid.

64. "Excellency of Christ," 19:590.

65. Ibid., 19:573–74.

66. Ibid., 19:590.

67. Edwards, "Sinners in Zion," in *Works*, 22:279.

68. "Sorrows of the Bereaved," 22:468.

CHAPTER 5

1. In *Religious Affections* Edwards refers to both the operations of the spiritual sense and the work of divine taste in speaking of our virtuous dispositions. Both terms are very much in keeping with

Hutcheson and Shaftesbury and, as I contend in this chapter, have an implicit relation to Hutcheson's moral sense.

2. Alasdair MacIntyre contends that although Hutcheson believed he was in keeping with Aristotle's account of the virtues, he was in error: Hutcheson's "discussions often follow Aristotle closely, and Hutcheson refers his readers to 'Aristotle and his followers' for a more 'copious explication,' but there are significant differences in the list of virtues, in the delineation of some particular virtues, and in the understanding of what a virtue is." MacIntyre, *Whose Justice? Which Rationality?* 262; see also 275ff.

3. Hutcheson wrote at a time when the study of Cicero was common; in turn, Cicero's writings were heavily influenced by Stoicism: in *De officiis* Cicero explains that "the teaching of ethics is the peculiar right of the Stoics.... I shall, therefore, at this time and in this investigation follow chiefly the Stoics, not as a translator, but, as is my custom, I shall at my own option and discretion draw from those sources in such a measure and in such manner as shall suit my purpose" (1.2.6). P. H. Clarke calls Hutcheson's view "Christian Stoicism"; see Clarke, "Adam Smith, Stoicism, and Religion in the Eighteenth Century," *History of the Human Sciences* 13, no. 4 (2000): 51. Likewise, the influence of the Roman Stoics on Hutcheson's precursor, Shaftesbury, has long been accepted. In his introduction to Shaftesbury's *Characteristics of Men, Manners, Opinions, and Times*, Lawrence E. Klein notes the extensive influence of the Roman Stoics upon Shaftesbury (see xxv–xxvi). This opinion is generally accepted among twentieth-century scholars: as early as 1923 Esther Tiffany affirmed that it is "generally recognized that the background of Shaftesbury's thought is classical . . . deriving both from Stoicism and from Platonism and neo-Platonism" via the Cambridge Platonists. See Tiffany, "Shaftesbury as Stoic," *Publications of the Modern Language Association* 38, no. 3 (1923): 642–44. The influence of the Roman Stoics on Shaftesbury's thought indicates that they would necessarily have influenced Hutcheson as well. In his book *Shaftesbury and Hutcheson* (London: Sampson, Low, Marston, Searle, and Rivington, 1882), Thomas Fowler notes that when Hutcheson published his first two essays, he connected his name on the title page with Shaftesbury's name; Fowler concludes, "There are no two names, perhaps, in the history of English moral philosophy, which stand in closer connexion" (183). Henning Jensen's *Motivation and the Moral Sense in Francis Hutcheson's Ethical Theory* (The Hague: Martinus Nijhoff, 1971) likewise affirms Hutcheson's explicit interest in defending and building on Shaftesbury's ethic (35–38), as does MacIntyre, who observes that Hutcheson was "greatly impressed" by Shaftesbury and that Shaftesbury is more or less the source for Hutcheson's moral sense. MacIntyre, *Whose Justice? Which Rationality?* 268.

4. *Work of Redemption*, 9:320. A similar argument could be made about other virtues of this type (e.g., denying lust, which Edwards also mentions in this text as a virtue that Christ does not possess), although it is less clear in Edwards's writings. In a certain sense the argument is epistemological: we know that we should resist lust after we have apprehended God and recognized both that he is morally praiseworthy and that he is not lustful. Nevertheless, it is most straightforward to focus on "repentance" in developing my argument because repentance is more explicitly a part of conversion, and conversion, in turn, is more explicitly connected to the receiving of a spiritual sense that enables us to pursue true virtue.

5. *Distinguishing Marks*, 4:252.

6. *Religious Affections*, 2:276–77. Hereafter cited parenthetically.

7. *Work of Redemption*, 9:320.

8. "If a man before his conversion, was by his natural constitution, especially inclined to lasciviousness, or drunkenness, or maliciousness; converting grace will make a great alteration in him, with respect to these evil dispositions; so that however he may be still most in danger of these sins, yet they shall no longer have dominion over him; nor will they any more be properly his character." *Religious Affections*, 2:342.

9. Michael J. McClymond, *Encounters with God: An Approach to the Theology of Jonathan Edwards* (Oxford: Oxford University Press, 1998), 51.

10. These are specified in Avihu Zakai's *Jonathan Edwards's Philosophy of History: The Reenchantment of the World in an Age of Enlightenment* (Princeton: Princeton University Press, 2003). Zakai explains, "Edwards owned and read many works of Enlightenment moral theorists, such as Hutcheson's *Inquiry into the Original of Our Ideas of Beauty and Virtue* (1725) and *An Essay on the Nature and Conduct of the Passions and Affections with Illustration on the Moral Sense* (1728)" (312).

11. Paul Ramsey, "Appendix Two: Jonathan Edwards on Moral Sense, and the Sentimentalists," in *Ethical Writings*, vol. 8 of *Works*, 703–4.

12. Zakai, *Edwards's Philosophy of History*, 320.

13. Fiering, *Edwards's Moral Thought and Its British Context*, 129.

14. Edwards himself says that *The Nature of True Virtue* "is principally designed against that notion of virtue maintained by My Lord Shaftesbury, Hutcheson, and Turnbull; which seems to be most in vogue at this day." Edwards, "To the Reverend Thomas Foxcroft," February 11, 1757, quoted in Zakai, *Edwards's Philosophy of History*, 307, 322.

15. William K. Frankena, "Hutcheson's Moral Sense Theory," *Journal of the History of Ideas* 16, no. 3 (1955): 371.

16. Jensen, *Motivation and the Moral Sense*, 55–59, 114. Jensen cautions against a "Naively Realistic" reading of the moral sense theory such that "we have a moral sense which reveals to us an objective quality which exists independently and just as we perceive it. On this theory [which Jensen rejects], ethical judgments are cognitive" (50).

17. Knud Haakonsen, *Natural Law and Moral Philosophy* (Cambridge: Cambridge University Press, 1996), 67.

18. Ibid., 72–73. Haakonsen is not isolated in this view; Jurgen Sprute suggests that human perceptions of beauty involve a cognitive act, so that our notions of beauty can be seen legitimately as descriptive of the world rather than simply as expressing our own emotions. See Sprute, "Hutchesons Grundlegung der Asthetik," *Zeitschrift für philosophische Forschung* 56, no. 1 (2002): 48–71.

19. Francis Hutcheson, *A System of Moral Philosophy*, book 1, chapter 4.1, in Hutcheson, *Philosophical Writings*, ed. R. S. Downie (London: Everyman's Library, 1994), 149.

20. "We cannot therefore say an action is judged good because it gains to the agent the pleasure of self-approbation; but it gains to him this pleasure because it was antecedently good, or had that quality which by the constitution of this sense we must approve." Ibid., 150–51.

21. "All men feel something in their own hearts recommending virtue, which yet it is difficult to explain." Francis Hutcheson, *Essay on the Nature and Conduct of the Passions and Affections*, in *The British Moralists*, ed. L. A. Selby-Bigge, 2 vols. (New York: Dover, 1965), 1:393.

22. Francis Hutcheson, *Illustrations on the Moral Sense* (1728, 3d ed. 1742), sec. 1, in Hutcheson, *Philosophical Writings*, ed. Downie, 132.

23. Hutcheson maintains that "there could not be any moral obligation in a society of purely rational beings, none of whom had sentiments or desires. There would be simply no point to morality in such a society." Beiser, *Sovereignty of Reason*, 316.

24. Some sort of "senses, instincts, or affections must be necessarily supposed to account for our approbation or election." Hutcheson, *Illustrations on the Moral Sense*, in Hutcheson, *Philosophical Writings*, ed. Downie, 127.

25. Hutcheson calls "our power of perceiving the beauty of regularity, order, harmony, an internal sense; and that determination to approve affections, actions, or characters of rational agents, which we call virtuous, . . . a moral sense." See Francis Hutcheson, *An Inquiry Concerning the Original of Our Ideas of Virtue or Moral Good II: Concerning Moral Good and Evil*, preface, in *Moral Philosophy from Montaigne to Kant*, ed. J. B. Schneewind (Cambridge: Cambridge University Press, 2003), 506.

26. See Clarke, "Adam Smith, Stoicism, and Religion," 54–55, 59.

27. Hutcheson, *Passions and Affections*, 1.1, in Selby-Bigge, *British Moralists*, 1:394.

28. "Nature itself will incline us to benevolence. . . . Virtue itself, or good dispositions of the mind, are not directly taught or produced by instruction; they must be originally implanted in our nature by

its great Author, and afterwards strengthened and confirmed by our own cultivation." Hutcheson, *An Inquiry Concerning the Original of Our Ideas of Virtue or Moral Good II*, in Schneewind, *Moral Philosophy from Montaigne to Kant*, 2.7.2, p. 521.

29. To underscore his claim that the moral sense "is natural, and independent of custom and education" (*An Inquiry Concerning the Original of Our Ideas of Virtue or Moral Good*, 4.6, in Selby-Bigge, *British Moralists*, 1:125), Hutcheson observes that we can see evidence of the moral sense in children, even before they have had time to be shaped by education and custom (1:127). Beiser likewise observes that for Hutcheson, moral principles "depend upon the *universal* and *invariable* facts of human nature itself.... The same moral sentiments are found in everyone whose sensibility has not been corrupted by the forces of prejudice and tradition." Beiser, *Sovereignty of Reason*, 315.

30. Hutcheson, *Inquiry Concerning the Original of Our Ideas of Virtue or Moral Good II*, preface, in Schneewind, *Moral Philosophy from Montaigne to Kant*, 506.

31. This end of the public good is linked to benevolence. Francis Hutcheson, *An Inquiry Concerning the Original of Our Ideas of Virtue or Moral Good* (1725, rev. 4th ed. 1738), 2.3, in Hutcheson, *Philosophical Writings*, ed. Downie, 79.

32. Francis Hutcheson, *Illustrations on the Moral Sense*, in Raphael, *British Moralists*, 1:310.

33. Jensen, *Motivation and the Moral Sense*, 67–68.

34. Hutcheson, *Passions and Affections*, 1.2, in Hutcheson, *Philosophical Writings*, ed. Downie 117.

35. "The virtuous benevolence must be an ultimate desire, which would subsist without view to a private good." Hutcheson repeatedly reiterates the point that benevolence is not something we exercise or feel merely because of our self-interest. See, for example, ibid., 120, and Hutcheson, *Inquiry Concerning the Original of Our Ideas of Virtue or Moral Good*, 2.4–5, in ibid., 81–82.

36. Hutcheson, *Inquiry Concerning the Original of Our Ideas of Virtue or Moral Good*, in ibid., 75.

37. Hutcheson, *Illustrations upon the Moral Sense* (1728, 3d ed. 1742), in Selby-Bigge, *British Moralists*, 1:404.

38. "We often do actions which we do not approve, and approve actions which we omit." Ibid., 403.

39. "Our moral sense, though it approves all particular kind affection or passion, as well as calm particular benevolence abstractedly considered; yet it also approves the restraint of limitation or all particular affections or passions, by the calm universal benevolence. To make this desire prevalent above all particular affections, is the only sure way to obtain constant self-approbation." Hutcheson, *Passions and Affections*, 2.2, in Hutcheson, *Philosophical Writings*, ed. Downie, 123.

40. Hutcheson, *Inquiry Concerning the Original of Our Ideas of Virtue or Moral Good*, 2.10, in ibid., 84.

41. Francis Hutcheson, *An Inquiry into the Original of Our Ideas of Beauty and Virtue, Treatise II: Concerning Moral Good and Evil*, sec. 1.8, in Raphael, *British Moralists*, 1:269, 270, 295.

42. "But the Spirit of God in his spiritual influences on the hearts of his saints, operates by infusing or exercising new, divine and supernatural principles; principles which are indeed a new and spiritual nature, and principles vastly more noble and excellent than all that is in natural man" (2:207).

43. Roger Ward, *Conversion in American Philosophy: Exploring the Process of Transformation* (New York: Fordham University Press, 2004), 10–11.

44. Stephen Wilson argues that according to *Religious Affections*, "Only the *fixedness* of the habit of love—not merely an occasional demonstration—qualifies as the real love distinguishable from non-religious affections." Wilson, *Virtue Reformed*, 67.

45. "Indeed allowances must be made for the natural temper: conversion don't entirely root out the natural temper: those sins which a man by his natural constitution was most inclined to before his conversion, he may be most apt to fall into still" (2:341).

46. "A transformation of nature is continued and carried on . . . to the end of life; till it is brought to perfection in glory. Hence the progress of the work of grace in the hearts of the saints, is represented in Scripture, as a continued conversion and renovation of nature" (2:343).

47. See Paul Lewis, "The Springs of Motion: Jonathan Edwards on Emotion, Character, and Agency," *Journal of Religious Ethics* 22 (Fall 1994); and James Gilman, *Fidelity of Heart: An Ethic of Christian Virtue* (New York: Oxford University Press, 2001).

48. Danaher, *Trinitarian Ethics of Edwards*, 143; see also Edwards, *Religious Affections*, 2:295.

49. Danaher, *Trinitarian Ethics of Edwards*, 151–54.

50. Wilson, *Virtue Reformed*, 68.

51. *Treatise on Original Sin*, 3:191. Subsequent citations given parenthetically.

52. *Religious Affections*, 2:394. Hereafter cited parenthetically.

53. In *Adam Smith and the Rhetoric of Priority* (Albany: State University of New York Press, 2006), Stephen J. McKenna contends that Hutcheson's moral sense is functionally equivalent to his sense of beauty or taste: quoting from Hutcheson's *Inquiry into the Origin of Our Ideas of Beauty and Virtue*, he affirms, "The moral sense is just such an internal sense, one fully analogous to the sense of beauty—Hutcheson even refers to the moral sense, after Shaftesbury, as 'this Moral Sense of Beauty in Actions and Affections'" (62).

54. "Thus a holy person is led by the Spirit, as he is instructed and led by his holy taste, and disposition of heart; whereby, in the lively exercise of grace, he easily distinguishes good and evil, and knows at once, what is a suitable amiable behavior toward God, and toward man"(2:282).

55. Edwards writes, "Thus in that great goodness of God to sinners, and the wonderful dying love of Christ, there is a natural good, which all men love, as they love themselves; as well as a spiritual and holy beauty, which is seen only by the regenerate" (2:277).

56. "And though I hundreds of times renounced all pretences of any worth in my duties, even in the season of the performance of them, and often confessed to God that I deserved nothing for the very best of them but eternal condemnation: yet still I had a secret, latent hope of recommending myself to God by my religious duties." *Life of David Brainerd*, 7:106. Subsequent citations given parenthetically.

57. O'Meara, "Virtues in the Theology of Aquinas," 254–58, 265.

58. Aquinas, *Summa theologiae* I.II.65, article 3.

59. O'Meara, "Virtues in the Theology of Aquinas," 261.

60. Aquinas, *Summa theologiae* II.II.Q8. For additional discussion, see Charles Bouchard, "Recovering the Gifts of the Holy Spirit in Moral Theology," *Theological Studies* 63 (2002): 539–58.

61. *Religious Affections*, 2:281.

CHAPTER 6

1. Julia Annas observes that an emphasis on the impartiality of love is a distinctive feature of Stoic virtue theory. See her *Morality of Happiness*, especially 128, 174, and 265.

2. *Nature of True Virtue*, 8:561. Hereafter cited parenthetically.

3. "Indeed most of the duties incumbent on us, if well considered, will be found to partake of the nature of justice. There is some natural agreement of one thing to another, some adaptedness of the agent to the object; some answerableness of the act to the occasion; some equality and proportion in things of a similar nature, and of a direct relation one to another" (8:569).

4. See Annas, *Morality of Happiness*, 12–13.

5. See Diana Fritz Cates, *Choosing to Feel: Virtue, Friendship, and Compassion for Friends* (Notre Dame: University of Notre Dame Press, 1997).

6. "There is no more virtue in a man's thus loving his friends merely from self-love than there is in self-love itself, the principle from whence it proceeds" (8:579).

7. "For sin, as was observed, is not only against a spiritual and divine sense of virtue, but is also against the dictates of that moral sense which is in natural conscience. No wonder that this sense, being long opposed and often conquered, grows weaker" (8:614).

NOTES TO PAGES 134–145

8. "What they are essentially defective in is that they are private in nature.... But yet agreeing with virtue in its general nature, they are beautiful within their own private sphere.... If that private system contained the sum of universal existence, then their benevolence would have true beauty; or, in other words, would be beautiful all things considered; but now it is not so" (8:610).

9. Susan Schreiner, *The Theater of His Glory: Nature and the Natural Order in the Thought of John Calvin* (Durham, N.C.: Labyrinth Press, 1991), 1.

10. John Calvin, *Institutes of the Christian Religion*, trans. Henry Beveridge (Peabody, Mass.: Hendrickson, 2008), 1.14.20.

11. John Calvin, *Commentary on the Psalms*, trans. James Anderson, 5 vols. (Grand Rapids: Christian Classics Ethereal Library, 1999), vol. 4, commentary on Psalms 104:24, 96:10, and 104:31.

12. Calvin, *Institutes of the Christian Religion*, 1.14.21.

13. Schreiner, *Theater of His Glory*, 78.

14. John Calvin, *Commentary on Romans*, trans. and ed. John Owen (Grand Rapids: Christian Classics Ethereal Library, 1999), commentary on Romans 2:15.

15. Ibid.

16. Schreiner, *Theater of His Glory*, 77.

17. John Calvin, *Commentaries*, trans. Joseph Haroutunian, with Louise Pettibone Smith (Philadelphia: Westminster Press, 1958), 132.

18. Ibid.

19. Schreiner, *Theater of His Glory*, 78.

20. Calvin, *Institutes of the Christian Religion*, 2.8.1.

21. John Calvin, *Commentary on John*, trans. William Pringle, 2 vols. (Grand Rapids: Christian Classics Ethereal Library, 1847), vol. 1, commentary on John 5:17.

22. Schreiner, *Theater of His Glory*, 3, 22, 30, 37, 79, 81, 87.

23. Calvin, *Commentary on the Psalms*, vol. 5, commentary on Psalm 145:16.

24. Ibid., vol. 4, commentary on Psalm 96:10.

25. For discussion of this concept, see Crisp, *Edwards and the Metaphysics of Sin*, 130–31.

26. Clarke, *Discourse Concerning the Unchangeable Obligations of Natural Religion*, 1:194–95. Hereafter cited parenthetically.

27. "The *existence* of the *things themselves*, whose proportions and relations we consider, depend entirely on the mere arbitrary will and good pleasure of God; who can create things when he pleases, and destroy them again whenever he thinks fit" (1:213).

28. "Now for the same reason that God who hath no superior to determine him, yet constantly directs all his own actions by the eternal rule of justice and goodness; it is evident all intelligent creatures in their several spheres and proportions, *ought* to obey the same rule according to the law of their nature; even though it could be supposed separate from that additional obligation, of its being the positive will and command of God" (1:213).

29. "In like manner; in men's dealing and conversing one with another; it is undeniably more fit, absolutely and in the nature of the thing itself, that all men should endeavour to promote the universal good and welfare of all; than that all men should be continually contriving the ruin and destruction of all" (1:193).

30. *End for Which God Created the World*, 8:421.

31. Fiering, *Edwards's Moral Thought and Its British Context*, 103–4.

32. "Now what these eternal and unalterable relations, respects, or proportions of things, with their consequent agreements or disagreements, fitnesses or unfitnesses, absolutely and necessarily *are* in themselves; *that* also they *appear to be*, to the *understandings* of all intelligent beings" (1:198).

33. "And by this understanding or knowledge of the natural and necessary relations, fitnesses, and proportions of things, the *wills* likewise of all intelligent beings are constantly directed, and must needs be determined to act accordingly; excepting those only . . . whose wills are corrupted by particular interest or affection, or swayed by some unreasonable and prevailing passion" (1:199).

34. "As the goodness of God extends itself universally over all his works through the whole creation, by doing always what is absolutely best in the whole; so every rational creature *ought* in its sphere and station, according to its respective powers and faculties, to do all the good it can to all its fellow-creatures" (1:209).

35. Fiering, *Edwards's Moral Thought and Its British Context*, 343–44.

36. *End for Which God Created the World*, 8:421. Hereafter cited parenthetically.

37. Lee, *Philosophical Theology of Edwards*, 199.

38. Holmes, "Does Edwards Use a Dispositional Ontology?" 100, 104–5.

39. Lee, *Philosophical Theology of Edwards*, 223, 225–26.

40. See, for example, Morimoto, *Edwards and the Catholic Vision of Salvation*; Gerald R. McDermott, *Jonathan Edwards Confronts the Gods: Christian Theology, Enlightenment Religion, and Non-Christian Faith* (Oxford: Oxford University Press, 2000); and Pauw, *Supreme Harmony of All*.

41. *End for Which God Created the World*, 8:429–30. Hereafter cited parenthetically.

42. Richard Price, *A Review of the Principal Questions of Morals* (1758, 3d ed. 1787), in Raphael, *British Moralists*, 2:132–33, 158.

43. It is possible that Edwards was aware of this argument in some other form; earlier thinkers more contemporary to Edwards, such as the British divine John Balguy, had made arguments that were similar to Price's. For discussion, see Jennifer A. Herdt, *Religion and Faction in Hume's Moral Philosophy* (Cambridge: Cambridge University Press, 1997), 55.

44. Edwards makes this point about both natural conscience (8:589) and private affections (8:602). He suggests later in this text that self-love is a principle that gives rise to sin, making the origins of justice and private loves suspect: "all sin has its source from selfishness, or from self-love, not subordinate to Being in general" (8:614).

45. "And as this sense of equality of natural agreement extends to all moral good and evil, so this lays a foundation of equal extent with the other kind of approbation and disapprobation, which is grounded upon it, arising from an aversion to self-inconsistence and opposition" (8:594).

46. "Thus natural conscience, if the understanding be properly enlightened, and errors and blinding stupefying prejudices are removed, concurs with the law of God, and is of equal extent with it, and joins its voice with it in every article" (8:594).

47. Gerald McDermott develops a similar argument about Edwards's account of patriotism in "Poverty, Patriotism, and National Covenant: Jonathan Edwards and Public Life," *Journal of Religious Ethics* 31, no. 2 (2003): 229–52. McDermott recognizes that, for Edwards, natural loves "fall far short of love for universal being" (240) and therefore fail to be truly virtuous. Throughout *The Nature of True Virtue*, Edwards is clear that "love for only a fraction of universal being is inferior and defective" (233). But McDermott nevertheless characterizes Edwards's conception of patriotism as an "inferior virtue, but a virtue nonetheless," an attribute that contains "positive good" (238). McDermott bases this reading on features of patriotism similar to those we see in partial loves and justice: patriotism has a relative beauty, takes part in "something of the nature of love," and shares "common moral goals" with those who exercise true virtue (238).

CONCLUSION

1. See Alasdair MacIntyre, *Dependent Rational Animals: Why Human Beings Need the Virtues* (Chicago: Open Court, 1999), 72–77, 81ff., and 110 for discussion of these virtues.

2. Ibid., chapter 3.

Works Cited

WORKS BY JONATHAN EDWARDS

Quotations from Edwards are taken from the multivolume critical edition of his works *The Works of Jonathan Edwards*, 26 vols. to date (New Haven: Yale University Press, 1957–). Full titles of the volumes I use are listed below in chronological order of publication.

Volume 1: *Freedom of the Will*. Ed. Paul Ramsey. 1957.
Volume 2: *Religious Affections*. Ed. John E. Smith. 1959.
Volume 3: *Original Sin*. Ed. Clyde A. Holbrook. 1970.
Volume 4: *The Great Awakening*. Ed. C. C. Goen. 1972.
Volume 7: *The Life of David Brainerd*. Ed. Norman Pettit. 1985.
Volume 8: *Ethical Writings*. Ed. Paul Ramsey. 1989.
Volume 9: *A History of the Work of Redemption*. Ed. John F. Wilson. 1989.
Volume 10: *Sermons and Discourses, 1720–1723*. Ed. Wilson H. Kimnach. 1992.
Volume 14: *Sermons and Discourses, 1723–1729*. Ed. Kenneth P. Minkema. 1997.
Volume 18: *The "Miscellanies," Entry Nos. 501–832*. Ed. Ava Chamberlain. 2000.
Volume 19: *Sermons and Discourses, 1734–1738*. Ed. M. X. Lesser. 2001.
Volume 21: *Writings on the Trinity, Grace, and Faith*. Ed. Sang Hyun Lee. 2002.
Volume 22: *Sermons and Discourses, 1739–1742*. Ed. Harry S. Stout and Nathan O. Hatch, with Kyle P. Farley. 2003.

OTHER PRIMARY SOURCES

Ames, William. *The Marrow of Theology*. 3d ed. Trans. John E. Eusden. Boston: United Church Press, 1968. Reprint, Grand Rapids: Baker, 1997.
Aquinas, Thomas. *Summa theologiae*. 2d rev. ed., 1920. Trans. Fathers of the English Dominican Province. http://www.newadvent.org/summa/index.html.
Aristotle. *Nicomachean Ethics*. In *The Basic Works of Aristotle*, ed. and trans. Richard McKeon, 935–1126. New York: Random House, 1941.
Augustine. *Of Faith and the Creed*. Trans. S. D. F. Salmond. In *Nicene and Post-Nicene Fathers*, 1st ser., ed. Philip Schaff, 14 vols., 3:321–33. Buffalo: Christian Literature Publishing, 1886–89. Reprint, Edinburgh: T & T Clark, 1986–89.
———. *On the Morals of the Catholic Church*. Trans. Richard Stothert. In *Nicene and Post-Nicene Fathers*, 1st ser., ed. Philip Schaff, 14 vols., 4:41–63. Buffalo: Christian Literature Publishing, 1886–89. Reprint, Edinburgh: T & T Clark, 1986–89.
———. *On the Trinity*. Trans. Arthur West Haddan. In *Nicene and Post-Nicene Fathers*, 1st ser., ed. Philip Schaff, 14 vols., 3:1–228. Buffalo: Christian Literature Publishing, 1886–89. Reprint, Edinburgh: T & T Clark, 1986–89.

———. *Tractates on the Gospel of John*. Trans. John Gibb and James Innes. In *Nicene and Post-Nicene Fathers*, 1st ser., ed. Philip Schaff, 14 vols., 7:7–456. Buffalo: Christian Literature Publishing, 1886–89. Reprint, Edinburgh: T & T Clark, 1986–89.

Butler, Joseph. *Fifteen Sermons*. In *The British Moralists, 1650–1800*, ed. D. D. Raphael, 2 vols., 1:325–77. Oxford: Clarendon Press, 1969.

Calvin, John. *Commentaries*. Trans. Joseph Haroutunian, with Louise Pettibone Smith. Library of Christian Classics 23. Philadelphia: Westminster Press, 1958.

———. *Commentary on John*. Trans. William Pringle. 2 vols. Grand Rapids: Christian Classics Ethereal Library, 1847.

———. *Commentary on the Psalms*. Trans. James Anderson. 5 vols. Grand Rapids: Christian Classics Ethereal Library, 1999.

———. *Commentary on Romans*. Trans. and ed. John Owen. Grand Rapids: Christian Classics Ethereal Library, 1999.

———. *Institutes of the Christian Religion*. Trans. Henry Beveridge. Peabody, Mass.: Hendrickson, 2008.

Cicero, Francis Tully. *De officiis*. Trans. Walter Miller. Cambridge: Harvard University Press, 1990.

Clarke, Samuel. *A Discourse Concerning the Unchangeable Obligations of Natural Religion, and the Truth and Certainty of the Christian Revelation*. 1706. 7th ed. 1728. Selected passages in *The British Moralists, 1650–1800*, ed. D. D. Raphael, 2 vols., 1:191–225. Oxford: Clarendon Press, 1969.

Cudworth, Ralph. "The Digression Concerning the Plastick Life of Nature, or An Artificial, Orderly, and Methodical Nature." In *The Cambridge Platonists*, ed. C. A. Patrides, 288–325. Cambridge: Harvard University Press, 1970.

———. "A Sermon Preached Before the House of Commons." 1647. In *The Cambridge Platonists*, ed. C. A. Patrides, 90–127. Cambridge: Harvard University Press, 1970.

Hutcheson, Francis. *Essay on the Nature and Conduct of the Passions and Affections*. In *The British Moralists*, ed. L. A. Selby-Bigge, 2 vols., 1:392–402. New York: Dover, 1965.

———. *Illustrations on the Moral Sense*. 1728. 3d ed. 1742. Selections in *The British Moralists, 1650–1800*, ed. D. D. Raphael, 2 vols., 1:305–21. Oxford: Clarendon Press, 1969.

———. *Illustrations on the Moral Sense*. 1728. 3d ed. 1742. Selections in Hutcheson, *Philosophical Writings*, ed. R. S. Downie, 126–48. London: Everyman's Library, 1994.

———. *Illustrations upon the Moral Sense*. 1728. 3d ed. 1742. Selections in *The British Moralists*, ed. L. A. Selby-Bigge, 2 vols., 1:403–18. New York: Dover, 1965.

———. *An Inquiry Concerning the Original of Our Ideas of Virtue or Moral Good*. 1725. 2d ed. 1726. In *The British Moralists*, ed. L. A. Selby-Bigge, 2 vols., 1:69–177. New York: Dover, 1965.

———. *An Inquiry Concerning the Original of Our Ideas of Virtue or Moral Good*. 1725. 4th ed. 1738. Selections in Hutcheson, *Philosophical Writings*, ed. R. S. Downie, 67–113. London: Everyman's Library, 1994.

———. *An Inquiry Concerning the Original of Our Ideas of Virtue or Moral Good II: Concerning Moral Good and Evil*. 1725. 4th ed. 1738. Selections in *Moral Philosophy from Montaigne to Kant*, ed. J. B. Schneewind, 505–23. Cambridge: Cambridge University Press, 2003.

———. *An Inquiry into the Original of Our Ideas of Beauty and Virtue, Treatise II: Concerning Moral Good and Evil*. 1725. 4th ed. 1738. Selections in *The British Moralists, 1650–1800*, ed. D. D. Raphael, 2 vols., 1:261–99. Oxford: Clarendon Press, 1969.

———. *A System of Moral Philosophy*. 1755. Selections in Hutcheson, *Philosophical Writings*, ed. R. S. Downie, 149–51, 189–204. London: Everyman's Library, 1994.
Luther, Martin. *Lectures on Romans*. Trans. and ed. W. Pauck. Library of Christian Classics 15. Philadelphia: Westminster Press, 1961.
More, Henry. *An Antidote Against Atheism: Books I and II*. In *The Cambridge Platonists*, ed. C. A. Patrides, 213–87. Cambridge: Harvard University Press, 1970.
———. "An Hymn upon the Resurrection of Christ." In *Philosophical Poems of Henry More, Comprising Psychozoia and Minor Poems*, ed. Geoffrey Bullough, 167–68. Manchester: Manchester University Press, 1931.
———. "The Purification of a Christian Man's Soul." In *The Cambridge Platonists*, ed. C. A. Patrides, 200–212. Cambridge: Harvard University Press, 1970.
Price, Richard. *A Review of the Principal Questions in Morals*. 1758. 3d ed. 1787. Selected passages in *The British Moralists, 1650–1800*, ed. D. D. Raphael, 2 vols., 2:131–98. Oxford: Clarendon Press, 1969.
Shaftesbury, Anthony Ashley Cooper. *An Inquiry Concerning Virtue, or Merit*. 1699. 2d ed. 1714. Selected passages in *The British Moralists, 1650–1800*, ed. D. D. Raphael, 2 vols., 1:169–88. Oxford: Clarendon Press, 1969.
Smith, John. "The Excellency and Nobleness of True Religion." In *The Cambridge Platonists*, ed. C. A. Patrides, 145–99. Cambridge: Harvard University Press, 1970.
———. "The True Way or Method of Attaining to Divine Knowledge." In *The Cambridge Platonists*, ed. C. A. Patrides, 128–44. Cambridge: Harvard University Press, 1970.
Whichcote, Benjamin. "The Manifestation of Christ and the Deification of Man." In *The Cambridge Platonists*, ed. C. A. Patrides, 62–76. Cambridge: Harvard University Press, 1970.
———. "The Use of Reason in Matters of Religion." In *The Cambridge Platonists*, ed. C. A. Patrides, 42–61. Cambridge: Harvard University Press, 1970.

SECONDARY SOURCES

Adams, Robert M. *Finite and Infinite Goods: A Framework for Ethics*. New York: Oxford University Press, 1999.
Annas, Julia. *The Morality of Happiness*. Oxford: Oxford University Press, 1993.
Beiser, Theodore. *The Sovereignty of Reason: The Defense of Rationality in the Early English Enlightenment*. Princeton: Princeton University Press, 1996.
Bouchard, Charles. "Recovering the Gifts of the Holy Spirit in Moral Theology." *Theological Studies* 63 (2002): 539–58.
Bowlin, John. *Contingency and Fortune in Aquinas's Ethics*. Cambridge: Cambridge University Press, 1999.
Brown, Peter. "The Saint as Exemplar in Late Antiquity." In *Saints and Virtues*, ed. John Stratton Hawley, 3–14. Berkeley and Los Angeles: University of California Press, 1987.
Burns, J. Patout. *The Development of Augustine's Doctrine of Operative Grace*. Paris: Etudes Augustiennes, 1980.
Burrell, David B. "Creation or Emanation: Two Paradigms of Reason." In *God and Creation: An Ecumenical Symposium*, ed. David B. Burrell and Bernard McGinn, 27–37. Notre Dame: University of Notre Dame Press, 1990.

Cates, Diana Fritz. *Choosing to Feel: Virtue, Friendship, and Compassion for Friends*. Notre Dame: University of Notre Dame Press, 1997.

Chai, Leon. *Jonathan Edwards and the Limits of Enlightenment Philosophy*. Oxford: Oxford University Press, 1998.

Clarke, P. H. "Adam Smith, Stoicism, and Religion in the Eighteenth Century." *History of the Human Sciences* 13, no. 4 (2000): 49–72.

Cooper, John. "Eudaimonism, the Appeal to Nature, and 'Moral Duty' in Stoicism." In *Aristotle, Kant, and the Stoics*, ed. Stephen Engstrom and Jennifer Whiting, 261–84. Cambridge: Cambridge University Press, 1996.

Crisp, Oliver. *Jonathan Edwards and the Metaphysics of Sin*. London: Ashgate, 2005.

Danaher, William J. *The Trinitarian Ethics of Jonathan Edwards*. Louisville, Ky.: Westminster John Knox Press, 2004.

Darwall, Stephen. *The British Moralists and the Internal "Ought": 1640–1740*. Cambridge: Cambridge University Press, 1995.

Delattre, Roland. "Religious Ethics Today: Jonathan Edwards, H. Richard Niebuhr, and Beyond." In *Edwards in Our Time: Jonathan Edwards and the Shaping of American Religion*, ed. Sang Hyun Lee and Allen C. Guelzo, 67–85. Grand Rapids: William B. Eerdmans, 1999.

———. "The Theological Ethics of Jonathan Edwards: An Homage to Paul Ramsey." *Journal of Religious Ethics* 19, no. 2 (1991): 71–102.

Dockrill, David. "The Heritage of Patristic Platonism in Seventeenth-Century English Philosophical Theology." In *The Cambridge Platonists in Philosophical Context: Politics, Metaphysics, and Religion*, ed. G. A. J. Rogers, J. M. Vienne, and Y. C. Zarka, 55–78. Dordrecht: Kluwer, 1997.

Dunn, John. "From Applied Theology to Social Analysis: The Break Between John Locke and the Scottish Enlightenment." In *Wealth and Virtue: The Shaping of Political Economy in the Scottish Enlightenment*, ed. Istvan Hont and Michael Ignatieff, 119–36. Cambridge: Cambridge University Press, 1983.

Fiering, Norman. "Benjamin Franklin and the Way to Virtue." *American Quarterly* 30, no. 2 (1978): 199–223.

———. *Jonathan Edwards's Moral Thought and Its British Context*. Chapel Hill: University of North Carolina Press, 1981.

———. *Moral Philosophy at Seventeenth-Century Harvard: A Discipline in Transition*. Chapel Hill: University of North Carolina Press, 1984.

Forde, Gerhard O. "The Exodus from Virtue to Grace: Justification by Faith Today." *Interpretation* 34, no. 1 (1980): 32–44.

Fowler, Thomas. *Shaftesbury and Hutcheson*. London: Sampson Low, Marston, Searle, and Rivington, 1882.

Frankena, William K. "Hutcheson's Moral Sense Theory." *Journal of the History of Ideas* 16, no. 3 (1955): 356–75.

Gass, Michael. "Eudaimonism and Theology in Stoic Accounts of Virtue." *Journal of the History of Ideas* 61, no. 1 (2000): 19–37.

Gilman, James. *Fidelity of Heart: An Ethic of Christian Virtue*. New York: Oxford University Press, 2001.

Gregory, Eric. *Politics and the Order of Love: An Augustinian Ethic of Democratic Citizenship*. Chicago: University of Chicago Press, 2008.

Haakonsen, Knud. *Natural Law and Moral Philosophy*. Cambridge: Cambridge University Press, 1996.

Harrington, Daniel J., and James F. Keenan. *Jesus and Virtue Ethics: Building Bridges Between New Testament Studies and Moral Theology*. Chicago: Sheed and Ward, 2002.

Hauerwas, Stanley, and Charles Pinches. *Christians Among the Virtues: Theological Conversations with Ancient and Modern Ethics*. Notre Dame: University of Notre Dame Press, 1997.

Herdt, Jennifer A. "Affective Perfectionism: Community with God Without Common Measure." In *New Essays on the History of Autonomy: A Collection Honoring J. B. Schneewind*, ed. Natalie Brender and Larry Krasnoff, 30–60. Cambridge: Cambridge University Press, 2004.

———. "Cudworth, Autonomy, and the Love of God: Transcending Enlightenment (and Anti-Enlightenment) Christian Ethics." *Annual of the Society of Christian Ethics* 19 (1999): 47–68.

———. "Divine Compassion and the Mystification of Power: The Latitudinarian Divines in the Secularization of Moral Thought." *Annual of the Society of Christian Ethics* 21 (2001): 253–73.

———. *Religion and Faction in Hume's Moral Philosophy*. Cambridge: Cambridge University Press, 1997.

Holmes, Stephen R. "Does Jonathan Edwards Use a Dispositional Ontology? A Response to Sang Hyun Lee." In *Jonathan Edwards: Philosophical Theologian*, ed. Paul Helm and Oliver Crisp, 99–114. Aldershot, UK: Ashgate, 2003.

———. *God of Grace and God of Glory*. Edinburgh: T & T Clark, 2000.

Hursthouse, Rosalind. *On Virtue Ethics*. Oxford: Oxford University Press, 1999.

Jensen, Henning. *Motivation and the Moral Sense in Francis Hutcheson's Ethical Theory*. The Hague: Martinus Nijhoff, 1971.

Keys, Mary M. "Aquinas and the Challenge of Aristotelian Magnanimity." *History of Political Thought* 14, no. 1 (2003): 37–65.

Klein, Lawrence. "Introduction." In Anthony Ashley Cooper, Lord Shaftesbury, *Characteristics of Men, Manners, Opinions, and Times*, ed. Lawrence Klein, vii–xxxi. Cambridge: Cambridge University Press, 1999.

Langan, John P. "Augustine on the Unity and Interconnection of the Virtues." *Harvard Theological Review* 72 (1979): 81–95.

Lee, Sang Hyun. *The Philosophical Theology of Jonathan Edwards*. Princeton: Princeton University Press, 1988.

Leites, Edmund. "On the Origins of Some Modern Ideas of Conscience: The Cambridge Platonists." *Andover Newton Quarterly* 20 (March 1980): 181–90.

Lewis, Paul. "The Springs of Motion: Jonathan Edwards on Emotion, Character, and Agency." *Journal of Religious Ethics* 22 (Fall 1994): 275–97.

MacIntyre, Alasdair. *After Virtue: A Study in Moral Theory*. 2d ed. Notre Dame: University of Notre Dame Press, 1984.

———. *Dependent Rational Animals: Why Human Beings Need the Virtues*. Chicago: Open Court, 1999.

———. *Whose Justice? Which Rationality?* Notre Dame: University of Notre Dame Press, 1988.

Marsden, George M. "Challenging the Presumptions of the Age: The Two Dissertations." In *The Legacy of Jonathan Edwards: American Religion and the Evangelical Tradition*, ed. D. G. Hart, Sean Michael Larcas, and Stephen J. Nichols, 99–113. Grand Rapids: Baker Academic, 2003.

———. *Jonathan Edwards: A Life.* New Haven: Yale University Press, 2003.
McClymond, Michael J. *Encounters with God: An Approach to the Theology of Jonathan Edwards.* Oxford: Oxford University Press, 1998.
———. "Sinners in the Hands of a Virtuous God: Ethics and Divinity in Jonathan Edwards's End of Creation." *Zeitschrift fur neuere Theologiegeschichte* 2 (1995): 1–22.
McDermott, Gerald. *Jonathan Edwards Confronts the Gods: Christian Theology, Enlightenment Religion, and Non-Christian Faith.* Oxford: Oxford University Press, 2000.
———. "Poverty, Patriotism, and National Covenant: Jonathan Edwards and Public Life." *Journal of Religious Ethics* 31, no. 2 (2003): 229–52.
McKenna, Stephen J. *Adam Smith and the Rhetoric of Priority.* Albany: State University of New York Press, 2006.
Meilaender, Gilbert. *The Theory and Practice of Virtue.* Notre Dame: University of Notre Dame Press, 1984.
Morimoto, Anri. *Jonathan Edwards and the Catholic Vision of Salvation.* University Park: Pennsylvania State University Press, 1995.
Morris, William Sparkes. *The Young Jonathan Edwards: A Reconstruction.* Brooklyn: Carlson, 1991.
Murphy, Nancey, Brad J. Kallenberg, and Mark Thiessen Nation. *Virtues and Practices in the Christian Tradition: Christian Ethics After MacIntyre.* Notre Dame: University of Notre Dame Press, 2003.
Noll, Mark. *America's God: From Jonathan Edwards to Abraham Lincoln.* New York: Oxford University Press, 2002.
O'Meara, Thomas. "Virtues in the Theology of Thomas Aquinas." *Theological Studies* 58 (1997): 254–85.
Passmore, J. A. *Ralph Cudworth.* Cambridge: Cambridge University Press, 1951.
Patrides, C. A. "The High and Aiery Hills of Platonisme: An Introduction to the Cambridge Platonists." In *The Cambridge Platonists*, ed. C. A. Patrides, 1–41. Cambridge: Harvard University Press, 1970.
Pauw, Amy Plantinga. *The Supreme Harmony of All: The Trinitarian Theology of Jonathan Edwards.* Grand Rapids: William B. Eerdmans, 2002.
Porter, Jean. *The Recovery of Virtue.* Louisville, Ky.: Westminster John Knox Press, 1990.
———. "The Subversion of Virtue: Acquired and Infused Virtues in the *Summa theologiae*." *Annual for the Society of Christian Ethics* (1992): 19–41.
———. "The Unity of the Virtues and the Ambiguity of Goodness." *Journal of Religious Ethics* 21 (1993): 137–63.
Ramsey, Paul. "Appendix Two: Jonathan Edwards on Moral Sense, and the Sentimentalists." In *Ethical Writings*, vol. 8 of *The Works of Jonathan Edwards*, 689–705. New Haven: Yale University Press, 1989.
———. "Editor's Introduction." In *Ethical Writings*, vol. 8 of *The Works of Jonathan Edwards*, 1–121. New Haven: Yale University Press, 1989.
Roberts, James Deotis. *From Puritanism to Platonism in Seventeenth-Century England.* The Hague: Martinus Nijhoff, 1968.
Rogers, G. A. J. "The Other-Worldly Philosophers and the Real World: The Cambridge Platonists, Theology, and Politics." In *The Cambridge Platonists in Philosophical Context: Politics, Metaphysics, and Religion*, ed. G. A. J. Rogers, J. M. Vienne, and Y. C. Zarka, 3–16. Dordrecht: Kluwer, 1997.

Schlabach, Gerald. "Augustine's Hermeneutic of Humility: An Alternative to Moral Imperialism and Moral Relativism." *Journal of Religious Ethics* 22 (2002): 299–330.
Schneewind, Jerome B. *The Invention of Autonomy: A History of Modern Moral Philosophy.* Cambridge: Cambridge University Press, 1998.
———. "The Misfortunes of Virtue." *Ethics* 101, no. 1 (1990): 42–63.
———. "Voluntarism and the Foundation of Ethics." *Proceedings and Addresses of the American Philosophical Association* 70 (1996): 25–41.
Schreiner, Susan. *The Theater of His Glory: Nature and the Natural Order in the Thought of John Calvin.* Durham, N.C.: Labyrinth Press, 1991.
Spohn, William C. "Sovereign Beauty: Jonathan Edwards and the Nature of True Virtue." *Theological Studies* 42 (1981): 394–421.
Sprunger, Keith. "Ames, Ramus, and the Method of Puritan Theology." *Harvard Theological Review* 59, no. 2 (1966): 133–51.
Sprutem, Jurgen. "Hutchesons Grundlegung der Asthetik." *Zeitschrift für philosophische Forschung* 56, no. 1 (2002): 48–71.
Stout, Jeffrey. *Democracy and Tradition.* Princeton: Princeton University Press, 2004.
Tiffany, Esther. "Shaftesbury as Stoic." *Publications of the Modern Language Association* 38, no. 3 (1923): 642–84.
Tuveson, Ernest. "The Importance of Shaftesbury." *Journal of English Literary History* 20 (1953): 267–79.
———. "The Origins of the Moral Sense." *Huntington Library Quarterly* 11 (1947–48): 241–59.
Verwilghen, Albert. "Jesus Christ: Source of Christian Humility." In *Augustine and the Bible*, ed. and trans. Pamela Bright, 301–12. Notre Dame: University of Notre Dame Press, 1999.
Ward, Roger. *Conversion in American Philosophy: Exploring the Process of Transformation.* New York: Fordham University Press, 2004.
Wetzel, James. *Augustine and the Limits of Virtue.* Cambridge: Cambridge University Press, 1992.
Williams, Bernard. "Moral Luck." In *Moral Luck*, ed. Daniel Statman, 35–56. Albany: State University of New York Press, 1993.
Wilson, Stephen A. "Jonathan Edwards's Virtue: Diverse Sources, Multiple Meanings, and the Lessons of History for Ethics." *Journal of Religious Ethics* 31, no. 2 (2003): 201–28.
———. *Virtue Reformed: Rereading Jonathan Edwards's Ethics.* Leiden: Brill, 2005.
Wilson, Stephen A., and Jean Porter. "Taking the Measure of Jonathan Edwards for Contemporary Religious Ethics." *Journal of Religious Ethics* 31, no. 2 (2003): 183–99.
Zakai, Avihu. *Jonathan Edwards's Philosophy of History: The Reenchantment of the World in an Age of Enlightenment.* Princeton: Princeton University Press, 2003.

Index

actions, virtuous, 53, 103–4, 110–11, 121
Adams, Robert M., ix, 2
agency, moral. *See* moral accountability
"All God's Methods Are Most Reasonable," 56
"All That Natural Men Do Is Wrong," 56
Ambrose, 135
Ames, William, 12, 13
Annas, Julia, 50, 51, 183 n. 1
antivoluntarism, 23, 29, 174 n. 13
   God's centrality for morality, 25, 125, 143, 156
Aquinas, Thomas
   acquired virtues, 121
   animals, 168
   Aristotle and, 4, 13, 63, 121, 171 n. 7
   gifts of Holy Spirit, 121–22
   humility, 19, 63, 70, 76–79
   infused virtues, 14, 121–22
   magnanimity, 77–80
   pride, 77, 80
   pusillanimity, 80–81, 84
   temperance, 77
   virtue theory, ix, 1–2, 9, 10, 17, 21, 61, 79, 109, 121
Aristotle, ix, 7–9, 172 nn. 12, 14, 173 n. 35. *See also* habituation, Aristotelian
   emotions, 109
   eudaimonia, 50
   friendship, 131
   human excellences, 92, 93
   magnanimity, 77–78
   moral luck, 61, 168
   virtue theory, 13, 14, 21, 171 n. 11, 172 n. 28, 180 n. 2
   virtues, 2, 4, 22, 79, 92–93, 109
aseity, divine, 149–50, 175 n. 33
atonement
   practice of virtue, 74, 87
   salvific, 4, 64, 86–87, 174 n. 16, 177 n. 3
Augustine, ix, 14, 17, 21, 137
   fortitude, 80–84
   humility, 63, 70, 76–79, 179 nn. 38, 40
   original sin, 44, 45
   pride, 77, 80
   pusillanimity, 80–84
   splendid vices, 20, 124
   virtues, 21, 62, 92
Austen, Jane, 8, 171 nn. 10, 11

Balguy, John, 185 n. 43
Basil, 135
Beauty, 8, 66–67, 115, 120, 127, 153, 168–69
   apprehension and approbation of, 100, 105–6, 112–15, 119, 121–23, 154, 181 nn. 18, 25
   benevolence, 160, 184 n. 8
   in creation, 43, 101–2, 126
   divine, 2–3, 29–30, 56, 67, 88, 96–97, 117–18, 125, 149, 169, 175 n. 42
   incomplete virtues, 126–28, 133, 158, 185 n. 47
   love, 42, 183 n. 55
   moral sense, 102, 183 n. 53
   proportion, 126–30
   secondary, 124, 126–27, 134
   true virtue, of, 124, 127, 156, 157–58
Beiser, Theodore, 173 n. 2, 174 n. 16
Benevolence, 3, 6, 11, 72, 100, 102–5, 129, 152, 159, 182 n. 39
   beauty of, 126–27, 160, 184 n. 8
   common good, 182 n. 31
   justice, 128–30, 132, 145, 163
   natural, 132, 145–46, 163, 181 n. 28
   true virtue, ix, 41–42, 125, 126, 133–34, 146, 156, 164, 182 n. 35
boldness, 83–84
Brown, Peter, 76
Burgerdicius, 171 n. 12
Butler, Joseph, 44, 50, 53

Calvin, John, 17, 51, 60
Cambridge Platonists, 23, 28, 173 n. 2
conscience, 137–40, 158
creation, 135–36, 146, 147, 151, 152
divine providence, 134, 160
natural law, 20, 125, 131, 134–40, 146
original sin, 132–33, 156–57, 166

INDEX

Calvin, John (*continued*)
  salvation, 55, 177 n. 3
  voluntarism, 18, 24, 125
Calvinism, 60
Cambridge Platonists, 17, 22–28, 56, 143, 173 nn. 2, 10, 174 n. 16, 177 n. 33
  creation, 47–48, 55, 140
  happiness, 49, 52
  latitudinarianism, 132–33, 174 n. 15
  original sin, 45, 54, 55, 57, 145
  Shaftesbury, 173 n. 9, 180 n. 3
  true virtue, 41, 46, 95
  virtue, practice of, 43–46, 60
  voluntarism and, 18, 100, 125, 173 n. 12
Cates, Diana Fritz, 131
charity. *See also* true virtue; love
  Christian happiness, 49–54
  Christian love, 177 n. 38
  distinguished from other loves, 41, 42
  divine nature, participation in, 43, 47–49
  Edwards's understanding of, 40–43
  practice of, 56, 61, 66
Charity and Its Fruits, 31, 33, 58, 59, 99
"Christian Happiness," 52
Cicero, 95, 137, 146, 180 n. 3
Clarke, P. H., 180 n. 3
Clarke, Samuel, 20, 98, 134, 155
  creation, 147–48, 154
  moral law, 54, 156
  rationalism, 125, 140–46, 152, 156
  voluntarism, 153
common good, 103
common sense, 110, 137
communication, divine, 48–49, 150–52, 165. *See also* emanation, divine
compassion, 67, 68, 131, 164
complacence, 48, 129, 133–34
condescension, 67, 85, 88–93
conscience, 44, 130, 156–57, 158–63, 185 nn. 44, 46
  approval, 83, 102, 104, 181 n. 20, 182 n. 39
  benevolence, 159–60, 164
  Calvin, John, 135, 137–40
  Clarke, Samuel, 143–44
  conversion, 96, 116
  formation of, 156, 163
  moral sense, 99, 133, 162
  reason, 53, 176 n. 7
constancy, 68, 109–10, 182 n. 44
"Continuing God's Presence," 70
conversion, 19, 56, 94, 96, 180 n. 8
  caused by God, 5, 16, 55, 119

change of nature, 121
continual, 182 n. 46
elect, 19, 105, 120
Life of David Brainerd, The, 17, 116–18
moral formation, 20, 95, 111–12
repentance, 180 n. 4
revelation of God, 117–18
sin, 57, 71, 97, 98, 182 n. 45
sin, awareness of, 98, 116
spiritual sense, 96, 105–11, 118, 167
virtue, practice of, 66, 100, 115, 124
virtuous repentance, 94, 106
Cooper, John, 176 n. 24
courage, 172 n. 28
creation, theology of, 31, 102, 127
  Cambridge Platonists, 44, 47, 125
  divine glory and goodness, 147–52
  Edwards's, 146–57, 165
  emanation, 48–49
  incomplete virtues, 5, 19, 20, 125–26
  intellectual background for Edwards's view, 134–46
Crisp, Oliver, 36, 37
Cudworth, Ralph, 23, 26–27, 173 nn. 2, 9

damnation, 34–37, 175 n. 51
Danaher, William, 2, 109
Delattre, Ronald, 2, 48, 55, 176 n. 17
deserved rewards (deserts), 89–91, 159, 175 n. 51
Discourse on the Trinity, 31
Distinguishing Marks of a Work of the Spirit of God, The, 32, 54, 68, 70, 82, 178 n. 15
divine activity
  human acceptance of, 130, 169
  loving, 31, 33, 35–36
  model for human virtue, 60, 145
  necessity and, 18, 37–38, 142
  providence, 139, 166
  reasonable, 56
divine perfections, 48, 85, 88, 117, 136
"Divine and Supernatural Light, A," 108
duty, 27, 52, 120, 130, 138, 141, 145–46, 183 n. 3
  imperfect, 10
  religious, 116, 183 n. 56

ecclesiology, 13
elect
  conscience, 116
  conversion, 19, 105, 106, 109
  dispositions, 112, 120, 123
  guided by Holy Spirit, 113–14, 121
  humility, 74, 90

INDEX

love, 62
redemption, 34–35, 57
spiritual sense, 64, 107–8, 112, 115, 118
true virtue, x, 54, 60, 111
election, 13, 34, 36, 56, 181 n. 24
emanation, divine, 30, 48–49, 149, 174 n. 33, 178 n. 26
End for Which God Created the World, The
creation, theology of, 135, 137, 139, 147, 154, 156, 178 n. 26
divine nature, 30, 47–48, 51, 72
loves, partial, 134
natural goodness, ix, 165
sin, 20, 36
telos, 171 n. 11
Enlightenment, ix, 6, 7–8, 125, 167
eudaimonia, 50–51, 176 n. 24
evil, 56, 180 n. 8
conscience, 159, 162
discerning, 114, 137–38, 144–45, 176 n. 7, 183 n. 54
God incapable of, 21, 38
good and, 25, 110, 120, 140–41, 154–55, 185 n. 45
justice, 127–28
original sin, 46
sin and, 26, 44, 97, 115–16, 118
turning from, 35
virtues and, 75, 81, 94
excellence. *See also* beauty; Jesus Christ
God's being, 29–30, 62, 175 n. 42
God's moral excellence, 32, 38, 41, 49, 97, 150, 175 n. 42; apprehension and approval, 112–13, 116–17, 123
human excellences, 4, 62, 79, 84–93
"Excellency of Christ, The"
incarnation, 64–65, 85, 88
virtues, 68–70, 89–90

Fiering, Norman, 17, 99–100, 113, 143, 147
fitness. *See* moral standards, eternal
fortitude, 80–84, 89
Fowler, Thomas, 180 n. 3
Frankena, William, 101
Franklin, Benjamin, 171 n. 10
freedom, divine, 18, 21, 37–39
freedom, human, 11, 15–16, 119–21, 165–66
Freedom of the Will, 38
friendship, 42, 131, 172 n. 28

Gass, Michael, 51
Gilman, James, 109
"God Amongst His People," 30

God, doctrine of, 2, 3, 32, 174 n. 15
goodness, divine, 23–31, 84, 125
contra voluntarism, 140
creation, 102, 135, 148–49, 150–52, 185 n. 34
emanation, 48, 165, 167, 178 n. 26
human related to, 5, 49, 51–52, 116, 119, 122–23
virtues and, 37, 43, 50, 125
goodness, natural
emanates from divine goodness, 165–66
incomplete virtues, 3, 5, 20, 161, 164
justice, 124–25, 134, 157, 162
loves, partial, 124–25, 134, 157, 161–62, 183 n. 55
sin, 20, 147, 152–57, 163, 168–69
grace, 57, 118, 121, 137, 168–69, 174 n. 16, 183 n. 54
benevolence, 129–30, 132
conscience, 116, 138
conversion, 16, 55, 66, 106, 108–9, 180 n. 8, 182 n. 46
gifts of Holy Spirit, 122
human dependence on, 2, 5, 11–12, 59, 120, 156–57
infused virtues, 3, 122
love, 56, 62
humility, 67, 71, 75
original sin, 37, 145
repentance, 96, 100, 115
salvation, 117, 172 n. 17
selective bestowal of, 34, 60
sin, overcoming, 46, 58
spiritual sense, 61, 107, 114, 167
telos, 55, 66
virtue, true, 18, 58, 60, 99, 126, 156
virtues, incomplete, 20, 124, 152, 154
virtues, practice of, 25–26, 53, 56, 105, 119, 147, 158, 164
gratitude, 132, 134, 160, 162–64
Gregory, Eric, ix
Grotius, Hugo, 9, 10

Haakonsen, Knud, 101, 181 n. 18
habit, 1, 12. *See also* constancy
habituation, Aristotelian, 15, 22, 95, 129, 133, 145, 165, 168. *See also* moral formation
grace, conflicts with theology of, 105–6, 109–12, 118, 121, 123
repeated acts, 12–13, 19
happiness. *See also* eudaimonia
Christian, 49–54
divine, 72, 152, 178 n. 26
human, 43, 145
telos, 13, 53
virtue produces, 44, 47, 55, 103

INDEX

Harrington, Daniel, 79–80
Hauerwas, Stanley, 13, 121, 172 nn. 28, 29, 179 n. 57
heaven, 33, 44, 91
hell, 14, 35, 44
Herdt, Jennifer, 174 nn. 13, 15, 185 n. 43
History of the Work of Redemption, A
   humility, 70, 73, 82, 90–91
   redemption, 91, 177 nn. 2, 3
   repentance, 95, 97
   salvation, 119
   virtues, Christ's, ix, 64, 67, 69, 70, 82
   virtues, divine, 3, 18
   virtues, human, 4, 5, 17, 167
Hobbes, Thomas
   moral knowledge, 144
   natural law, 9, 143
   voluntarism, 23–24, 32, 100, 125, 140
Holmes, Stephen, 31, 55, 150, 174 n. 33, 177 nn. 2, 3
Holy Spirit. *See also* love, divine
   elect guided by, 113–14, 182 n. 42, 183 n. 54
   grace imparted by, 121–22, 174 n. 15
   human response, 120, 122
   love, equivalent to divine, 17, 21
   virtue caused by, 13, 16, 96, 107
   virtue, true, in humans, 47, 55, 84, 175 n. 42
   will, divine, 21, 31, 37, 46
Homer, 14
Hume, David, ix, 8, 10, 61, 175 n. 60
humility, 11, 66, 69, 82. *See also* Jesus Christ
   Christ as exemplar of, 62–63, 87, 178 n. 15, 179 n. 40
   Christ embodies, 4, 54, 67, 72–76, 79, 86, 94
   classical views of, 14, 76–79, 171 n. 7, 179 n. 38
   creaturely excellence, 18, 85
   moral formation, 66, 93
   pride, resistance to, 70–73
   self-renunciation, 19, 69–84, 178 n. 31
   virtues, corresponds to divine, 88–93, 122, 123
Hutcheson, Francis
   apprehension and approbation, 19, 95, 111–12
   benevolence, ix, 182 n. 35
   classical thought and, 51, 95, 180 nn. 2, 3
   moral formation, 95, 98–105, 110, 115, 182 n. 28
   moral sense: natural, 181 nn. 24, 25, 182 n. 29; spiritual sense, 99, 118; virtue, cultivation of, 100–105, 113, 123, 182 n. 39
   moral theory, 17, 94, 181 nn. 10, 14, 23
   reason, 100–105
   sin, 44, 96
   taste, 114, 180 n. 1, 183 n. 53
   virtue, acquisition of, 15, 95, 100–105
   virtue, pursuit of, 106, 153

"Impending Judgments Averted Only by Reformation," 35
incarnation. *See* Jesus Christ
incomplete virtues. *See also* justice; love
   goodness, natural, 20, 125, 157
   grace, 152, 167
   infused virtues, distinct from, 67
   moral accountability, 164–66
   natural, 3, 5, 153
   true virtue, connected to, 124, 147, 156
intentionality, 18, 89, 150
intuition. *See* moral sense

Jensen, Henning, 101, 103, 180 n. 3, 181 n. 16
Jesus Christ. *See also* humility; redemption; true virtue
   condescension, 89–92
   creation distinguished from, 150
   creatures, renewed by, 176 n. 17
   excellences, embodies divine and human, 5, 62, 67, 84–90
   exemplarity, 62–69, 70, 86–88, 92, 109
   grace, source of, 121, 172 n. 17
   humility, 63, 69, 76–77, 81–82, 84, 89–91, 94. *See also* humility
   incarnation, 62, 65, 68, 86, 88–92
   love. *See* love, Christ's
   meekness, 74, 82–84
   natures of, 86–87, 91, 95
   redemption, 47, 55, 63–65, 96, 130, 174 n. 15, 177 n. 3
   righteousness, 64, 119
   self-revelation, divine, 10, 57, 63–65, 92
   virtues of, ix, 4–5, 19, 38–39, 67–68, 80, 83–84, 180 n. 4
judgment, moral, 101, 103, 104, 114, 144
justice, 5, 20, 59, 114, 122, 129, 137, 144
   beauty, 126–30, 134, 158
   benevolence, 128–30, 132, 134, 145
   damnation, 36, 175 n. 51
   divine, 27, 34–35, 141, 143, 149
   law, divine, 130, 142, 184 n. 28
   love, 21, 126–28
   proportion, 126–29, 183 n. 3
   pursuit of, 157–64
   sin, 185 n. 44
   virtue, incomplete: love, form of, 21, 185 n. 47; meritorious, 124–26, 133, 152, 161–65
   virtue, true, related to, 147, 151, 156
"Justice of God in the Damnation of Sinners, The," 34
justification, 55, 106, 177 n. 33

INDEX

Kant, Immanuel, ix, 8, 10, 11
Keenan, James, 79
"Keeping the Presence of God," 70
Keys, Mary M., 78
Klein, Lawrence E., 180 n. 3
knowledge. *See also* understanding
   divine, 48, 143
   human, 67, 115, 138, 155, 184 n. 33
   moral, 9, 18, 100, 144, 146
   sensory, 100, 101, 105
   spiritual, 108, 112, 114

latitudinarianism, 24, 25, 132–33
law, divine
   eternal standards, 142
   knowledge of, 144, 159, 185 n. 46
   virtue and, 54, 130
   voluntarist understanding of, 23
law, moral, 25, 52, 143, 156
Lee, Sang Hyun, 149–50, 174 n. 33
Lewis, Paul, 109
Life of David Brainerd, The, 17, 30, 111, 116–18
Locke, John, 24
love. *See also* benevolence; charity; incomplete virtues; love to God; self-love; true virtue
   Augustinian, 21
   benevolence, 129, 133
   Christian, 4, 40, 59, 62, 177 n. 39
   Christ's, 4, 68, 73, 82–83, 91, 178 n. 15, 180, 183 n. 55
   complacence, 129, 133
   divine: Cambridge Platonists, 25, 27–28, 46–47, 174 n. 15; divine being constituted by, 25, 27–28, 37, 63, 92; God identified with, 22, 32, 123; human love related to, 5, 61, 62; Trinitarian, 28–37, 72; virtues, 17–18, 63, 69. *See also* Holy Spirit
   human: Christ, of, 64; divine love, participation in, 47–49, 62, 94; gift of Holy Spirit, 122; sin and, 26, 77; virtue and, 8, 55
   impartial, 183 n. 1
   justice and, 126–28
   law, natural and, 10
   partial, 20, 90, 104–5, 122, 129, 131–32, 134; incomplete virtue, 124–26, 152, 156, 161–65; private, 126, 130–34, 145, 185 nn. 44, 47; pursuit of, 157–64; virtue, true and, 42, 123, 147, 151
   repentance and, 5, 97, 98
   universal, 42, 145–46
love to God, 66, 97, 111, 161
   charity, 177 n. 38

Christ's, 67, 68, 73
loves, partial and, 5, 131, 158
repentance and, 94
sin and, 138
spiritual sense, 112, 115
virtue, true and, 4, 41–43, 75, 82, 96, 126, 145, 148, 157, 176 n. 2
lust, 5, 46, 81, 144, 180 n. 4
Luther, Martin, 12, 18, 23, 172 n. 17

MacIntyre, Alasdair
   After Virtue: A Study in Moral Theory, 6, 7–8, 13
   Aristotelian ethics, 14, 121, 180 n. 2
   classical virtue theory, return to, 9, 10, 11, 171 nn. 10, 11
   history of virtue, 6, 180 n. 3
   human dependence, 168
magnanimity, 13, 14, 77–80
Malebranche, Nicolas, 173 n. 35
Marsden, George, 17, 28, 173 n. 10, 177 n. 2
"Mary's Remarkable Act," 70
Mather, Cotton, 12, 13
McClymond, Michael, 34
McDermott, Gerald, 185 n. 47
McKenna, Stephen J., 183 n. 53
meekness
   Christ as exemplar, 4, 62, 73, 74, 83–84
   related to humility, 66–67, 82, 84
Meilaender, Gilbert, 13
mercy
   divine, 19, 52, 58, 84–93, 94
   humans and, 56, 63, 175 n. 51
   salvation, 34–35, 76, 116
merit, 20, 38, 61, 74–76, 78, 90, 168
   Christ's, 64, 89, 91
   God's, 86, 117
   grace independent of, 118
   human, inadequacy of, 11, 18, 55
   salvation, 116, 172 n. 17
Miscellanies, 36, 172 n. 12
Miscellany 704, 36
moral accountability
   agency, divine, 21, 37, 39, 40, 51, 165
   agency, human, x, 20, 37–39, 94, 152–57
   authorship of actions, 60–61, 118–23, 167, 169
   freedom and necessity, 15–16, 18, 22
   grace necessary for good actions, 2, 12
   providence, divine, 11, 16, 152
   responsibility, x, 1, 12, 16, 40, 169
   sin, 54–55, 58
   virtues, ix, 47, 95 164–66

INDEX

moral faculty, 100, 155
moral formation, 100, 105, 110–15, 120, 157–58, 163–64, 169, 181 n. 28, 183 n. 54
  accountability and, 93, 122
  approbation and assent, 115, 123
  Aristotelian thought, 12, 14–15, 93, 95
  conversion, 108–9, 111–12
  divine activity in, 119, 122, 165
  grace necessary for, 11, 49
  habituation, 12, 19, 110, 168
  spiritual sense, 113, 98–107, 110, 113–14, 158–59, 179 n. 1
  virtue, reception of, 94–95, 172 n. 12
moral knowledge, 9, 18, 100
moral luck, 61
moral sense
  apprehension and approbation of virtue, 104–5, 113, 181 nn. 16, 25
  beauty, 183 n. 53
  conscience, natural, 133, 162
  goodness, perception of, 103, 182 n. 39
  moral agency, 118
  moral formation, 123
  Shaftesbury and, 180 n. 3
  spiritual sense, 19, 94, 99–100, 180 n. 1
  virtue, pursuit of, 102, 111, 153
moral standards, eternal, 141–44, 147–49, 151, 154–55, 184 nn. 32, 33
More, Henry, 23, 27, 45–46, 173 n. 10, 176 n. 16
Morimoto, Anri, 12, 109
Morris, William Sparkes, 171 n. 12, 173 n. 35
motives
  divine, 72, 91
  natural, 5, 104, 147
  self-love, 96, 159–60
  virtuous, 50, 53–54, 138, 148, 175 n. 60

natural affections, 131, 133–34, 157–61, 162–64
natural faculties, 5, 67, 101–2, 107, 120, 132, 161, 165, 182 n. 29, 183 n. 7
  Calvin, John, 137
  capacities of, 25, 44, 58, 132, 133, 137, 143, 167
  virtues, incomplete, 20, 122, 124, 132, 158, 165
  virtue, pursuit of, 100, 106, 163, 166, 176 n. 8
natural law, 9–10, 101, 125, 131, 137, 146
  Calvin, John, 20, 131, 135–40, 147, 160–61
  Clarke, Samuel, 141–43
Nature of True Virtue, The. See also benevolence; charity; incomplete virtues; true virtue
  justice, 126, 162
  grace necessary, 59, 126

partial loves, 126, 162
rationalism, 153
spiritual sense, 154
virtue, incomplete, 147, 185 n. 47
virtue theory, 56, 181 n. 14
virtue, true, ix, 41, 46, 59, 79, 131, 133, 185 n. 47
negative moral goodness, 124, 157, 162–63
Neoplatonism. *See also* Cambridge Platonists
  Christianity and, 14, 29, 40, 47, 62
  creation, 31, 149, 152
  divine exemplarity, 22, 84
  divine nature, 1, 2, 14–15, 29–31
  emanation, 174 n. 33, 178 n. 26
  virtue and, 40, 126, 131
Nietzsche, Friedrich, 7
Noll, Mark, 12
Norris, John, 23

obedience
  Aristotle and, 172 n. 28
  Christ's, 38, 45, 73
  salvation, 4, 64, 178 n. 3
O'Meara, Thomas, 121
original sin, 20, 26, 44–45, 54–58, 84, 138, 141. *See also* sin
  Calvinist view of, 44, 132–33, 135, 156–57
  Cambridge Platonists, 45, 145, 173 n. 2
  Christian doctrine of, x, 18, 20, 40, 54–55, 58, 132
  conscience, 137, 156
  goodness, coexistence with, 131, 147, 157
  moral accountability, 15
  overcoming, 108, 121
  permitted by God, 36–37
  pusillanimity, 82
  salvation, 23, 47
  virtue, creaturely, 66–67
  virtue, practice of, 25, 62, 90, 105, 130
  will, distortion of human, 4, 46, 124, 135, 166

Passmore, J. A., 173 n. 9
Patrides, C. A., 27, 46
patriotism, 132, 185 n. 47
Pauw, Amy Plantinga, 31, 32, 34, 175 nn. 41, 42
Pelagianism, 11, 133, 174 n. 16
phronesis, 14
Pinches, Charles, 13, 172 n. 28, 179 n. 57
pity, 60, 132–34, 160, 163–64
Plato, ix, 144
"Pleasantness of Religion, The," 52
Plotinus, 150
Porter, Jean, 14, 171 n. 1
predestination, x, 23, 169, 173 n. 2

200

INDEX

Price, Richard, 153, 185 n. 43
pride
  first sin, 77
  human nature, distortion of, 131–33, 163, 179 n. 38
  humility and, 63, 69–75, 77
  magnanimity and, 78–79
providence, divine
  creation, theology of, 125, 134–46, 152
  happiness, 50–51
  human responsibility and, x, 1, 11, 118
  natural affections constructed through, 158–61
  natural law, 160–61
  rational nature of, 56, 123
Pufendorf, Samuel, 10
punishment, 54, 96, 159, 162. *See also* damnation
pusillanimity, 80–84

Ramsey, Paul, 2, 30
Ramus, Peter, 12
rationalism
  British, 15, 20, 140, 146, 155
  Clarke, Samuel, 125, 134, 143, 156
  creation, 147, 156
  sentimentalism, 153
reason
  conscience, 53, 160
  creation, theology of, 134–46, 152
  Hutcheson, 100–105, 110
  human, 143–46, 174 n. 16, 176 n. 7
  knowledge, 23, 114–15
  right, 77–79, 143
  sin, 56, 77
  virtue and, 13, 44, 51, 154
redemption. *See also* Jesus Christ
  Christ's exemplarity, 63–65, 67, 81
  Christ's perfect virtue, 86–87
  conscience, 57
  design for world, 177 n. 2
  elect, 34, 56, 119
  human response to, 130
  incarnation, 91, 177 n. 3
  love, virtuous human, 47
  natural good, 48, 96
  sin and, 45, 63–64
Religious Affections, The
  apprehension and approbation, 111–12, 115, 118
  conversion, 106, 108, 180 n. 8
  human dependence on God, 120
  love, 182 n. 44
  moral excellence, 175 n. 42

moral formation, 12, 109
repentance, 96, 97, 98
spiritual sense, 99, 113, 179 n. 1
virtues and, 17, 53, 66, 75, 82
repentance, virtuous, 94, 96, 115–18
  apprehension and approbation of God, 19, 116
  conversion, 5, 94–98, 180 n. 4
  cultivation of, 94, 105–19
  sin and, 19, 35, 96–97
  sin, hatred of, 94, 159, 160
  sin presupposed for, 94
  spiritual sense, 94, 96, 105, 115–18
  virtue, corollary of true, 11, 96–97, 100, 122–23
reprobate, 34, 35, 36, 175 n. 51
revelation
  Cambridge Platonists, 25
  Christ's exemplarity, 63–65, 68
  God's self-revelation, 19, 66, 115, 118, 138–40, 174 n. 16
  moral norms, 5, 57, 84, 151
  scriptural, 174 n. 33
righteousness
  Christ's, 69, 72, 91–92, 119
  conscience, 44
  divine, 36, 82, 149, 172 n. 17
  virtue, 64, 81–82
Roberts, James Deotis, 174 n. 16

salvation
  Calvinist view of, 55
  Cambridge Platonists, 23, 57
  Christ's divinity, 87, 177 n. 3
  Christ's exemplarity, 4, 65
  Christ's virtue, 64, 119
  conversion, 57, 95
  divine will and, will, 31, 58–60
  elect, 34–35
  grace, 116–19, 169, 172 n. 17
  moral formation, 165
sanctification, 2, 55, 106, 119, 177 n. 33
Schlabach, Gerald W., 76
Schneewind, J. B.
  antivoluntarism, 25, 143, 156, 173 n. 12, 174 n. 13
  modern moral thought, 8–11, 17–18, 23, 26, 29, 34, 125
  virtue, history of, 6, 23
  voluntarism, 17–18, 24–26, 29, 32, 34, 58, 125
Schreiner, Susan, 135, 137, 139
self-examination, 71
self-interest, 50, 53–54, 103, 182 n. 35
self-love
  divine self-love, 42–43, 72

self-love (continued)
  motive, 96, 131–33, 159–60
  natural affections, 158, 160–61, 183 n. 6
  sin, leads to, 138, 156–57, 185 n. 44
  virtue and, 104, 146, 163
self-renunciation, 19, 69–84, 88–90, 92
sentimentalism, 131, 153–54
Shaftsbury, Anthony Ashley Cooper, 95, 99, 180 n. 3, 181 n. 14
  Cambridge Platonists, 24, 173 n. 9
  moral judgments, 103
  moral sense, 100, 180 n. 1, 183 n. 53
  motives, virtuous, 50, 53
  taste, 113
sin. See also original sin
  atonement, 64
  aversion to, 106, 115–16, 123, 160
  awareness of, 96–98, 116–18
  Calvinist view of, 139–40
  Cambridge Platonist view of, 44–45
  Christ's lack of, 39
  conscience, 96, 156, 159, 183 n. 7
  conversion, 55, 98, 108, 180 n. 8
  counter to scripture and inner light, 44, 144
  creation, distortion of, 84, 140
  damnation for, 36–37, 175 n. 51
  doctrine of, 54, 63
  habituated, 45
  human nature affected by, 26, 47, 55–58, 65, 80, 82, 84–85, 131–32, 138, 152–57, 158, 162–63
  members of church, 91–92
  pride, 71, 77
  pusillanimity, 80
  repentance, 94, 96
  self-love, 133, 156, 161, 185 n. 44
  virtue and, 54, 138
  virtues, incomplete, 19–20, 157
  virtues, presupposed for some, 5, 67, 94, 95
"Sinners in Zion," 91
Smith, Adam, 10
Smith, John, 23, 27
Some Thoughts Concerning the Present Revival of Religion in New England, 71, 74
"Sorrows of the Bereaved Spread Before Jesus, The," 68, 92
sovereignty, divine
  human action, relation to, 59, 122, 156, 169
  human freedom, relation to, 11, 15, 119
  sin and, 36–37
  voluntarism, 23, 24, 28
Spinoza, Baruch, 150

spiritual sense, 99, 105, 126, 154–55, 179 n. 1. See also conversion
  apprehension and approbation, 19, 56, 64, 100, 113
  conscience, 159–60
  moral accountability, 118–23, 153–54
  moral formation, 111–15
  repentance, 94, 96, 97, 115–23, 180 n. 4
  virtues, incomplete, 158
  virtue, pursuit of, 58, 61, 133, 157, 164
splendid vices, 20, 124, 157. See also Augustine
Spohn, William, 2, 30
Sprute, Jurgen, 181 n. 18
Stoicism, 8, 50, 54, 126, 176 n. 24, 179 n. 57, 180 n. 3, 183 n. 1
Stoics, Roman, 51, 95, 176 n. 24, 180 n. 3
Stout, Jeffrey, 8, 171 n. 11
"Sweet Harmony of Christ, The," 85
suffering, 54, 68, 73–74, 82–84, 91

teleology, 1, 7, 8, 149, 173 n. 35
telos. See also true virtue
  charity, 47
  grace necessary for, 66
  happiness, 53
  human nature, 1, 47, 171 n. 12
  virtue and, 7, 22, 51, 55, 93
temperance, 21, 77
temptation, 68, 69, 70, 83, 85
"Terms of Prayer, The," 30
Tiffany, Esther, 180 n. 3
"Torments of Hell are Exceeding Great, The," 34, 175 n. 51
Treatise on Original Sin
  habituation, 12, 109–10
  sin, 36, 55, 56
  virtues, 17, 65
Trinity
  divine glory, 64, 117
  love among, 2, 4, 27–37, 72, 175 n. 42
  pride, 133
  virtue, divine, 26, 42, 84
true virtue, 2–3, 8, 11, 21, 22, 27–28, 40–41, 66, 95–96, 131–33, 155–56, 164. See also benevolence; charity; love; love to God
  accomplished through grace, 57, 58–60
  beauty, 127, 133, 154, 157–58
  benevolence, ix, 128, 133
  charity, 18, 40–43, 59
  Christ embodies, 4, 63, 67–68
  complacence, 133

202

conscience, 159, 160
creation, 153, 163
divine being, constitutive of, 62, 67, 92, 125, 155
divine being, participation in, 63, 84, 88, 94
elect, limited to, x, 34, 60
excellence, 22, 62, 175 n. 42
grace needed for, 15, 25, 57–60, 129, 158, 167
happiness, 47, 49–54, 72
human, 18, 62, 155
justice, 145, 147, 151
love of self, 92, 163
love to God, 4, 41–43, 176 n. 2
loves, natural, 132–33, 157, 160
loves, partial, 134, 145, 147, 151, 162
pursuit of, 158, 180 n. 4
received, 58, 153, 167
repentance and, 94, 97, 100, 112
sentiment, 154
spiritual sense, 106, 158
telos, 4, 44, 46–60, 66
virtue, incomplete: distinct from, 20, 122–23, 165; inferiority of, 124–26, 152, 162, 164, 185 n. 47
will, divine, 31, 153, 156
Turnbull, George, 176 n. 16, 181 n. 14
Two Dissertations, 5, 17, 99, 124–25, 133

understanding, 56–57, 115, 144–45, 184 n. 33
conscience, 185 n. 46
divine being, 32
faculty of, 107–8, 112–13, 132, 155

Verwilghen, Albert, 76
virtue ethics
Aristotelian, 15, 79, 109
Christian, 13–14, 16–17, 79–80, 111, 172 n. 28
doctrine of God in, 2–3
human dependence on God, 60–61, 121
modern, 7, 11, 37, 80

premodern, 8
twentieth-century, ix, 1, 169
voluntarism
Calvinist, 23–24, 32
faculties, created, 47, 58
goodness, natural, 148, 152–57
Hobbes, 32, 100, 140
modern, 18, 23, 125, 142, 147
Schneewind, 25–26
will, divine, and, 27, 28–29, 31, 34

Ward, Roger, 108
Whichcote, Benjamin, 22, 43–45, 174 nn. 15, 16
will
divine, 18, 21, 153; Clarke, Samuel, 141–43, 145; creation, 140, 184 n. 27; freedom and necessity, 38–39; Holy Spirit, 46; justice, 130; knowledge of, 60; loving by nature, 31–33, 37, 169; moral law, 156, 184 n. 28; salvation, 58–60; sin opposes, 116; voluntarism, 23, 26–28, 34, 100
human, ix, 13, 120; corrupt, 140, 157, 184 n. 33; governance of, 144–45, 156; justice, 137; knowledge and, 112–13, 114; moral sense, 103, 105; sin and, 20, 56, 132, 135, 166
Williams, Bernard, 61
Wilson, Stephen
Aristotelianism, 15, 109–10, 173 n. 35
Cambridge Platonists, 173 n. 2, 174 n. 15, 177 n. 33
love, 182 n. 44
Turnbull, George, 176 n. 16
wisdom
Christ, 65
of creation, 136, 147
divine nature, 32, 143, 149, 151, 163
human, 45, 127

Zakai, Avihu, 99–100, 181 n. 10

www.ingramcontent.com/pod-product-compliance
Lightning Source LLC
Chambersburg PA
CBHW021404290426
44108CB00010B/386